Lives of Passion, School of Hope

Lives of Passion,
School of Hope

HOW ONE PUBLIC SCHOOL IGNITES A LIFELONG LOVE OF LEARNING

Rick Posner, Ph.D.

SENTIENT PUBLICATIONS

First Sentient Publications edition 2009
Copyright © 2009 by Rick Posner, Ph.D.

A paperback original

Cover design by Kim Johansen, Black Dog Design
Cover photo by Kevin Kenerick
Book design by David Kirby, Creative Connection

Library of Congress Cataloging-in-Publication Data

      Posner, Fredric, 1948-
      Lives of passion, school of hope / Fredric G. Posner.
        p. cm.
      ISBN 978-1-59181-084-1
      1. Jefferson County Open School (Lakewood, Colo.) 2. Alternative schools--Colorado--Lakewood. 3. High school students--Colorado--Lakewood--Anecdotes. I. Title.
      LD7501.L3513P67 2009
      371.0409788'84--dc22
      2009015003

Printed in the United States of America

10 9 8 7 6 5 4 3 2 1

SENTIENT PUBLICATIONS
A Limited Liability Company
1113 Spruce Street
Boulder, CO 80302
www.sentientpublications.com

Contents

Contents

For those who have left us with the spirit of the school:

> *Dagnia*
> *Josh*
> *Judy*
> *Levi*
> *Mike*
> *Nicolas*
> *Tara*

And for my dad, who finally came to understand it.

Preface

This book is for anyone, in any walk of life, who believes that education can be a joyous, lifelong love affair. For those of you who are not so sure, I hope the book will ignite your passions. If nothing else, I hope to inspire you to take another look at what is possible for our schools and our children and to motivate you to act for change.

I will introduce you to a very unusual school. Jefferson County Open School in Lakewood, Colorado, is a public, alternative school that goes against the grain of high-stakes testing, standardization, and the narrowing of the curriculum. It is a school of life, really, offering an education that can truly last a lifetime. In this book, the alumni of this school talk about their experience with a very different kind of education—one that nurtures enthusiasm, plants seeds of hope, and insists that everyone deserves a personalized, well-rounded education. Their education has enabled them to continue to pursue their interests throughout their adult lives.

Many of the stories about Open School alumni that I share deal with values and priorities: Exactly what is important to them and how have their lives and worldviews been shaped by the school? Do they feel that their education helped them develop skills, attitudes, and characteristics for leading happy, fulfilled lives?

By presenting their answers, I want to show you what is possible for our public schools as we begin to meet the challenges of the twenty-first century, and what we can learn from a real educational community that inspires and supports lifelong learning. I'd like you to see what self-directed, sustainable education looks like through the words and stories of these impressive alumni.

Ian (class of 1997) tells a story of struggle, determination, and hope—the pursuit of happiness—that illustrates the power of a school to inspire its students. When Ian was thinking about coming to the Open School, he had to confront an enormous obstacle. He had lived his life in a wheelchair, and the school building was not wheelchair accessible. Cerebral palsy had previously dictated the kind of education he had received; now, he was getting ready to assert himself by choosing the school he would attend. It was a gutsy decision! How would he negotiate the concrete stairs of a school that was built in the 1920s? How would he fit into a program that seemed to be the diametric opposite of the ones he had attended?

Ian was determined. He had decided to leave the physically disabled program behind. He was tired of being rolled from one adjacent classroom to another, spending his days in a controlled, sterile environment. Ian put it succinctly:

> I was profoundly unhappy. I did not, in any way, enjoy learning. I was only going to school out of routine and obligation. And I was angry because of how stifled and ridiculously flat my experiences were. Feeling trapped in an antiquated system added to my unease. I felt excluded. I was dying, dehydrated, and damn thirsty! I did not see the value of learning in my life. I threatened to drop out of school. My loved ones were understandably worried. I had to find something new.

Ian (class of 1997) ten years after graduation

At this point, he was desperate. He vowed to negotiate the stairs of the school on his own terms. He would literally crawl up to the second floor on his hands and knees just to get a chance at a different kind of education. Once he arrived, he knew it was the worth the effort:

> When I came to the Open School, it was like an oasis in the middle of the desert. I finally got to drink! I was allowed to be passionate. I no longer felt segregated and pigeonholed. I found I was now the stakeholder in my education. I felt truly supported. I learned to take risks and welcome challenge. I left the four walls of the classroom behind. The doors of my mind and soul that had been closed to intellectual curiosity were now wide open!

Ian opened doors at the Open School as well when he consulted for a building renovation to make the school accessible.

Before long, Ian took off like a rocket. Where he was once a sheltered, disabled boy who had never even spent the night away from home, he soon became a world traveler, an avid explorer of life:

> I never looked back! The world was no longer defined by a set of meaningless assignments to be completed for some outside entity; rather, it was open to the questioning mind. At last, I was able to investigate, reflect, and internalize based on my own personality and learning style. The Open School helped me set a new personal standard. From then on, I was going to expect to be stimulated and challenged by my teachers and my schools.

Eventually, Ian went on to graduate with honors from Guilford College in North Carolina. There, he was the student body vice president and chairman of the diversity committee. Since graduating, Ian has become the assistant director of education at the Association for Retarded Citizens in Denver. Eventually, he plans to get a law degree, along with a license in educational administration.

But much more than all of his accomplishments, it is the kind of person he is that makes Ian special. He has become a warm, compassionate human being who is not afraid to speak truth to power and follow his own heart through his experience at the Open School. There are many stories like Ian's in this book—tales of struggle and hope, personal journeys. For when a school centers on more than academics, it nourishes the heart and soul.

I tell my own odyssey of personal growth alongside the students' stories, for as a teacher and advisor at the school for many years, I, too, am an alumnus. The paths of my family and professional lives have traced a meandering course on the way to writing this book. I come from a long line of lawyers and businessmen. When I first moved to Colorado, I became a school bus driver. Back in the Midwest, at the country club, my father was telling people that I was in the "transportation business" and that I had my own fleet of buses. I was the first in my family to go into the public sector. Thus, for me, the personal part of this book includes my family's reluctant acceptance of my life as an educator at an alternative school.

At first, I struggled mightily to find my own identity as a teacher. After teaching special education for many years at conventional schools, I began to burn out. I felt like the defense attorney my dad always wanted me to be, advocating and plea bargaining for kids who didn't fit into the system. When I transferred to the Open School in the early eighties, I was giving myself one more chance to reconnect with my original love of teaching. I got lucky. I found something to believe in, a place where everyone supported kids. At this school, all the students were considered "special."

This rejuvenation catalyzed me. I had found my passion in a new kind of education. I went back to finish my Ph.D. dissertation, focusing on the modern rites-of-passage curriculum used at the Open School.

I taught at the school for nineteen years, finishing my tenure there as an administrator. I never looked back. I knew I had found my home. My only child entered the school in preschool and graduated in 2002. The school changed me and my family profoundly. That is why you will read my stories as well as those of the alumni; I have gone through the same kinds of transformations there as those who have gone before and after me.

Accordingly, I do not pretend to present a fair and balanced look at the Jefferson County Open School. I am of extreme prejudice and bias. There! I admit it! I am an unabashed lover of the school's philosophy, and I'm proud of it.

The pages that follow do not present a statistical or experimental study. The percentages and numbers stated in this book are based on 431 responses to detailed questionnaires and personal interviews conducted between 2002 and 2006. This sample was not randomly selected; instead, I tried to contact as many former students as I was able to locate through email addresses, school district graduation lists, *classmates.com* groups, and, of course, word of mouth. My intent was to solicit as many responses as possible from an extensive network of 865 former Open School students, and I personally interviewed or surveyed about 43 percent of the total number of graduates from the first graduating class in 1976 through 2002. When I use the term *alumni* in this book, I am referring to those former students who have responded to my surveys and interviews. For a detailed breakdown of the data, please see the graphs and charts in this book or contact the author. Also, please note that some of the names have been changed according to the wishes of the alumni involved.

It's my wish that these stories of love and zeal will encourage the dreams of those who want something more from their schools, something personal and lasting for their children. Hope springs eternal throughout these stories; passion is hope's wellspring.

Introduction—
Educare and the Pursuit of Dreams

*Once we believe in ourselves, we can risk
curiosity, wonder, spontaneous delight or any
experience that reveals the human spirit.*
—e.e. cummings

*For me, it was all about confidence and the
strength and courage to take some chances
with my learning and my life.*
—Bill, class of 1978

Today, we hear an awful lot about education and schools. Everyone seems to have an opinion about how schools are performing and what changes need to be made. Rarely, however, do we hear a thoughtful examination of what education really means.

What is the particular educational philosophy of your neighborhood school? If you walked down the halls of the school, would anyone (students, staff, or administration) be able to tell you what it was? Everything except the straightjacket of standardized testing is a little blurry and tenuous.

What is clear is that the climate in public schools is foreboding to many children, parents, and educators. High-stakes testing and its ensuing pressures and limitations are just part of the gloomy picture. School violence, student alienation, and a general lack of engagement (even from straight-A students) are widespread. Dropout rates are rising, fewer students are going on to higher education, and employers complain about young workers' lack of experience and self-motivation. Anger, fear, and frustration mark the educational landscape, while the political powers that be keep pushing for more testing, homework, and narrowly defined academics.

Both of the killers in the Columbine High School massacre were products of this large, impersonal system. In fact, they were considered good students by most conventional school measures—good grades, high test scores, probably college bound. However, because of the avoidance of real issues and the lack of attention to the social and personal needs of students, these angry boys were able to hide out. The exclusive focus on only one domain of learning, the intellectual, has significant pitfalls. Isn't it possible for our public schools to provide a well-rounded education? As the education theorist Art Combs once asked, "Why, in our schools, do we have to make a choice between smart psychotics or well-adjusted dopes?"[1]

With so many of our public institutions in disrepair, the time is ripe to take a good look at some alternatives to the large, impersonal schools that breed so much anger and disaffection. For example, might a school with an empowered student government, where every student had at least one positive connection with an adult, help mitigate the violence and alienation that pervade our schools today? Would students from this kind of school turn out to be—as the education reformer John Dewey hoped—socially conscious, actively engaged citizens in our democratic society? [2]

This book examines the effects of just such a school, a public-education alternative with a nongraded, experiential, and student-directed curriculum that has thrived for over thirty-five years. It explores the effects on students of an educational program that is devoid of artificial rules, limitations, and grades and that encourages young people to follow their passions, not just prepare for standardized tests. The book asks how the alumni of this kind of school are doing as adults, and it asks them how they feel about their school's influence on their lives.

An educational program should be measured by its outcomes, and the graduates of a school should model the program's goals and mission. Too often, conventional schools have nebulous mission statements or merely give lip service to the social and personal development of their students. The Open School, with its emphasis on these domains, should turn out well-rounded, productive members of adult society. These people should also be self-directed, joyful, lifelong learners who see change and personal growth as the framework for their lives.

Unfortunately, there is very little information on the long-range impact of public open-school alternatives. Over sixty years ago, the Eight-Year Study, the seminal study of alternative schools in this country, asked the question: what are the long-term effects of a curriculum that "[helps] students confront prominent social issues while helping them develop in accordance with their particular interests, abilities and needs"?[3] This study match-paired nearly 1,500 conventional and experimental school graduates and followed them for eight years after high school. (The experimental schools in the study were nongraded, experiential schools much like Jefferson County Open School.) This study found that the experimental school graduates did quite well in college and went on to establish productive, well-rounded lives as young adults. Eventually, World War II, the Cold War, and the enduring stubbornness of the conservative educational establishment wiped the promising results of these educational experiments from the national memory. The experimental schools faded away as the Sputnik era ushered in a wave of stiff international competition in math and the sciences. The schools soon got back to business-as-usual and resorted once again to delivering the curriculum exactly like they had done for over one hundred years.

Now, with even more uniformity and standardization of the curriculum on the rise, the same questions that the Eight-Year Study asked need to be posed again. At this time of high-stakes testing and a narrowing curriculum, a fresh look at the effectiveness of alternatives to the mainstream seems crucial to educational reform. While conservative educational theorists like E. D. Hirsch try to tell us what every fourth grader should know, more parents and kids are looking for something else from their education than just the facts. As parents and students ask for schools that build character and develop a confluence of the mind, heart, and spirit, a detailed portrait of the former students of such a school becomes even more important. An understanding of the lives of these adults might provide a vision of hope for the future of our educational system.

This is the first book in over fifty years to provide an in-depth look at the graduates of a nongraded, experientially based, democratically run public school. These graduates paint a vivid picture of a school of heart and soul that allows parents and children to take their education back from the politicians and the educational bureaucrats. Here are stories to encourage all of us who believe that a real education, based on personal growth and challenge, is not only possible, but essential in a dynamic and diverse democratic society.

The Jefferson County Open School—or Open School, as it is usually called—is a school that confronts the current standardization trend in educational practice. For over thirty-nine years, the Open School has thrived as a public alternative to conventional schooling. This prekindergarten through twelfth grade school is self-paced, does not use any grading system, and promotes learning through experience. No grade point averages or academic credits cloud its approach to the education of the whole child. Every student has an advisor on the staff and an individual learning plan with goals in the social, personal, and intellectual domains.

Just the idea of a school like this may provoke a change in perspective about what education really means. Therefore, please be warned that this book may force you to reexamine your life, the lives of your children, and your ideas about education and its connection to everything that is important to you. While reading it you may think about the influence of education on your own life, and what it means to be educated. If you are a parent, you might find yourself asking what it is you want from your children's schools. You may even wonder about what kind of person you want your child to be like when she leaves school.

When you look back on your own school experience, what comes to mind? You may think about the fun you had in school or the individual teachers who inspired you. You may be able to say that your school experience prepared you for life after graduation, or maybe not. Would you send your own children to the same school you went to? Perhaps, like many of us, you rarely think about your own education at all, let alone relate it in any way to your life as an adult.

What does it really mean to educate someone anyway? Perhaps we should start with the root of the word *education. Webster's New World Dictionary* shows *educare* as the Latin root, meaning "to lead, draw out, or bring out." This is a far cry from the common idea of education, which is to give out knowledge or fill up young minds with what we think they should know.

Some educators believe that we are born with a searing passion for learning. Many also feel that it is pounded out of us by our standardized, depersonalized system of education. How often do students get to identify their interests and actually pursue them? Many parents and educators feel that American schools have failed students in this regard.

Throughout the book I have included what I call Profiles of Success. These are stories of former students who have their own idea of what it means to be successful—living up to the goals and vision of their school. These profiles add substance to the argument for a sustainable education that builds character and influences students throughout their lives.

My hope is that this book will make you think about these graduates, who have been so deeply affected by their school experience that for many of them it is still the center of their lives. We all want what is best for children. Here, we have a picture of what is possible: education that focuses on the whole person and, in many cases, helps make dreams come true.

What Kind of Weird School
Is This Anyway?

*We wanted more from our schools. We wanted
something creative and comfortable for our kids,
not a factory approach to education.*

—Founding parent of the Open Living School, 1970

*I remember my first day of school. I saw an
overweight, weird-looking kid on the playground
and expected the taunting and name calling to
begin. It never did, and I saw that this kid was
accepted, even welcomed at this school. I knew
I was in a very different place.*

—Jean Anne, class of 1979

The description of the elements of an Open School education in this chapter
should provide some useful background and context for the stories of
alumni that follow. These basic aspects of a well-rounded education may
also be seen as a framework for change in our public schools—guidelines that
show us what is possible for our kids and our future.

Mission: Developing Wholeness

It was 1970 and the country was divided. The Vietnam War was still raging. New
ideas and changing perspectives abounded. It was a time to confront the status

quo, and many parents began questioning the educational establishment. They were looking for a more humane place for their kids, one that paid attention to the whole child.

Some parents in Jefferson County, Colorado, approached the school district about creating an alternative program; they discussed their vision of a school that paid heed to more than just the academic part of education. Their plan included a mission statement that advocated a holistic approach, a well-rounded perspective based on personal growth in a variety of areas.

The mission of the school—to create a safe, stimulating, and supportive environment that fosters the personal, social, and intellectual growth of each student—has changed little over the years. The school still emphasizes helping each student reach his unique potential within a community of learners. The program still focuses on self-directed learning, personal and social responsibility, and the commitment to lifelong learning. Experiential learning is still considered paramount. Developing the whole person remains the goal.

Goals to Live By

The basic goals of the school were formed by the high school staff and students in the seventies, from discussions about the most important outcomes of the new educational program they were creating. It was really an outcomes-based approach before the term even entered the educational vernacular. "'What do we want kids to look like when they leave our program?' That question was the key to the goals," says one staff member from that era. The five goals that emerged were:

• Rediscover the joy of learning.

• Engage in the search for meaning in your life.

• Adapt to the world that is.

• Prepare for the world that might be.

• Help create the world that ought to be.

Five basic outcomes were elucidated for every student. Every student was expected to become an effective communicator, a complex thinker, a responsible citizen, an ethical person, and a quality worker.

The Elements of an Open School Education

The basic idea of the school is to facilitate growth in the personal, social, and intellectual domains of learning and to encourage the development of well-rounded, competent, and compassionate human beings. An Open School education has several interrelated components, all of which reflect a vision that can serve as a model for educational reform.

A Community of Learners

The school provides a supportive, nurturing environment where everyone is perceived as a learner first and foremost. This includes each member of the school community: the staff, teaching assistants, parents and other volunteers, custodians, and secretaries, as well as the students. In such a community, everyone has a stake in the outcome and a share of the responsibility for each member. Also, each person contributes what he can to support every other member's growth.

This is a democratic community in which students have a voice equal to the staff's regarding the philosophy and everyday operation of the school. Students are proportionally represented on hiring committees for staff and administration. School governance meetings are held regularly to debate, vote on, and decide important issues such as setting group norms, reevaluating the entire curriculum, selecting the hiring committee for a new principal, and determining the kinds of classes offered. These meetings are led by students from a voluntary (not elected) leadership class. The idea is to empower everyone and develop a sense of ownership of the school. This kind of school governance is also a good practice ground for active citizenship in a democratic society.

A school governance meeting

Self-Directed Learning

The school relies heavily on experiential and self-directed learning: the ability to use one's innate sense of curiosity and personal experiences to discover how to learn and to internalize what is learned. For example, a student who is keenly interested in fishing might shape most of his curriculum around it, thereby learning many academic and interpersonal skills. The process of learning becomes familiar to him this way, and he can apply it to other areas of interest.

The self-directed learning at the center of the school's philosophy reflects the integrated learning advocated by John Dewey, the client-centered psychology of Carl Rogers[4], and the application of humanistic psychology to education promoted by Art Combs[5]. Combs argues that the hallmark of authentic education is to treat students as people, not as things, and he outlines six principles of learning that make it such a powerful experience:

• People learn best when they have a need to know.

• Learning is a deeply personal, affective experience.

• All behavior, including learning, involves self-concept.

• Learning is governed by the experience of challenge or threat.

• Feelings of being cared for and belonging have vital effects on learning.

• Effective learning requires personal feedback.

For Combs, then, the richness of the learning process is related to the learner's overall self-concept and ownership. With support and a sense of belonging, anything is possible. One does not go it alone in this process.

Thus, self-directed learning is not synonymous with independent learning. It is not learning that takes place in a vacuum; it is in fact interdependent and relies on a supportive, interconnected community. One of the prime qualities of a self-directed learner is that he knows how to connect with other learners and when to ask for help. Other characteristics, developed over time by staff and students, include:

• Has a vision and goals for learning

• Is able to develop a strategic plan for education

• Is willing to take calculated risks

• Is determined and persistent

• Has organizational skills

• Is able to develop a solid support network

• Is self-motivated and self-disciplined

• Takes initiative and is action oriented

• Is self-assessing (is able to evaluate self clearly and honestly)

• Has positive self-esteem, confidence, and self-efficacy

Learning Environments

The school understands that learning occurs in a variety of settings and thus has identified and supports four distinct quadrants of learning:

	Formal Learning	Informal Learning
In School	Planned learning in-school formal learning that occurs in classrooms, lecture halls, laboratories, workshops, presentations, etc.	Unplanned learning in-school informal learning that occurs in spontaneous discussions, socialization in the halls and cafeteria, or unexpected events in formal settings such as a laboratory project that does not go as planned, etc.
Out of School	Planned learning out-of-school learning that occurs at conferences, field trips, internships, apprenticeships, family trips, work, etc.	Unplanned learning out-of-school learning that occurs through time spent with friends and family, travel without formal agendas, sports activities, playing, reading, etc.

Most people say that the informal, out-of-school quadrant is the one they thrived most in. For instance, I learned a lot of math and language arts skills by collecting baseball cards as a kid. The school attempts to facilitate learning experiences in this informal, out-of-school area as much as possible. For example, a student's work might focus on her hobbies, relationships with family, or her soccer skills.

Trips, apprenticeships, and out-of-school projects are all staples of the school. Alumni consistently say that much of their most important learning occurred outside of formal classroom settings. These peak learning experiences are ones that they appreciate dearly for the long-lasting effects on their lives as adults.

Advising

The centerpiece of an Open School education is advising. Every student has a counselor or coach, someone who will be there consistently to help him with personal and social issues as well as academic ones. That first relationship at the school is the crucial launching pad for personal growth. Building trust is the key. Many students, especially those coming from conventional schools, have never had a trusting, positive relationship with an adult outside their family. Hopefully, after this first important relationship is established, the student is ready to branch out and make more connections in and outside the school community, knowing that his advisor is always there as a guide, an advocate, and a friend.

The advising system is, in fact, the crux of the school. Every teacher is an advisor, first and foremost. In other words, a math teacher's primary focus is to act as a mentor for her advisees. Teaching math comes later.

Each advisor helps to create a Mutually Agreed-upon Program (MAP) with each advisee. This is a schedule of classes, plus an individual plan, that takes the whole child into consideration. Each student's MAP is part of her broader

Individualized Learning Plan (ILP), which encompasses goals, strategies, and evaluation techniques in a variety of areas relevant to personal, social, and intellectual growth. Students meet individually with their advisors periodically to reconnect, reassess, and make new plans. All of the advisees of a particular advisor also meet together with the advisor in regular group meetings.

Students also meet in smaller groups, called triads, which are subgroups of each advising group. These support groups, composed of first-, second-, third-, and fourth-year students, provide extra connections for students as they progress through the program.

Having a personal advisor is a powerful aid for students in making their way through childhood and adolescence. Becoming an adult takes mentoring and modeling from adults. The advisory system is an expression of the school's conviction that building meaningful relationships is essential for a full, healthy life.

The Rites-of-Passage Curriculum

The curriculum is based on growth in the personal, social, and intellectual domains. The idea is that education is a journey of individual growth and that equal attention must be paid to the three domains in order to shape a well-rounded person ready to take on the challenges and responsibilities of an adult citizen in a democratic society.

The elementary, middle school, and high school students all have experiential, self-directed, project-based curricula. The high school curriculum, which builds on Maurice Gibbons's ideas about a modern rites-of-passage curriculum,[6] is called the Walkabout Program. The Walkabout Program consists of self-directed projects, called Passages, in six distinct areas of learning. Each student at the high school is expected to plan, execute, and defend his Passages (see Appendix A for detailed outlines of Passages). The six Passage areas are:

> **Practical Skills**: Learn how to do something that the student can use in everyday life. Practical Skills Passages may involve building a car, learning to speak Spanish, or learning ways to control anger.

> **Career Exploration**: Explore a career and its related field. This may include working in an apprenticeship or internship, conducting job interviews, following someone on the job, or using the student's own on-the-job. As part of the process, each student creates a personal profile, which is a list of personal strengths and aptitudes, along with a summary of personal challenges. The student conducts his own aptitude assessment through self-reflection and journaling. One alumnus worked with a cartoonist for a local paper; another did an internship at the local police department.

Creativity: Create something unique. The student completes a creative work and documents the process he goes through as he works on his project. One alumnus created a wall of beer bottles and caps that reflected his recovery from alcohol abuse. Others have composed original pieces of music and performed them for the school.

Logical Inquiry: Conduct an original piece of research using the scientific method. Projects have ranged from studying the eating habits of rare birds to examining the effects of video games on teens.

Global Awareness: Help create the world that ought to be, by taking on an issue that is important to you. This typically includes writing a research paper on the subject, educating others in your community, and actually doing something about the issue by volunteering and getting involved. Examples include promoting awareness of the AIDS epidemics and working for women's reproductive rights.

Adventure: Engage in a personal quest like the "hero's journey." Demonstrate a willingness to step outside of your comfort zone and use self-reliance, courage, and good decision-making skills to find what you are looking for. One student found his biological parents; another climbed a "fourteener."

As you will see when you hear their stories, Passages are a way of life for the alumni. Whether they are age twenty or fifty, alumni have a special framework to mark their transitions from one stage of life to another. The idea of constant rites of passage is prominent in the narratives of the graduates.

Classes and Trips

Classes are diverse, intimate, and characterized by the infectious enthusiasm of staff and students alike. You may see normal math, science, English, and social studies classes on the schedule as well as more unusual ones like Film Noir, I Hate Reading, or Calculus for Poets. Student input is critical, and many classes are student taught. Most are the result of students' needs and aspirations, and those of the staff. On a typical day, however, you may notice that there are many students working in apprenticeships, out on extended trips, or just working on their Passages.

Almost any topic, issue, or destination can become the basis for a class or extended trip (see Appendix B for a partial list of school trips). I gathered a group of like-minded kids and staff and started doing Blues Cruise classes in conjunction with trips down to the Delta region of Mississippi. The classes were devoted to history, culture, art, and science. We studied everything from the history and legacy of the Civil War to southern barbeque. One student created a cookbook and journal with the thumbprints of famous barbeque pit bosses imprinted cleverly in the recipes for their sauces.

Students did projects on African-American music and its effect on American culture. One music-loving student produced a wonderful paper on the history of the Stax Recording Company. Others studied wildlife, geography, and the environmental impact of development along the Mississippi River. We even took a two-hundred-mile canoe trip down the Big Muddy before I retired. I had one student lead me on an animal-tracking expedition on the island where we camped in the middle of the Big Muddy. It reminded me that I was just another learner in the Open School community.

With as many as thirty trips a year organized by the students, their schedules are often filled with trip planning classes. These are intensely focused sessions, where students and staff alike share the responsibility for the schedule and curriculum for the trips. Students are directly involved in fundraising; they pay for their trips themselves, but there are grants, loans, and travel funds available for those who need assistance.

Students in the Palace of Versailles

Also, students work on personal, social, and intellectual goals on trips. One student might be developing social skills while working in a cooking group; another might be involved in a wellness program by exercising and eating healthy foods. Others might be working on Passages. I once had a student do an internship in which he built a royal canoe in Mississippi as part of his Career Exploration

Passage. He was an intern for the river guide, an Open School alumnus, with whom we eventually took the trip. The student then helped lead the trip while we paddled in the boat that he had helped build.

How does a student know what classes or trips to take or what she needs to learn? This is up to the advisor and the student and is ideally based on the student's educational plan. If a student and advisor perceive a need to learn math skills, then the advisor encourages the student to develop those skills. The advisor, who should know his advisee well, plays an important role as a consultant. Nothing is forced. Everything is negotiated.

Graduation Expectations

Each student must address a set of graduation expectations in the three domains. Students are expected to have acquired experience and to develop competence in a number of key skills in each domain. Being able to assess and take responsibility for one's own emotional, physical, and mental wellness is an example of a key skill in the personal domain. Being able to confront others effectively and positively in relationships is an important skill in the social domain. Honing one's critical thinking is a crucial skill in the intellectual domain. (See Appendix C for a complete list of graduation expectations.)

I had one advisee who wanted to become a chef. After gaining exposure by working in the cafeteria at school, he went on to take a culinary arts class at a local vocational school and eventually did an internship at a well respected restaurant. The feedback from his mentors indicated that he had achieved competence in "integrating work experience as part of his school experience," as well as many other skills such as "meeting commitments" and "developing problem-solving skills." In other areas, such as math, he achieved the level of "experience" because he struggled with some of the math involved in measuring. Students often meet many of the graduation expectations through one single, powerful experience.

Authentic Assessment

The school does not have grades or credits. Thus, many people ask, "How do you know they're learning?" The response to this question is another question: "What do you mean by *learning*?" At the Open School, the word takes on an expanded, and I believe, richer meaning.

The issue of how to measure growth in the personal and social areas brings to mind Albert Einstein's classic statement, "Not everything that can be counted counts, and not everything that counts can be counted." All three areas of growth are assessed by the student, the advisor, and the larger school community in a qualitative manner. The typical hierarchical relationships of assessment are broken down. There is no top-down, external authority telling kids what they should be doing or how well they are doing it.

The school has always focused on the development of self-assessing learners. Students personally evaluate everything they do—classes, trips, advising, and their Passages—on a very consistent basis. Most evaluations ask the learner: what did I learn about myself, and what did I learn in the three domains?

The emphasis on self-assessment does not mean that feedback from others is not important. Every evaluation of a class or trip or Passage is responded to, not just by a staff member or teacher of the class, but often by the students' peers or fellow trip members.

For instance, after trips, a processing session is held where each trip participant has a chance to assess each other's role and performance on the trip. These sessions are seen as invaluable lessons in meaningful assessment by alumni as they look back at their education. Most say that the ability to take a good honest look at themselves through the eyes of others is one of the greatest assets of their school experience.

Evaluation is not just a judgment call on the part of advisors. It is, in fact, a much more informed assessment than that of a math teacher evaluating exam scores. The process might be compared to a full-body CAT scan. Learning is not limited to one area of the spectrum; instead, the evaluation looks at the student as a whole person, as a naturally curious, social human being. As one former staff member puts it:

> We know the students are learning because we get to know them
> so well through the advising program. We get a close look at their
> strengths and the issues that they need to tackle in the three domains
> of learning. Through a negotiated process with their advisors (and
> even in their advisory groups), students learn how to gauge their
> own progress and get what they need to grow and thrive. Ultimately,
> we are trying to get the students themselves to know when and what
> they are learning—to become reflective and self-assessing, which
> are sustainable skills for creating a well-rounded, fulfilling life.

Thus, there is a kind of negotiated assessment that continually occurs between advisor and advisee based on each student's individual learning plan and feedback from the community. Advisors and triads meet regularly to assess growth, and midterm and year-end evaluations summarize growth in all three areas.

Students are also constantly asked to demonstrate competence in their skills and behaviors on trips, at Passage wrap-ups, and in governance meetings, classes, and advising sessions. The focus is on performance in the real-world setting.

I had students who were scared stiff of assessments. They would sometimes break down at parent conferences because they were so accustomed to negative feedback. It took some time for them to become comfortable with the idea that they are the ultimate judges of their own personal growth. Once they realized this, they were like birds set free from their cages. They could fly freely without fear. They even began to take some risks with their learning.

Final Transcripts

A student is ready to graduate when her advisor and the larger school community agree with her assessment that she has demonstrated the development of important skills in a variety of areas and that she is ready to join the adult community. This is a negotiation of sorts based on educational plans, graduation expectations, Passage completion, and a bit of natural instinct. There is no magic time or age for graduation. Readiness for the adult world is the key.

It is at this time that students write their final transcripts. This document includes a narrative description of the student's life at the school, including all the trips, classes, Passages, and experiences that constitute their time of growing up. Transcripts include a personal statement, which is a summary of the student's educational journey. This is frequently a voluminous document (some are eighty pages long) in which the student emphasizes certain themes in his growth in the three domains. Trip evaluations, classes, journal entries, and Passage summaries are all gleaned from the student's personal portfolio.

Imagine trying to write the story of your life when you are eighteen! Many alumni say that they refer periodically to their transcripts in order to get a handle on the directions their lives have taken. Students do this not just from nostalgia; they find that these transcript documents are useful.

Final Support Groups

Although there is a wonderful open-air ceremony for the entire school community to celebrate graduation each year, the real graduation comes at the student's final support group. The student runs the show and invites friends, family, staff, and just about anyone who has been part of his life during his time at the school.

At the meeting, the student reviews his Passages, and he highlights growth themes. Then each member of the group gets a chance to give the graduate feedback. Some of these meetings can last for hours. There are lots of tears, and laughter and revelations. It's worth it. I had more than a couple of advisees break down and tell their parents that they loved them (seemingly for the first time). Alumni report that, for many of them, this was a major point of transition in their lives.

Transitioning to the Real World

In the first ten years of the school, there were regular meetings for students who were graduating and ready to transition to the "real world." These sessions were considered useful by alumni from that era in helping to mitigate some of their fears

and misconceptions about the world outside of the school. Discussions addressed
the difficulties of living in a world that does not often share the school's values
of love and trust, along with the ways that graduates could continue to use and
develop the community-building skills they had acquired. However, these kinds
of meetings became less frequent over the years, and many generations of Open
Schoolers went without them. Only recently have graduate transition sessions
been reinstituted.

Open School Lingo

Here are some terms particular to the school that may be useful as you read
this book:

Wilderness trip: Sometimes called an intentional disorientation,
this challenging weeklong backpacking trip is required for all
students new to the high school. It is a way to learn about the school
and the classroom beyond its walls as well as an excellent way to
bond with one's new advising group. Veteran students act as trip
leaders.

Boundary Waters trip: A trip that became institutionalized at its
inception, this canoeing adventure takes kids to the Boundary Waters
area of Minnesota. This is a tough, physically challenging trip so it
is often remembered by alumni as a major turning point in their lives
and an excellent way to transition from the school as a graduating
student.

Teacapan trip: In this biennial trip to a small Mexican fishing
village south of Mazatlan, students engage in home visits with
Mexican families while they learn about language, culture, science,
and much more. Some students study the marine life of the
estuary. Others work on their Spanish. Home stays lead to lifetime
friendships. Picking chilies with local families can be an experience
that shapes a student's world forever. Teacapan has become what it
was intended to be—a satellite campus in the Third World. Many
students and staff from the small village have also traveled to
Colorado to a take classes and workshops at the Open School.

Community service: Service work is not a strict requirement, but
it shows up as a prominent graduation expectation. Community
service work supports the Global Awareness Passage and the goal
of helping create the world that ought to be. Some service projects

involve everyone, like the Caulkathon, where the entire school helped caulk the homes of low-income senior citizens. More often, students participate in small-scale projects like working at a soup kitchen or doing a community service project on a trip.

Support groups: These are groups called together to deal with a student's need, crisis situation, or any concern. Friends, triad members, family, staff, and anyone who wants to help are invited.

Group processing: This is a Gestalt kind of exercise after trips and in support groups, where each participant discusses her role and learning during the experience and then gets feedback from the other participants.

Students building a trail for the disabled in Colorado

Next, I will review the history of the school, to further understanding of the different trends, pressures, and transformations that have affected the perceptions of its former students. Let these stories illustrate the trials and triumphs of making authentic changes in our public schools and providing a sustainable, long lasting education for all of our children.

The Easy Livin' School,
Happy Hippie High, and
Other Convenient Myths:
A Brief History of the Open School

The school is organic in its nature. That's why it has withstood the enormous pressures of time and change. It makes sense, and, most importantly, it works.

—David, class of 1991

It is a great tribute to the school that it has outlasted so many political, social, and cultural changes. Three wars, seven U.S. Presidents, and many school superintendents later, it still thrives. Although the basic vision has remained intact, it should be noted that the alumni from different eras may have had experiences that were unique to their time periods. Accordingly, alumni perceptions of the school and its influence on their lives vary in their emphases and focus.

The Seventies: The Halcyon Days

In 1970, a concerned group of parents, students, and educators asked the Jefferson County School District (the largest in Colorado) to respond to their needs. What they wanted was a district-wide alternative elementary school that represented their philosophy of education and life—that allowed students to pursue their ambitions and connect to a community that was at once democratic and supportive. The original intent of the founding fathers and mothers was to provide an environment where:

• The growth of the whole child is always respected.

• The curriculum is designed according to student needs.

• Individuality and diversity are honored and nourished.

- Creativity is given as much attention as intellectual development.
- Personal discovery is a key element in a student's education.
- The school climate is flexible and informal.
- Learning from real experience is essential; the world is the classroom.
- The teacher acts more as a guide, coach, observer, and facilitator than as an instructor.
- The entire community is involved in the program: "It takes a village to raise a child."
- Assessment of student progress is authentic, personal, and self-reflective.
- The human spirit is constantly celebrated in the joy of lifelong learning.

The district responded by authorizing a school on a pilot basis. It was initially located in Arvada, a suburb just north of Denver. Two hundred students, aged three to twelve, and ten staff members pioneered the program. In 1973, the school was approved for a three-year run with a review at the end of the three years. Seventh and eighth grades were added.

The Open School community began to discuss forming a high school that would graduate students with a Jefferson County diploma. In 1975, this wish became a reality as Mountain Open High School was launched on a pilot basis.

After a national search was conducted, Arnie Langberg was hired as principal. Arnie describes his interview as involving a "cast of thousands," including parents, kids, teachers, and community members. His previous experience at the Village School, an alternative school on Long Island, gave Arnie the perfect background. As it turned out, Arnie had the incredible blend of charisma, intelligence, and courage that allowed him not only to get the high school off the ground, but also to sustain its spirit through the trying times of its fledgling beginnings.

The early days of the high school were filled with excitement, sometimes tempered by frustration and confusion. As Ron (class of 1976) puts it:

> Sometimes it was overwhelming as a high school kid to have so
> much responsibility for everything from hiring staff to creating a
> curriculum. We had lots of heated discussions about what direction
> the high school should go in. It definitely wasn't easy, but it was a
> learning experience.

The first years were the halcyon days of creating from scratch, arguing about philosophy, and hiring staff who had like-minded ideas of challenging the existing paradigm of education in the seventies. Vietnam was a recent nightmare,

Nixon had just resigned in shame, and real change was in the air. Susie, one of the first staff members, describes it: "We wanted to create a different kind of atmosphere, one where it was safe to make mistakes and it was okay to trust each other."

Initial staff members were hired by the same mix of kids, parents, and community members. Arnie recalls that the decisions to hire certain people were based on their passion for learning and creating, and perhaps most of all, their willingness to take risks.

Other early high school staff remember that they had to restrain themselves at times from taking too much control away from the kids during the formation of the school. Everyone was exuberant about the possibilities. The feeling was "if we didn't like the way things were going, we could change everything the very next day!"

The new students were different, too. An important aspect of the first group at Mountain Open High School was that nearly 80 percent of the students came in from conventional schools. These kids came for different reasons: some because they had failed at their schools, others because they felt that they didn't fit into the system. For many it was the court of last resort as far as high school was concerned.

> Our population was different than other alternative schools in those
> first years. Some kids came to us because they just couldn't keep
> up with the pace of conventional school; others came because the
> pace was too slow for them. What both groups agreed on, however,
> was that the social and personal aspects of the normal school setting
> were toxic. They didn't like how people treated each other in the
> school culture.
> *—Arnie Langberg, principal, 1975–1986*

These refugees from conventional schools were mixed in with the kids who had come up through the Open "farm system," meaning the kids who had started at the Open elementary school. Arnie Langberg says that these farm system kids helped tremendously with the modeling and philosophical underpinnings necessary for the formation of an open kind of high school. "In this sense, it made us special as an alternative school because we already had some kids and families who were acculturated in our philosophy and way of doing things," Arnie recalled.

When the new alternative high school opened in my town, Evergreen, I was a school bus driver for Jefferson County and a teacher at a conventional high school. One of the stops on my route was a pick-up at the Open Living School, as it was called at the time. My fellow drivers called it the Easy Livin' School, reflecting the attitudes that many in this conservative mountain town held toward progressive schooling.

The popular notion was that these kids were mountain hippie kids, with their long hair and colorful clothing—the offspring of hippie parents who allowed them to do whatever they wanted. They were considered wild and wooly, but the irony for me was that they were by far the best-behaved kids on any of my routes. A few other drivers began to concur. The image of the school was malleable; it was certainly subject to real experience with the kids. As members of the mountain community began to settle in with the idea that this school was something different and even necessary in a school system that ignored or marginalized some of their own children, their attitudes began to change.

Alumni from this time period remember having to constantly defend and explain the school:

> I spent a lot of my time defending the reputation of the school. "It's not for dropouts or losers," I would say. After a while I got tired of trying to change peoples' minds. What counted was how I felt about the school.
> *—John, class of 1976*

"It took time to change our image," a former staff member remembers. The idea that the school was an integral part of the mountain community was an important factor. The school initiated service projects with local programs such as the senior center, and internships and apprenticeships with local businesses and craftsmen helped to change minds and influence people. Slowly but surely, students at Mountain Open (the high school component of the Open Living School) came to be seen simply as "just good kids."

The first graduates, from 1976, recall that the school was a little chaotic but mostly just what they needed to recoup their losses at conventional school. Some say that they never would have completed high school without the option. One alumna puts it this way:

> I quickly discovered that learning was fun again. What a relief to just follow my bliss and rejuvenate my sense of what was important and meaningful in my life.
> *—Sue, class of 1976*

Those first four years of the high school were fairly wide open in terms of the curriculum. Classes were offered by staff and students according to what were perceived as the prevailing interests. Projects and trips were sometimes created on a whim. Everything seemed spontaneous and often improvised.

An advisory system was put into place at the very beginning, and it served as the ultimate anchor in the seas of constant change during those first years. Every student had a personal advisor whom she could go to about any issue in her life. Students would meet with their advisors in small groups of fellow advisees on a regular and as-needed basis. Individual meetings with advisors occurred regularly.

This personal relationship between the student and an adult member of the community was the crux of the school. It was the beginning of every possibility the school had to offer, and it was the glue that held everyone together. The decision about whether a student was ready to graduate was based heavily on the opinion of the advisor. As one advisor noted, "We had to trust our instincts as to when students were ready to graduate; it could get tricky at times."

School governance was also a critical aspect of the school at this time. Important decisions had to be made. A formal governance meeting was created, which involved every community member as an equal partner in decision making. Debates and discussions were open-ended and often intense. The idea was to empower everyone.

Alumni from this time period tend to have a purist vision of an open school education:

> We had to face up to the idea that we alone were responsible
> for creating our own education. Anything went as long it had
> some relevance for us. Everything revolved around advising and
> governance. We got used to creating our own structure from chaos.
> *—Kate, class of 1977*

The Eighties: Walkabout

In 1980, several staff members, searching for a framework for the curriculum, came upon a self-directed educational program created by the Canadian education pioneer Maurice Gibbons. It was called the Walkabout program, a modern rites-of-passage curriculum that involved a series of self-directed projects called Passages that would demonstrate an adolescent's readiness for the adult world. Gibbons noted the dearth of rituals and transitions in our modern culture and borrowed from the Aboriginal walkabout in Australia, where the tribe would send youngsters into the outback to show that they were ready to be accepted as adults.

The new system was not welcomed by everyone. Some immediately saw it as constrictive and anti-open education because some of the choices were being taken away from the kids. Others saw the opportunity to give the program some backbone and perhaps more legitimacy in the eyes of a dubious public.

In any case, the Walkabout program was phased in and by 1983 became institutionalized as the main part of the curriculum. Some alumni from this era reflected on the frustrations and confusion of yet another change:

> I really balked at the Passages at first because I saw it as limiting my freedom to design my own program. As time went on, however, I began to see the value in doing these projects. I even began to enjoy the challenge of completing and defending them in front of others.
>
> *–John, class of 1982*

Trish (class of 1986), Sergeant First Class, U.S. Army, 2006

Alumni who were students during the remainder of that decade experienced the early stages of Walkabout, a time when a lot of trial and error went on in refining the program. These were my first years at the school, too and, as a new advisor, I can remember having trouble deciding what a legitimate Passage really was. A lot of it had to do with how to couple good advising with the Walkabout program. If you really got to know a student well, you could tell what an appropriate level of challenge and relevancy was for him.

It wasn't easy, and the feeling was that some students got away with manipulating the system because of everyone's inexperience with the program. I feel that I learned some valuable lessons as an advisor in this time period. Some students from this era felt that some of their peers cheapened the program by getting away with easy Passages. I did observe, however, that some of those kids were merely working at their particular levels. In any case, the alumni from the eighties have a somewhat conflicted view of the Walkabout program.

The Nineties: The Merger

The nineties were marked by a major change: the merger, in 1989, of the high school with the middle and elementary schools in Lakewood, a suburb west of Denver. These were rather turbulent times as internecine conflict threatened the whole idea of a prekindergarten-through-twelfth-grade program situated in one building. The problems had to do with philosophy, leadership, mutual responsibilities, and the usual jealousies and anxieties of teachers at different levels. Some of the staff looked at the merger as a forced marriage.

At the same time, in the early part of the nineties, the pressures the parents exerted on the school were changing. The idea that the school should become more college-oriented and academically focused was promulgated. The clientele began to change as the mountain influence waned and the percentage of students who were urban or suburban grew.

Some of the alumni from this transitional period are critical of the school for being too lax academically and generally not structured enough. However, these feelings are often mixed with a positive recognition of the value of a prekindergarten-through-twelfth-grade program and some hope for its future.

As the nineties progressed, the staff became more comfortable with the Passages and more adept at gauging the appropriate level of difficulty for each of their advisees. In my case, I know that I got much more skillful at facilitating a comprehensive webbing or integration of all of the Passages for each student, as both an advisor and a Passage consultant.

The end of this decade was characterized by the onslaught of high-stakes achievement testing. While most staff and students resented the increased importance of the testing, some parents welcomed it. These external and internal pressures may have forced a greater emphasis on academic skills. The new testing climate renewed the perpetual debate about the balance among the three domains of learning. Were we giving short shrift to the intellectual domain?

More academically specific classes, such as Algebra II and English Grammar, were added to each schedule, and

The archeology trip became an important part of the curriculum in the nineties

academic expectations were raised. Graduates from the end of the nineties have more positive perceptions of the school, especially where academic preparedness is concerned. Although more time spent on classes meant less time for advising, a healthy respect for the advising process still permeates the responses from alumni from this era.

The Twenty-First Century

The challenges of high-stakes testing continued and increased as No Child Left Behind appeared on the horizon of the educational landscape. Individual schools now have to stake their existence on one single set of test scores. Curricula are being narrowed nationwide to eliminate classes that do not deal with the material on the test. Art classes and even social studies are becoming relics of the past in the new age of school accountability. Schools have no choice: pass the test or be closed down or converted into state-run charters. The pressure to "teach the test" is enormous, even on the Open School.

Yet the school continues to pass the test despite resisting, as best it can, the institutionalizing of a culture wherein the entire school year is spent gearing up for the state exam. Alumni from the beginning of this decade begin to reflect some anxieties and fears about The Test. Mostly, they fear for the school and its future, not for themselves and their lack of preparedness for the rigors of the academic world.

Inevitably, there are still times when it is necessary to explain and defend the school. Staff members, too, have to do some educating about the value of self-directed education. Even after speaking to my own father for many years about the school, I don't think he really understood it until he came out for his granddaughter's Open School graduation right before he died. Some alumni, regardless of what era they are from, have noted that this is an important part of their education:

> I think that having to defend and explain the program has made me stronger, more articulate, and more resolute in my beliefs about education and life in general.
> —*Nat, class of 1990*

Finally, it is encouraging that the responses of the alumni from four very different decades of the school's history, each with its own unique challenges and pressures, have remained somewhat consistent. The core values of the school appear to be rock-solid. At a gathering of fifteen alumni from the New York area—all from different time periods at the school—in a Manhattan location for a video interview, I was struck by how much they had in common as they talked about their bonds with one another and the school. They discussed the importance of advising and the profound relationships they had developed. They also shared stories from programs like the Boundary Waters trip that spanned four decades in history.

The students' love and respect for the unique educational experience that they shared was powerful, even exhilarating. In fact, as they left the interview, discussing plans to keep in touch with one another, I was deeply moved and motivated to continue my alumni follow-up project.

Now, thirty-nine years after the inception of the Jefferson County Open School, we are still explaining and defending our way of doing things. Regardless, it is clear that the Open School remains a fixture in Colorado's largest school district. Based on the reports from alumni, we have reason to be proud for having provided such a successful option in our public schools.

All schools would do well to heed the Open School's course. Building meaningful relationships has been the glue that has kept it alive and well along the way. This is where real change begins and, eventually, sustains itself.

Relationships: The Skills of Life

● ● ●Ninety-six percent of Open School alumni report that they feel that relationships are very important to them and their lives as adults.

● ● ●In a 2004 poll, 25 percent of American adults reported that they have no one to confide in, up from 10% in 1985 (American Sociological Review).

● ● ●Fifty percent of the alumni said that having meaningful relationships was the most important thing in their lives.

The Open School inspired me to open up to other people in ways that I was always scared of and intimidated by before. The school emphasized building meaningful relationships as an important life skill.

—Jay, class of 1995

No Child Left Behind and its accompanying high-stakes testing pay no attention to building meaningful relationships in school settings. The socialization process is not on the test.

As school systems scramble to adapt to the strictures of federally and state-mandated student achievement tests, the real purpose of education becomes lost, subordinated to the One Big Test Score and academic achievement. Electives are cut. Physical education: out. Classes in the arts: not required. Social skills, so crucial for success and happiness in life, are ignored as *extracurricular*, another word for unimportant.

Kids get the message all too well. The pressure to achieve mounts like a frightening storm. Smart kids crack. Kids who don't fit in simply give up. The Test takes over, and many young people are left out in the cold.

> The pressure I feel to do well on the tests and get good grades is enormous. I think about it all the time. I have no life, and sometimes I feel completely alienated from what I am supposed to be learning. Meanwhile, the things that are really important to me, like my relationships with friends, family, and the world, seem to be considered totally unimportant.
>
> *–Debbie, a student in a conventional high school in Marin County, California*

Advising is a trusting, supportive relationship

Those who choose to play the game develop what the columnist David Brooks calls "a prudential attitude" toward learning: one cannot allow oneself to be obsessed or passionate about a subject that is not measured by the test. One learns to avoid risks. A student's passion is drained and homogenized. The system, Brooks observes, "whittles kids down into bland, complaisant achievement machines."[7]

Relationships? Social skills? Many educators think: "Who has the time? It's not the school's place to deal with these matters anyway," while many parents believe it's up to families and churches to handle them outside of school. But as we see through increasing dropout rates, gang participation, school violence, and numbers of disaffected youth, families and churches often aren't facilitating children's social development all that well.

In this brave new world of schooling, it's easy to lose track of what really matters: the life skills, what Brooks calls the keys to one's "worldly success." If we sit down and really think about it, what we should be aiming for in our schools is to develop well-rounded, smart kids who have the wherewithal to get along with people and maintain meaningful relationships.

My years at the school deeply affected my own ability to develop and sustain fulfilling relationships. When I first transferred to the Open School, I had already had some experience with being an advisor as a special education teacher in conventional schools. There, with a little ingenuity and more than a little freedom from scrutiny from the mainstream program, I was able to get pretty close to kids. The truth was that I was often the only advocate for my kids. Increasingly, I felt like a defense attorney for these poor souls who felt trapped in a system that did not respond to their desires or needs.

When I came to the Open School, it didn't take long to realize that everyone was treated as special and that relationships were paramount in importance. I quickly saw that I could really do what I had always thought teaching was all about: get to know kids on a profoundly personal level and help them to achieve their own goals. Advisors were actually encouraged to take the time to pursue these relationships, not to look at them as distractions from the "real" curriculum. As a teacher, I was in heaven!

For me, the school's focus on relationships put all of my own personal connections in a more prominent light. My family, friends, and community became important. I began to feel that I needed to pay closer attention to all the people in my life and to their hopes and dreams.

I was also reminded of a Yiddish word that I learned from my father: *haimisch*. It meant *down home* or *family*. I began to see that the feeling at the school was one of family—the closeness and support that appear to be absent in so many lives today. For many alumni, this is one of the school's greatest gifts.

> It's like one big extended family, with all the joys, sorrows,
> celebrations, and struggles that go with it.
> –Marsh, class of 1987

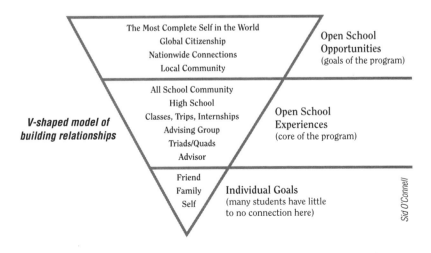

A Foundation to Build On: The Advisor-Advisee Relationship

In some ways, the school is *all* about relationships. In fact, one of the few requirements is that each student has at least one trusting, supportive relationship to start with—the one with his advisor. This connection with an adult in the community is really the starting point for everything that happens at the school. The advisor acts as an advocate and guide through the self-directed journey that is the Open School.

Self-directed does not imply independent. A student does not go it alone. Instead, the idea is to expand from the initial advisee-advisor relationship and build social connections incrementally to include the wider school community and then, ideally, the world at large. The progression of personal relationships and connections looks like a V, with the student at the bottom. As the student develops personally, socially, and intellectually, he begins to branch out. The initial connection with the advisor becomes the starting point for the adventure at hand: one's journey of personal growth.

The importance of this first relationship is rarely lost on new students, especially those coming from conventional schools. More often than not, these kids arrive from large, anonymous schools where it is easy to get lost or hide out. The Columbine tragedy offers a sobering example of the depersonalized environment common in many large schools today. The killers were angry, alienated boys who either were ignored because they got good grades or were persistently harassed because they didn't fit in with the popular cliques. They had no personal connections at the school; there was no one who really knew them or cared. Who knows what having a personal advisor would have done for them?

For many of the new students at the Open School, this is the first time they have been asked to be connected with anyone in a school environment, let alone with a teacher. Accordingly, they are suspicious of adults and wary of the requirement to create a relationship with an advisor. Obviously, the building of trust is essential, and it takes time to develop. Some of the alumni say that it took them years to establish that first connection. Often, they remember a series of successes and setbacks as part of their growth in the social area.

When Don first came to the school, he was shy, insecure, and very angry. He actually talked about doing harm to some of his past teachers and schools. His trust level with adults was at zero. Initial meetings with his parents revealed deep emotional wounds and a long history of dysfunctional relationships.

Slowly, almost imperceptibly at first, Don and I began to connect. The school's environment afforded us the time and opportunity to really get to know each other. A strong bond developed, but Don was not ready to expand beyond it. His first foray into the world of relationships outside of our advisor-advisee relationship was a disaster, a school trip where Don reverted to his angry, alienated behaviors.

This first setback was not the last. However, Don learned quickly that he would not be slammed down for his mistakes. Instead, he would be allowed to learn from them.

At least he knew that he had one person whom he could rely on—someone who would support him and advocate for him. Don soon got himself together, and with much encouragement, went on another trip. This time everything clicked. He found that there were other kids with the same issues, people whom he could trust and relate to. Many former students identify such an experience as a turning point that gave them the confidence to reach out to others, to finally trust themselves to be themselves.

Don and I are still close. We have maintained our relationship over twenty years now. I have seen him struggle, stumble, and grow. The bottom line is that we have been there for each other throughout the years. Sometimes, Don thinks about what he would have done without the Open School. He says that he probably would have dropped out or, much worse, might have turned into someone like one of "those Columbine kids."

When new students arrive, they are still trying to meet the most basic needs identified by the developmental psychologist Abraham Maslow in his hierarchy of needs.[8] Kids who have not had security and trust needs met are pretty hard to reach, especially if you are trying only to teach them advanced algebra. Maslow contended that all social systems should address the basic needs of safety, shelter, and health before moving up to higher-level needs such as intellectual development, and eventually, achieving one's potential as a well-rounded human being. His model was aptly shaped like a pyramid.

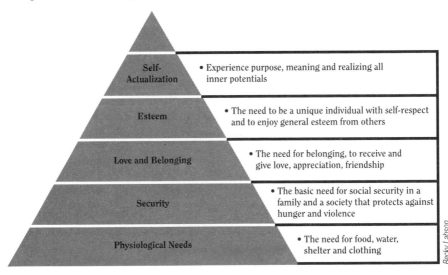

Maslow's heirarchy of needs

The Open School philosophy, much like Maslow's model, is driven by the idea that the personal and social domains must be addressed first and foremost. The idea is that these domains of learning deserve equal time with the intellectual domain. That first trusting relationship with an advisor sets the stage for all that follows in all three domains of learning.

As an advisor, I quickly learned that my role had changed dramatically. One of my first experiences at the school woke me up immediately to the challenges and gifts of teaching in this new environment. I was about to begin the "disorientation," or wilderness trip—a fairly tough backpacking trip into the mountains taken by each new group of kids—when a student who previously had seemed quite gung ho and prepared for the trip stopped in his tracks about twenty feet into the trail. He threw down his expensive pack and gear and yelled that he couldn't make it and that he wanted to call his dad to pick him up. What was I to do, a new teacher at the school, unsure of my role as an advisor and probably just as fearful about the trip as this frustrated boy in front me? Immediately my assistants, who were veteran students, came to the rescue. They volunteered to carry his pack and coaxed him along through that difficult first day's hike.

He made it through the five-day trip and was very proud of himself. Most importantly, he made some new friends and could sense that, with support and caring, he could do almost anything. I was struck by the focus on encouragement and trust displayed by these kids as they helped me form an advising group built on strong personal relationships. The purpose of the trip, to show that school didn't just take place in the confines of a classroom, was not lost on me.

Open School students are asked to do something that many adults find downright scary. They are asked to become a part of a real community, a family of learners. For many, at first it feels like a hopeless task. Usually, however, a slow but steady change starts to take place. The same student who seemed so alienated and separated begins to speak up in small groups, then in larger settings like classes or governance meetings. Soon it may be hard to recognize this student as the shy, withdrawn kid he once was.

Also, having ownership and control in one's community through a process of community government is a key point of connection, especially for kids who had no sense of responsibility before. Suddenly, formerly isolated and withdrawn students are serving on hiring committees where they have an equal vote with the staff. They quickly learn that along with strong relationships comes much responsibility. Kids learn that reciprocity is part of the social process.

Kara was a prime example of a student who benefited from forging relationships within the school community. When she first came into my advisory group, she was painfully shy, afraid to talk with anyone about anything. As our relationship developed, she started to reach out little by little. First she made some connections with a small group within the advisory group. Then, with added confidence, she spoke up from time to time in the larger group. Before too long, Kara was taking leadership classes and running the governance sessions for the entire high school.

> As I began to feel that I was in a safe, supportive environment, I
> began to feel it was okay to share my thoughts and feelings. When
> I reached the point of really caring about the school community,
> I started to see that it was my responsibility to express myself and
> even to become a leader.
>
> *—Kara, class of 1983*

All of the school's trips and group activities contribute to its focus on social skills and relationships. Many former students mention the group processing that occurs after school trips and group projects—wherein each participant gives and receives feedback regarding her role within the group—as having changed the way they look at themselves as members of an interconnected community.

> In processing, we practiced giving and receiving compliments and
> criticisms, which are vital aspects of any working relationship. I
> learned how to listen to others and take seriously what they had to
> say to me, and I also learned how to communicate compliments and
> criticisms in a positive way so as to be encouraging to someone,
> rather than discouraging.
>
> *—Andrew, class of 1997*

With so much emphasis placed on the social domain, it is not surprising then to hear alumni talk about the importance of relationships in their lives. Many hearken back to the connection with their first advisor. Most have learned to value the enriching qualities of mentoring relationships in their lives while others have become advisors themselves, in either a formal or informal sense.

> I often think of my advisor and how connected we became. As a
> result, I think I have learned how to take advantage of having many
> mentors in my life. Also, I have acted as an advisor or mentor for
> others in my roles as a family member, friend, and worker.
>
> *—Matt, class of 1979*

Many alumni say that developing a sense of accountability to themselves and their advisors, school, and community made for a genuine lesson in life. With all the talk about school accountability these days, no one seems to be asking about a student's accountability to herself and her responsibility for her own education. And who is accountable to the individual student? At a conventional school, who does a parent call to find out about how his child is doing? His child's math teacher? The school counselor? Sometimes, you're lucky if anyone even knows your child by name. At the Open School, a parent knows who to call—the advisor.

The advisory system is designed to build confidence and encourage the social and personal skills a student needs to pursue goals and to participate actively in the community. Students gain a sense of empowerment that extends to and is supported by the school community, and they learn invaluable skills that they can carry through their lives as adults. Some kind of advising or mentoring program should be the starting point for all schools that wish to transform students' lives and build for the future.

A School that Fosters Healthy Relationships

I wonder how many of us would look back on our high school education as a major influence on our ability to develop meaningful relationships. For Open School alumni, the influence is prominent, sometimes even profound.

Various themes emerge from alumni responses about relationships, some having to do with skills and attitudes, others dealing with social roles and obligations. The feeling that relationships are central to a happy and meaningful life is widespread among former students, and many report that the value placed on relationships by the school had a powerful effect on their adult lives. For some, it was a pleasant surprise:

> I remember finding it shockingly refreshing that a school would
> even allow us to recognize our own social needs, much less consider
> them a part of life that needed to be honored and factored into a
> balanced life. Until that point, it seemed my social activities had
> been viewed (by teachers and parents alike) as something to be
> tolerated and minimized as much as possible, please. It was such
> a relief to have social interactions respected as a perfectly natural
> need, not just a frivolous distraction. Accepting that this was a part
> of life then allowed us to put the social domain into perspective—
> not letting it overshadow other areas of life, but not neglecting
> it at the expense of other areas either. Was I always successful at
> maintaining this balance? Of course not. Am I now? A little bit more
> so, but not always. What matters is that we were taught to value
> balance, and that we were supported in our fledgling attempts at this
> lifelong tightrope act.
> *–Anne, class of 1990*

Trust and Compassion: We Know How to Relate

A theme that resounds in alumni feedback is that trust is the centerpiece in building strong relationships. It gives people the freedom to be themselves, and it allows them to feel compassion for others without the fear of getting burned. Many alumni point to specific episodes that made them aware they were in a trusting, caring environment.

> My early elementary school experiences had been socially
> disastrous in many respects, and my family was in no way able to
> provide healthy examples of healthy relationships. I came to the
> Open School fundamentally alienated from my peers, furious with
> authority figures, but also desperately eager to please. I was terribly
> lonely, yet longing for self-sufficiency. I was struggling with feelings
> of inadequacy, frustrated with myself and anyone who didn't
> understand me. In short, I was roundly mad at a world that I felt I
> was not made for. I was only ten!
> *—Corrine, class of 1997*

At school one day, Corrine learned firsthand that she was at a different kind of place, one that valued relationships and the trust that formed them. Realizing that a friend had run away from school, she quickly left the grounds without permission to seek her out and comfort her. When her advisor found out that Corrine was missing, he followed her off campus. When he discovered what she was up to, instead of getting mad and reporting her, he commended her on her effort to help a fellow student. From that time on Corrine knew that relationships were at the center of the curriculum. She understood that building trust was something she would be allowed to work on as part of her education, not something left for after school. As a result, Corrine incorporated relationships into everything she did at the school. The effects did not diminish in adulthood:

> I won't say that I don't still struggle with these issues, but, after
> years of advisors giving me genuine affection, despite my bullshit,
> I gradually gained confidence in myself. Through the intense social
> experience of trip after trip, the outlandish notion that I was not
> entirely alone among my peers eventually became an accepted part
> of my life. Through my experiences at the school, I learned how to
> be genuinely self-sufficient without having a constant chip on my
> shoulder. With encouragement from the school community, I began
> to discover strengths and talents within myself that allowed me to
> express how I really felt about things. I started to share parts of my
> soul that I had felt necessary to hide before.

The advisor-advisee relationship comes up again and again in alumni responses as a focal point of change. Many alumni point to the trust and confidence they developed as part of gaining competence in building and maintaining relationships, especially as it pertains to relationships with adults.

> The relationships I shared with my advisors were by far the most meaningful. During my youth I struggled with my relationships with adults, and through a trusting, loyal, and honest process, I emerged challenged and changed. Not only was I more confident about facing adulthood, I was excited to do so.
> *—Pam, class of 1992*

Alumni frequently mention trips as turning points in their lives. Support from experienced students helps kids decide to take some chances with making friends. Kim, who went on to get her Ph.D. in math and computer science, remembers her first trip experience:

> When I was in junior high school, I was very shy. I felt that there was no way I could ever break into any of the more popular cliques and that I would have to become a different person in order to do that. I insisted to my parents that I wanted to change schools, and the Open School seemed like the best option. The first day of the wilderness trip I sat alone on a rock apart from the other kids to eat my lunch so that I wouldn't have to talk to anyone. One of the kids, a girl in a leather jacket and Mohawk, came over to me and said that I could join the group if I wanted to. She said that I probably wouldn't believe her, but that she used to be shy too, so she knew how it felt. She was right, I didn't believe her, and I finished my lunch on my own. But I was also deeply affected by her unexpected kindness and was able to join the group and form friendships by the end of the trip.
> *—Kim, class of 1985*

Empathy: We Can Walk in Your Shoes

Being able to put themselves in someone else's shoes is another theme that resonates with alumni. Building solid relationships depends on it. The school is credited with encouraging empathy and reminding kids consistently that they have the ability to reach out to others and make a difference. Trips and other experiences that foster a sense of community are safe, supportive training grounds for developing empathetic skills and sensibilities.

The extensive travel program at the school served to enhance this feeling of empathy. The trips to Third World countries were especially powerful. I remember picking chilies with a family in Mexico and cooking an impromptu dinner with a group in Colombia—we couldn't help but relate to the struggles and hopes of humanity through these experiences.

The ability to relate to others is something that all schools need to foster. It is part and parcel of the skill set for a global future that demands empathy and understanding on an ever-increasing level. Schools also need to present adult models who can show students how to reach out beyond their personal world.

Modeling: We Model Healthy Relationships for Each Other

Models of strong relationships are plentiful at the school. Both adults and kids focus on the importance of treating each other with respect and compassion. Kids learn to value these behaviors as they begin to actively engage in the community. Many alumni say that they were presented with strong empathetic adult models for the first time in their lives. Seeing adults engaging in healthy relationships showed them that it was safe for them to reach out to others without the fear of getting hurt or humiliated.

Tom (class of 1983) is the director of a well-known art museum in Manhattan. He says the exposure to positive role models in high school has increased his capacity to get along with different people on the job and in his personal life. Like many other alums, he says he is not afraid to reach out in honest and caring ways.

> The Open School provided an inspiring group of adult role models with excellent communication skills. I learned to communicate with them as peers; they called me on my bullshit and I called them on their bullshit. They refused to be manipulated. They were passionate people that loved their jobs. Sure, they could lecture very well, but I really learned the most from their example, the way they carried themselves in the world. All of the teachers genuinely cared about my opinion, point of view, and reason for being. They cultivated the idea of fleshing out meaning in life, creating a life, and finding meaning in one's relationships. It is still with me to this day.

My personal challenges with role models started early on. With a powerful patriarchal father and a rather introverted older brother, I searched for male role models who embodied compassion. I found these models in friends of the family and even uncles and in-laws. The Open School experience showed me more positive role models whom I could interact with as a peer. Immediately, I could see the benefits for the kids who had been searching for these kinds of relationships as I had.

Healthy modeling by teachers who are encouraged to be themselves should be an important part of a school's charter. Children need to know that healthy relationships are powerful and possible, and they need to learn to approach each other honestly and openly.

Conflict Resolution: We Can Confront and Mediate

Learning how to solve problems, confront difficulties, and compromise is a large part of the Open School experience. Many alumni say they gained valuable training in conflict resolution from the many forms of experiential learning and from having to solve problems within a community that was basically run by the students themselves.

They say they learned that respectfully and competently resolving problems is an important life skill that involves both knowing oneself and appreciating the perspectives of others. Once they were more confident in themselves, they were better able to confront others in positive, honest ways. The school governance process helped. I learned immediately that it was okay to confront, argue, and deliberate about all kinds of things in governance. Staff and students alike tried to solve problems from locker thefts to drinking on school trips to hiring principals. Students learned early on that they were expected to speak up and contribute to the problem-solving process.

> In preschool, if ever a pair or group of us got in an argument or
> fight, Pat would sit us down at a table and have us talk through the
> conflict, each giving our side and then thinking of solutions. Even
> though I don't remember these talks, I know that they had an effect
> on me, because that's exactly how I work to resolve conflicts now, as
> an adult.
> *—Andrew, class of 1999*

The process was not lost on me either. Here I was, a student activist from the sixties, and I was reluctant or sometimes too cynical to get involved. All of a sudden, the kids were modeling *their* courage and activism for *me*. Like many reluctant students I was becoming connected with the idea that it was my responsibility as a member of the community to confront issues and help solve problems. I became more confident and started to get involved. I even began confronting fellow staff members about issues regarding school governance and approaches to kids. I was changing and growing from the realization that it was possible to get involved without becoming angry or hurt. It was even all right to be confronted and to confront myself if it was done with love and compassion.

It was a great practice ground for citizenship and personal growth. Trips helped too. Conflicts were abundant in travel groups that lived with each other

24/7. Students were presented with conflicts such as how to discipline those who broke school trust rules, disagreements about travel plans, and angry confrontations between group members and sometimes even between teachers.

On one of my first trips with the school, my co-teacher and I relied on the kids to fill the gas tank, wash the van windows, and do the cooking and cleanup on the first night out. The next day we heard the kids having an impromptu meeting and before we knew it, they were confronting us about not pitching in and helping. My initial reaction was one of anger—distress, really—at losing control. I soon got over it and realized that I was part of the group and needed to share in the responsibilities. I had learned something about how the school operated, and I had become more aware of my own ability to look at confrontation as a win-win situation and not just a constant competition.

The school culture made this possible. Schools that encourage students to become empowered and open give us hope. Meaningful relationships depend on the ability to confront and resolve conflicts, and the world is increasingly dependent on these skills.

Responsibility: The Buck Stops Here

Students learn the reciprocity involved in relationships. Within the richly interconnected school community, the ability to make decisions, proceed with plans of action, and complete projects often depends on one's fellow students. For instance, Passage meetings do not take place unless the entire committee, which includes several fellow students, is present. Peer pressure to follow through with commitments is an essential part of the process.

Once kids buy into the idea of belonging to a real community, they will frequently help those who are seemingly disengaged and floundering. Kids who fail to attend governance or advising meetings are often sought out by connected students who try to bring them into the fold. This sense of responsibility and ownership translates into life skills that are highly valued by alumni.

> The school fostered a sense of ownership or responsibility in relationships. In an advising group, one had to be responsible for other advisees' learning by being part of their committees and support groups. Everything was interconnected. Expectations were high. Everything was evaluated in a community context. I became an "educational citizen," because in a community of learners, one has to be responsible for others' success.
> *—Ian, class of 1997*

Building relationships is hard work. Too often conventional schools assume that these connections will develop outside the school setting. No time is allotted for the development of social skills, and students don't learn that relationships are two-way streets. They are only held accountable for grades and credits, not for character development. When schools take the time and pay attention, the importance of personal responsibility for developing meaningful relationships will change the way students learn and grow.

Confidence: We Have the Courage to Connect

Many alumni say that when they came to the school, they were painfully shy and lacked any social confidence to speak of. Yet they were suddenly asked to dive into social engagement and do things that previously terrified them. Mark (class of 1989) said that at first, it felt like being thrown to the lions. He puts it this way:

> When I first arrived at the Open School, I was paralyzed by shyness. Truth be told, I was terrified of almost everyone and only sometimes marginally convincing at pretending otherwise. I felt I didn't understand the rules of engagement, and I found most social encounters insufferably stressful, so I would often go far out of my way to avoid unnecessary contact with humans other than my closest friends and the few other people who somehow managed to find their way onto my safe list.
>
> Exhibit A: I was terrified of the telephone even more than face-to-face conversations because I couldn't read the faces of the mysterious people on the other end to see how I was doing. Thus, in the preparatory stages for my first Open School trip (Bahamas 1987), naturally it was I who was gently volunteered by my skillful advisor Dan for the duty of cold-calling numerous venues on the road between Denver and Miami to (gulp) ask if they would put up a group of twenty or so students—for free, no less!
>
> The irony of this was not lost on me, and the culture of the school supported me from all sides to embrace the challenge as an opportunity for growth. I sat in the school office and gave myself a crash course in the Yellow Pages, and conducted my trembling telethon right there where everyone could hear just how inept I was on the phone, facing all my fears at once… and got it done! See, that wasn't so bad; in fact it was thrilling to face my fear, and I was ecstatic to overcome it. I was hooked, hooked on taking meaningful personal risks. I wanted to do it again and again and again, and I did, for the next three years and ever since.

It would be a bit of a stretch to say my school experience completely
and permanently cured me of all anxiety related to human
interaction, but this much is absolutely true: I still have the same
courageous attitude that I learned then. When I notice I'm feeling
nervous, I light up with inspiration and look forward to embracing
the challenges courageously, knowing I'll get through them, and it's
just a question of how to relax into the zone of ease and grace.

So if learning to navigate and eventually overcome social anxieties
were the attenuation of a negative, the other side would be the
amplification of the positive. And one of the clearest expressions
of that would be the fact that I have become a community builder!
Not only is my life centered on cultivating relationships of
mutual support in my own life, but it is also dedicated to creating
environments and experiences that bring others together in
meaningful, healing, and productive ways. It takes a global village...

Oh, and I have lived almost every year since then in various
community-living situations, creating live-in support situations
that are analogous to Open School advisory groups and other such
experiences in my home. My wife and I currently share a beautiful
house in Oakland with three close friends, including another Open
Schooler. We are also in touch with several alumni in the area.

Mark has gone on to work for the Dalai Lama, helping to create community
resource programs in India and the Third World. He carries his Open School ideals
with him as he continues to walk the talk of community and global harmony.
His confidence, courage, and commitment to strong personal relationships
drive him.

The development of personal confidence is really the goal of all good teachers.
School can provide a model community wherein members help each other to
challenge, learn, and grow. Strong personal relationships are at the core.

Acceptance: We Know How to Accept Ourselves and Others
Acceptance of self and others is mentioned frequently as a lasting influence of
the school.

When I came to the Open School, I was not too sure about who
I was, so it was hard for me to accept people who were different
from me. I found myself part of an advising group made up of very
diverse people. As I became more sure of myself, I started to like

being around different kinds of people. The school gave me so many opportunities—so much exposure to variety—that I grew to love it. As an adult, I love working with diverse groups and meeting different people.

—Leigh, class of 1988

The manner in which the school conducts its special education program is another example of dealing with diversity in relationships. Carsten first came to the school as a middle schooler. He was a tall, handsome young man who just happened to be labeled autistic. Up to this point, he had spent his school days in a small segregated special program for severe, multiply handicapped children. At the time, special education doctrine dictated that a place like our school would be anathema to a child like Carsten; it would be too distracting and disorganized for a person with his learning style.

Nevertheless, his mother, Anna, was looking for something different, someplace that gave real meaning to the term inclusion. She hoped that the Open School would be the place where Carsten could finally be welcomed into an authentic community:

As a teacher and parent at the Open School, I could see how it lent itself to the idea and realization of inclusion. The school emphasized individualized, self-paced learning, but not at the expense of community cohesion. The inter-age, nongraded curriculum and focus on support groups seemed to offer a fertile ground for inclusion.

Anna took the leap of faith. Almost immediately, Carsten became an integral part of the school community, attracting friends of all ages. He displayed many talents and his warm smile filled a room.

I discovered Carsten when he came to my advisory group in high school. My group became a perfect setting for him to take off, both personally and socially. I already had a diverse group of kids who loved and respected each other.

Carsten was an immediate star, and his light shone throughout the entire school. His artistic abilities in drawing and music were given ready outlets, and he soon was performing in front of the whole school. He took classes he was interested in, completed all of his Passages, and even learned to take the bus and keep a job. In truth, he became more self-sufficient than many typical high school students. Everything our advisory group did, Carsten was a part of. He taught us much more than we taught him about kindness, compassion, and acceptance.

When he graduated, Carsten gave a grand performance at the ceremony. It was highlighted with his funky, high-pitched singing, which brought the house down. As parting gifts, he left his drawings and some of his poems. One of his favorites reads:

Good, good tree
Applegrass. Sunny day.
Talk happy. Boat paddle.
I laugh and laugh.

Carsten's drawing, "Happy Tree"

The Open School is a place where anyone who wants to contribute can be honored by the community. Acceptance comes naturally when you value the community and its web of relationships.

Respect: We Know that Everyone Is Important

Offering respect is another aspect of good relationships that alumni learned in their school experience. One of the norms of the school is to remember to show respect for others. In conventional schools, kids often are not treated respectfully by their peers or their teachers, yet they are expected to be respectful in return. Alumni learned that respect has to be earned and reciprocated for it to be valued.

> Because we had so many caring adults at the school, I strive to be a caring teacher. I am a Montessori teacher, and I realize how much the Open School has influenced my way of teaching. I had many opportunities to cultivate positive relationships while a student there, which is wholly developmentally appropriate for adolescents. I strive to create meaningful relationships and convey respect for all people, especially children.
> *—Elizabeth, class of 1979*

Respect for others is a key issue in today's divisive, fractured world. There is lots of talk about acceptance and tolerance but not much discussion about real means for inclusion. I recently heard a black minister who was part of the civil rights movement say that they were not after mere tolerance or acceptance. They wanted to create an inclusive community in which each member would be responsible for the personal growth of the other.

This is what the school tries to do by focusing on the inter-connective power that enables members of the community to become their fullest selves. Schools that become powerful communities can help create a better world, where respect and love are not just possible, but predominant.

Effects on Parenting: We Pass It On

The school's focus on meaningful relationships directly affects alumni's ability to be thoughtful, caring parents. The communication skills that students learn are lasting.

> I think the relationships I had with both teachers and students were the most important part of my experience at the Open School. That experience led me to realize that relationships in my adult life are very important. It also gave me a greater ability to cultivate them. I believe it has helped me be a better parent as well, being able to teach my children many of the communication skills I learned as a child, along with the importance of valuing other peoples' feelings.
> *–Sharon, class of 1982*

Respect for self and others also translates into good parenting. Alumni have learned not to be intimidated by adults, and they transfer that sensibility to their children.

> The Open School experience taught me much about parenting with respect and love. My kid-adult relationships at the school showed me that children should not be intimidated by adults. Instead, they should learn to trust in their relationships and themselves.
> *–Patty, class of 1977*

I learned many things about parenting through letting go and allow things to happen. This was especially difficult for me, coming from a very controlling family, but once I became accustomed to allowing kids to make mistakes and solve their own problems, it helped me as a parent.

Schools that influence their students' parental attitudes and skills make an important contribution to an evolving, sometimes chaotic world. Allowing young people to be themselves takes courage and commitment, and a school's culture can make a big difference.

Effects on Marriage and Long-Term Relationships

Many alumni say that their commitment to making long-term relationships work can be attributed to their experience at the school. Being responsible and accountable to one's advisor and one's community makes a lasting impression.

I learned the values of commitment and responsibility at the school from being part of an extended "family." I have carried these on in my twenty years of marriage.

–Leigh, class of 1980

My long-term relationship is based on trust, compromise, and hard work. At the Open School, I learned that it takes constant effort to maintain meaningful relationships, but in the end it is worth it.

–Tom, class of 1984

Alumni learned early on what is required to develop and maintain long-term relationships, and so it may not be surprising that there are many inter-alumni marriages and long-term partnerships. Many such alums say that they appreciated the shared values and the "Open School way of communicating."

The Role of Families in the Schools

While there is much talk these days about family values, little of it has to do with schools. At many schools, both families and staff look at each other askance, with mutual distrust and anxiety. Most school communities keep a safe distance from the idea that they can have something to do with developing family values. Meanwhile, parents often feel unwelcome as partners in their children's education.

But families are not only welcomed as equal partners, they are expected to be part of the process at the Open School. Parents' involvement begins with a commitment to their choice to come to the school: parents and kids choose to be there. Along with that choice comes responsibility.

Most Open School families say that they felt like they were directly involved in developing sound family values such as respect, openness, and support, along with a good dose of loving and caring, as part of their children's education. Others say that the school's focus on meaningful relationships directly affected their family's values.

The impact of the school on our family was immediate; the school reminded us of the things that are really important: the human skills of compromise, compassion, and honesty.

–New parent at the Open School, 2001

Other families talk about their experiences as integral members of the school community. Many have taught classes. Quite a few have participated in trips as leaders, or just as learners.

> I learned so much about my daughter, the school, and myself on the
> trip! I think the experience reinforced my family's strong bond and
> made us more aware of what we valued as a family.
>
> *—Parent of a high school student, 1995*

Other alumni say that they sought out places like the Open School, such
as the Sudbury schools or Waldorf schools, for their children. Many others
considered home schooling networks or, if they were fortunate enough, public
school alternatives such as charter schools or Montessori models.

For me, having my daughter go to the school was a blessing. My wife and
I feel that it brought our lives together and enriched us as a family. The artificial
boundaries of work, friendships, and family melted away for us as we became part
of a powerful, supportive community. It gave us the sense that everyone was part
of raising our child. The feeling of being connected to a larger family is a very
joyous one.

Why can't schools become like family centers? The Open School shows
us that if the community is determined and involved, it can create schools
with which it has a perpetual connection. All it takes is a commitment to the
school's values and a desire to place family-style relationships at the heart of
the program.

In the thirty-nine years since the school began, a number of alumni have
gone on to send their own kids there, wanting the next generation to have the
rich educational opportunities they experienced and wanting to participate
actively in their children's learning. Over the decades, several families stand
out as examples of this strong connection between parents, kids, and the
school community.

The First Family of the Open School

One of the founding families of the Open high school program is the Sternberg
family of Evergreen, Colorado. In 1974–75, when their daughter was in a
conventional high school, Gene and Barbara Sternberg, along with some other
mountain families, sought a more personal and meaningful education for their
kids. They went searching for a philosophy and a leader who could make it come
to life. They found and hired Arnie Langberg, who had taught at the Village
School in Long Island. The rest, as they say, is history.

Their daughter Jennifer graduated from the Open School in 1977. Jenny's
son graduated in 2003. At his graduation ceremony, Jenny sang the same song
she had sung twenty-six years earlier at her own graduation, "Teach Your
Children."

Corrine McDermit

The Sternberg-Boone family

The circle had been completed. Barbara spoke about her feelings for the school and its influences on her family:

> For us, the school became a connecting point in our lives. Our
> relationships within the school and with each other were valued.
> The school became part of the fabric of our lives as a family and as
> members of the mountain community. To see our grandson follow
> the same path was inspiring and wonderful.

Jenny says her proudest moment came at her son's graduation, when she realized how synergistic a place the Open School could be:

> I began to see and feel all the connections between the past, present,
> and future. It made all of our family relationships even stronger because
> we understood that we shared the same values about the importance of
> relationships in our lives. My advisor was still on the staff, and my son's
> advisor recognized the rich history my family had with the school.

Jenny's son, Logan, cried openly when I interviewed the family. His tears were joyous:

> My love for my family was magnified by my own experience at the
> school! I went through so many of the changes that my mom went
> through. My spirit came alive. My connection with my grandparents
> took on added meaning, too. After all, they were some the founding
> parents of the school.

The Grand Family of the Open School
If the Sternbergs are the founding family, then the Durbins might be considered the "grand family." For three decades, Chuck and Madeline Durbin have sent all but one of their eleven children and grandchildren to the school. They have trusted the school to provide a place of joy and nourishment. Madeline puts it this way:

> Our family has been constantly enriched by the school. In fact, the Open School is like one big extended family: a support system of "brothers and sisters," "aunts and uncles," and even "grandparents" getting in on the act. We have always felt completely welcomed by the school community, so we have remained active throughout the years. One of our daughters teaches at the school, so we see the connection of relationships grow and change, always in joyously personal ways.

The Durbins: the grand family of the Open School

All in the Family: Other Family Connections
Ruby Gibson was part of the very first graduating class of 1976. As of 2008, all of her children have graduated from the school. She says:

> I see the school as promoting the values of family and community. The Open School taught me and my kids about a way to live life to the fullest, with love and support from family and friends.

Two of Ruby's children had the same advisor who had worked with Ruby in 1976. Her son Jinji puts it this way:

The connections were amazing! Of course, I had a different relationship with Jeff than my mom did, but it was very cool to feel like someone really knew my family and how it developed over the years, someone who cared about us as a family.

Here is an abbreviated transcript of Ruby's speech at her youngest child's graduation:

Community and Fearlessness *by Ruby Gibson*

Ruby at her son's graduation

Our son is graduating today. He's sitting right over there. I am so proud of him. How incredible to watch him bloom into a magnificent human being! Thirty-two years ago I sat in the same spot. And some of the same people sitting in the audience *then* are *again* sitting here today. My mother, my sisters, and some of the early pioneers of mindful education are also here. I have deep gratitude for all of you . . . for your mentoring, your wisdom, for being true to your dreams. With special thanks to Mateo's advisor for her sweet and delicate care of our son . . .

Mateo's father and I have produced five children and five JCOS graduates. We have been in this community a long time, and I feel as if I am graduating for the seventh time! What a joy to come full circle again. I stand here as an alumni, as a mother, a learner, a teacher, and a grateful community member. How did thirty-two years pass so quickly? And why are we all still here, year after year, returning to this annual celebration? Well, I didn't know back then. But I know now. It has taken me all this time to truly understand the magic that is happening here.

When I was sitting where my son is now, I was scared to death.
I didn't recognize it as fear. I only knew that I was being given
responsibility for my life. In 1976, I didn't face even a fraction of the
challenges that the class of 2008 will have to deal with. There was no
oil shortage, no endangered polar bears, no fear of global warming, no
genetically modified corn threatening to collapse our sustainability. I
didn't even know what a cell phone was! In 1976 my dreams were to
gather up my backpack, hammock, and harmonica and hitchhike my
way across the southwest. Which my sisters and I did!

But I was still afraid. When I found Arnie and the Mountain Open
High School, I was a bit of an outcast. A high school sideliner
consumed with risky adventure, drugs, and boys. But it was nothing
that a wilderness trip, an inspired staff, and the support of our newly
formed community couldn't cure, and I began to imagine that there
was more to life, and quite possibly, more to me. The one-year
thrust of community interaction was enough to propel me toward
my destiny. I have published two books, traveled around the globe,
healed thousands of suffering people, and have become a leader in
my circle. But I never forget my roots. In one short year, the Open
School community left an indelible mark on my heart and soul, and
in combination with my family of origin, established and sustained a
belief that I was never alone. What a comfort!

Ruby's beautiful speech echoes my appreciation of the collective weave
of the school family. She describes the possibility of family and school as a
hoop of hope, a way of connecting the best of our culture to the creation of a
better world.

Most staff members have sent their children all the way through the Open
School program. This strong faith in the philosophy of the school is much more
than just loyalty. It is a wonderful opportunity to form a powerful bond of family
relationships based on strong values and shared experiences.

When my daughter came to the school, I was elated. I realized that she would
share the same life-changing experiences and personal growth opportunities
that I had had. Over the years, I understood how this common bond helped
our family connect and grow. Our strong foundation was rooted in the school's
values of love, compassion, and following our dreams. Other staff families feel
the same.

We took our kids on school trips from the time they were in
kindergarten. They became acculturated in the Open School values

and ideas about learning and personal growth. They also became quite familiar with the adult world by being around older kids and staff members. The whole experience served to bring our family together in ways we never dreamed possible. The school became the center of our family life. We all felt like we were part of a large extended family, with all the joys, headaches, and support that come with it.

—Open School staff member and parent, 1976-2002

Effects on Relationships with Communities, the Environment, and the World: We Are All in This Together

The influence of the school on building relationships extends to the larger community, the natural environment, and even to the world as a whole. Many alumni say that their relationships to their communities are based on commitment and responsibility. They are involved in a wide variety of community activities, including political activism to promote the rights of immigrant workers, environmental action in the areas of water and wilderness preservation, and engagement with movements for peace and justice in the Third World.

Anna (class of 1979) echoes the sensibilities of the sixties when she says, "If you're not part of the solution, you're part of the problem." She has remained active in community affairs throughout her adult life.

> I learned at the school to take my commitment to community seriously. I learned to take advantage of my opportunities to become involved and empowered as a leader and activist. Now I am part of many communities in my life as an adult: my child's school, my political representation, even my neighborhood's housing group.
>
> *—Anna, class of 1979*

One former student describes himself as having been, at one time, "rather apathetic" about most community matters. Now, looking back, he says the school gave him the confidence to develop his leadership skills, which he soon got an opportunity to demonstrate.

> I became the president of my college student government and the coordinator for several social-justice activist groups in the community. The Open School helped me discover who I am, what my values are, and my sense of self-worth.
>
> *—Aaron, class of 1996*

Many former students report that they were surprised to extend their concept of relationships to the earth and the environment.

> On camping trips with the school, a deep respect for the environment was encouraged. We practiced a low-impact kind of hiking. We always tried to leave our campsites as clean as if we hadn't been there at all. We learned to appreciate the importance of our relationship with the earth.
>
> *—David, class of 1990*

On several trips, encounters with bears emphasized the importance of living with nature. On one wilderness trip, a bear chased a student through camp.

> I was scared out of my mind! I guess we learned that we are not alone in this world. We started using our bear bags to hang our

Disorientation: the wilderness trip shows that learning takes place everywhere

> food, and we weren't so careless and sloppy with our lives in the wilderness. We understood that we couldn't just do anything we wanted all the time. It was a lesson in responsibility and respect.
>
> *—Barb, class of 1984*

The many trips to other parts of the U.S. and other regions of the world enabled students to establish relationships with people whose lives looked quite different from their own, and yet who shared the same desires, needs, and aspirations. Students were able to stretch their sense of community to embrace the entire world.

> The Berlin trip is still with me every day! I learned so much about myself and how to relate to people in a different culture. It helped me become more connected, not so separated from current events. As a result, I have studied and lived in Germany as an adult. I consider myself a citizen of the world now.
>
> *—Michael, class of 1990*

On a trip to Mexico in 1985, Greg (class of 1986) told me:

> I finally realized that my Mexican-American heritage makes me
> part of a large global family with connections and relationships
> everywhere.

Profile of Success

IT'S ALL IN THE FAMILY!

Heidi McAllister, Class of 1978

Heidi's emblem of success is sleeping in the next room. Raising her young child
to follow his dreams seems most important to her now. Her son has an excellent
role model; Heidi was able to start her own pursuit of a full, engaged life at an
early age. She was, in fact, in the first wave of students in 1970, at the original
Open Living elementary school. She remembers the early days with the same
sense of wonder and joy that she has today.

> I recall that the love of learning was so important to everyone in
> those first years at the school. The idea of a good student was one
> who was always curious, always searching for solutions to problems.
> The stage was set for the concept that learning was cool. The school
> naturally cultivated a desire for the learning process itself.

She remembers that the qualities of honesty, fairness, and good citizenship
were valued highly. She says, "We learned to be honest because the teachers and
community members were honest with us."

Freedom was also important. Kids were allowed to play and explore. She
quickly learned that it was okay to take some chances and try new things, and to
be creative and improvise. No one yelled at kids for going out of the box. Today,
Heidi sees that this freedom enabled her to see life as a great adventure, one that
requires courage and innovation.

> The school set the stage for a successful life as something that was
> always challenging, but also an exciting and fulfilling experience.

Heidi soon found herself among another vanguard as she participated in the
creation of the Open High School in 1975. She felt that she was in on the ground
floor of something wonderful, but the responsibility of creating a school almost from
scratch was sometimes daunting. She was involved with the extensive search and

subsequent interviews for the principal's position and the staff. As a result, Heidi and the other Open Living students got to make some very important decisions about just what kind of school they wanted for the future.

> Being involved with hiring for the new high school was hard but
> rewarding work. We kids soon discovered that being a good citizen
> and community member meant taking the responsibility to make
> decisions. Now, I see that being a successful adult means doing the
> same thing.

Heidi soaked up as much experience and learning as possible. She credits the school with helping her make thoughtful choices by demanding that she constantly create her own curriculum. She was also expected to develop her critical thinking skills and not to just accept the status quo.

> The constant meetings to determine the way the school would work
> forced us to think about the ideal school and what we really wanted
> from our education. This, in turn, helped us to see that we needed
> to think critically about all the ideas out there. This is an invaluable
> skill in making your way through life's many challenges.

She remembers going on the first school trips to Mexico and Guatemala, and recalls how passionate her teachers were about everything from math to geography. She got involved in giving back to the wider community through service projects, internships, and work at museums and with environmental groups. These experiences convinced her that, for her, a meaningful life would involve service and educating others. She discovered her passions for the environment and teaching, and combining these in her pursuits became her lifelong goal.

As an undergraduate, she studied environmental education, leadership, and the natural sciences. During the summers, she worked as a volunteer at the natural history museum and taught classes on environmental issues to public school students.

Heidi continued her education at the Yale School of Forestry, where she studied environmental management and museum studies, particularly museum education programs. When she completed her master's degree, she applied for the Peace Corps. She had had a lot of experience going to other countries at the Open School, and she still wanted to fulfill her desire to travel and learn about more cultures. She says, "I really wanted to continue to challenge myself, see the world, and serve other people at the same time. The Peace Corps seemed ideal."

Heidi (class of 1977) with her pride and joy, Benjamin, 2007

Accepting a tough assignment in Paraguay, Heidi became immersed in the Peace Corps philosophy of giving back and helping to create the world that ought to be. Instead of treating it as a two-year phase in her life, Heidi went on to teach and train prospective Peace Corps candidates in Panama.

After this experience, Heidi left for Mexico, where she taught English in a small village. Soon after, she was recruited by Mexico's forestry service, where she became an advisor and instructor for the Mexican Department of Education, designing and conducting educational workshops on the environment.

After several years, Heidi returned to the Peace Corps to run the environmental education and training program. She looks back on her educational and career trajectory with much respect for the strong foundation she gained at the school.

> After twenty-five years of professional experience and three
> published books, I still think that I got the initial drive to follow my
> dreams from the Open School. The school provided me with the
> early confidence and wherewithal to really go for it. I have worked
> and lived in more than a dozen countries, but my home base is
> always the school.

Along the way, Heidi met her future husband and, after many years of trying, finally had her first child. Now, she reevaluates her life in terms of her core values. Viewing herself as a lifelong learner has motivated her as her life changed directions.

All of my academic honors and work experiences pale in comparison to the wonderful feeling of success I feel as a parent. My goals are always going to be there, but the Open School taught me that a full, meaningful life has heart, passion, and relationships at its roots. Now I have a ten-month-old baby upstairs sleeping, and I get to spend every minute with him. I couldn't be more passionate about anything.

Putting Things into Perspective

On April 22, 1999—two days after two students attacked their high school in Littleton, Colorado, killing twelve students and staff and, finally, themselves—the entire staff and student body of the Open School marched five miles to Columbine High School to pay their respects and show their support. No other school in Jefferson County joined them.

One month after the Columbine murders, a group of Jefferson County principals and administrators met to discuss strategies to prevent such tragedies in the future. The questions of the day: How could this have happened in one of the most affluent school districts in Colorado? Why didn't we see this coming?

Columbine was a large high school. It was easy for students to get lost or hide out. Then there were the cliques: the Jocks, the Goths, the Stoners, and others. Some kids felt they were outcasts. Many felt that there was no sense of school community except for the pep rallies for the sports teams, which only about 20 percent of the school participated in.

How could these kids have gone so far? After all, they were not bad students. Perhaps they were ignored because they got good grades and performed well on the standardized tests. Did anyone really get to know these boys?

At the principals' meeting, the question was raised: do we have a model for some kind of counseling program that can reach all kinds of kids? Only one of the principals offered a response. The director of the Open School stated that her school had been conducting an effective advising program for thirty years. She added that every student had an advisor whose job was to get to know him on a deep, personal level. No one at the meeting took much interest in the advisory program, and the discussion went on to consider some packaged, formulaic counseling programs. It was as if to say that the Open School was an anomaly that had nothing to offer the real world of conventional schools and education.

The aftershock of the Columbine shootings rocked the foundations of the education system across the country. Most of the talk was about metal detectors and searches. Some debate involved parental responsibility. Little of the discussion involved the idea of personalizing the educational system and getting to know kids. In fact, if anything, there was a retrenchment to a back-to-basics, impersonal approach to education and schools. The social and personal domains were, once again, given little attention. The importance of relationships and community responsibility was pushed back into the closet.

In the days after Columbine, many parents were afraid to send their kids to school. High school students, fearing a copycat incident, stayed home in huge numbers. Tensions were high. Meanwhile, the Open School went on with its business of building a safe, nurturing community in which to learn. Students actually used the school as a haven.

> I remember, the day after Columbine, I couldn't wait to go to
> school. I felt so safe and supported there. It felt like walking into
> my own living room with my family around a table. I don't think
> a Columbine could ever happen there. At the very least, we would
> have known that something was coming because everyone gets to
> know each other so well.
> *—Kelly, class of 1999*

Other alumni say that their issues with anger and alienation were brought to the fore by the Columbine incident. They credit the school with providing them with a supportive, safe environment in which to face these problems.

> I had anger, violent tendencies, and difficulty making and keeping
> friends. The explicit graduation requirements highlighted the
> importance of relationships and specific concepts that I was to work
> on and made it easier to discuss them with my advisor. The freedom
> I was given allowed me to work through many personal and social
> problems. Hence, in my present and recent past life, I have been able
> to cultivate scores of meaningful relationships and have worked with
> and met lots of people without the fear or conflict that afflicted me in
> earlier times.
> *—Dan, class of 2002*

The importance that the school places on building meaningful relationships is not a cure-all for today's educational problems. However, if we are looking for ways to personalize and humanize our approach to education, we can go far by taking some steps in that direction.

According to some educational reform experts, children need to be surrounded with meaningful, stable relationships in order to thrive in the twenty-first century. A 2007 UNICEF report that rated twenty-one First World countries on the status of their children's well-being ranked the United States eighteenth overall and twentieth in the "family and peer relationship" dimension.[9] This assessment included such factors as the amount of time parents spent with their children and how helpful and kind children found their peers. Apparently, many American children are starving for attention. As families falter in their support for young children, who is picking up the slack? It seems obvious that schools must start paying heed to the value of human relationships and the effect they have on students' ability to develop rich, satisfying lives.

Most Open School alumni say they wouldn't be the people they are today without the impact of that first connection with their advisors. From that point on, they were able to build and expand their relationships into a meaningful web, or extended family, that reached beyond themselves to the world at large.

But Do They Go to College?

● ● ● Ninety-one percent of the alumni who responded went
to college.

● ● ● Eighty-five percent of these respondents have completed
degree programs; the national average is 45 percent.

● ● ● Twenty-five percent have graduate degrees; the average
reported grade point average is 3.44.

● ● ● Eighty-nine percent say that the Open School has had
a positive influence on their college lives and academic
performance.

*The pressure of not just getting into college, but
getting into a "good college," is overwhelming.
It takes over your life!*

—Senior at a conventional high school, 2000

*When I sent my transcripts (fifty pages!) out to
seven different colleges, I received several replies
that indicated that the admissions departments
would not even look at them without grades.
I decided then and there that I didn't want to go to
a school that didn't want to take the time to get to
know me as a complete person.*

—Brian, class of 1990

"The school sounds great, but do they go to college?" So often, this is the first question that prospective parents ask. The question itself reflects all of the fears, pressures, and expectations related to contemporary education in America. Many parents see schools as nothing more than a training ground for the next step. Scores on standardized tests, grades, and scholastic awards make up the requisite package—the ticket to a good college.

Everything tends to be geared toward the college track. These days the pressure for academic achievement begins to crank up in preschool. The importance given to preparation for the rigors of kindergarten is like something out of a bad dream. Parents spend much time shopping for the right school for their four-year-olds. The competition to get in is fierce. The effect on children and their attitudes toward learning have yet to be examined, but you don't have to have a Ph.D. to consider the consequences.

The high school senior walks a precarious line between getting into the right school and having some kind of life. Grade point averages and SAT scores take over. The stakes soar. The pressure cooker can take its toll on young people who are just trying to get a grip on life and its many possibilities.

Despite this intense focus on preparing for college, only eighteen out of one hundred American ninth graders come out the other end ten years later with a college degree.[10] Many so-called dropouts say that they were already turned off to learning by the time they reached ninth grade, so why continue school when you can start working instead? Others see a gaping disconnect between success in school and their real lives. College just looks like another unreal, boring experience. Why prepare for something that you can't use anyway?

In fact, the author and columnist David Brooks[11] reminds us that the required documentation (good grades and high test scores) for college admission will never be needed again during one's lifetime. He further adds that once you reach adulthood, the key to success will not be demonstrating teacher-pleasing competencies across many fields; it will be finding a few things you really love and committing to them passionately. The traits you used to get good grades and get into a prestigious college might actually hold you back from pursuing your goals.

When I think about my own college experience, I realize how irrelevant the academic part really was for me. I went to college because I was expected to go, but I just drifted through it and was not particularly engaged. In fact, as I reflect back, I did have many interests, but they were, in effect, buried, because no one, including myself, took them seriously. Like so many others, I had to muddle my way through the academic world.

As a teacher and advisor at the Open School, with the freedom to fly with my passions, I began to uncover my love of learning. I started to see that my love of jazz, cooking, and even baseball were intellectual pursuits in their own right. Suddenly, the academic world was revitalized. I began to see the intellectual domain as a toolbox that would allow me to express myself in all the important areas of my life—another set of skills to develop my personal growth. For example, completing my dissertation allowed me to advocate more credibly for something I felt strongly about—the Open School.

It wasn't until I revisited my college alma mater for the first time since graduation that I realized how far I had come. I was on campus looking to interview two professors for my doctoral dissertation in education, when I realized that I didn't even know where the education building was located. I had not taken a single education class there! The irony was overwhelming and just served to emphasize how little real effect my college experience had had on me.

While many people find that their college years are irrelevant to their adult lives, most of the Open School alumni feel differently. They tend to understand when they begin their education that it is their own responsibility and that formal institutions are only guiding or stepping-off places on the journey of life. They understand how to shape their own programs and make sure that what they learn is relevant and meaningful. Furthermore, they often know what they are looking for in a college program.

Getting in Without Grades: A Tricky Business

For Open School students, selecting and applying to colleges involves confronting the conventional world again. What are the expectations and demands at different schools? What are the strengths and weaknesses of different programs? What is worth accommodating or compromising for? Applying to and getting into an appropriate college tends to be an involved, arduous process for every high school senior. For Open School students, this is a time when all their practice with decision-making comes in handy. Alumni have been confronting the college admissions issue for over thirty-five years, and most of them manage quite well.

Consider the current milieu of high-stakes college entry, where even straight-A students with 1600 SAT scores are denied admission to many universities. Now, ponder the fate of the senior who applies to colleges with nothing more than a fifty-page transcript, or narrative record, of her high school experience. This transcript is a comprehensive documentation of all of the classes, trips, Passages, and significant learning experiences of the student's life during her high school years. There are no grades or credits. The transcript includes an explanation of the school's philosophy and curriculum and several letters of recommendation. The document is usually divided into several themes of personal growth that are significant for that particular student. Marie, from the class of 1999, tells about her experience with the college application process:

When I applied to colleges, I sent my transcripts and several letters of recommendation. One college admissions officer asked about my grades and credits. When I called to explain that I didn't have any, she just laughed. She thought I was kidding. I ended up going out for an interview. They were so impressed with my personal skills and all of the wonderful experiences I had had at the Open School that they accepted me on the spot. Later, when they finally read my transcript, they were amazed. Now, I hear that they actually seek out some kind of portfolio or narrative documentation for admissions. I guess there are so many straight-A students out there that they are looking for something more from their applicants.

A few alumni felt frustrated about college admissions policies. One alumna thought the Open School should have provided her with more objective criteria on which the colleges she applied for could judge her application.

When I was applying to colleges, I wished that I had some documentation other than self-assessment. I think this hurt me with admissions because I couldn't be compared with other applicants who had grades or credits. I think it affected my chances of getting into some good theater schools. I think the whole self-assessment thing can be rather self-indulgent and harmful.
–Kristin, class of 1997

Some students used creative methods to get into the colleges of their choice. Kim was a brilliant math student who noted on her application to a state university that she was interested in majoring in mathematics. They replied that her transcript had no grades or credits and that one of the math courses she had listed was "Calculus for Poets." Was this a joke?

Kim received a letter stating that she had not been accepted, and in her desperation she went to her advisor. He suggested she use her pull with the governor of Colorado, with whom she had worked on his Education Task Force. A week later, Kim received another letter, this time an acceptance to the school. Apparently the governor had made some calls. Four years later, Kim graduated with honors from the university. Shortly thereafter, Kim received her Ph.D. in math and computer sciences. She has worked and traveled all over the world.

I remember when a curious admissions counselor once called me about a wonderful student of mine. He asked about his grades and requisite coursework. After I told him about the school, he finally asked about the student: would he be a good fit at the school? My answer: "If you were a basketball coach, would you want Michael Jordan on your team?" Although they still rejected him because of the lack of grades and credits, he went on to be the student body president and a magna cum laude scholar at another college.

Many Open School seniors take a more circuitous route to admission. If the school they really want to go to requires grades for admission, they go to community or junior colleges and gather their credits and grade point averages and then transfer out. Sometimes however, when they achieve their ultimate goal of admission to their schools of choice, they are disappointed.

> My goal was to go to this really good and hard-to-get-into school.
> I was determined to get there, so I took a year at a local school and
> got my grades and credits. I was accepted the following year and
> graduated with honors from there three years later. But what was
> interesting was that I really didn't fit in there. It wasn't progressive
> or alternative enough for me. I missed the kind of community of
> learners that I experienced at the Open School. Now looking back,
> I see that I just wanted to go to a prestigious school when I should
> have trusted my instincts.
> *—Mystelle, class of 1988*

Some alumni chose to leave college programs that did not fit their needs. Krista had no regrets about dropping out of a program where she felt inhibited from making her own choices and designing her own curriculum:

> I was working on my goals with modern dance, but the school was telling
> me that I had to do this, and I had to do that. They wanted me to choose a
> major. I said, "Why do I have to choose a major when I am getting what I
> need by taking a variety of classes?" They couldn't understand that I was
> accustomed to being in charge of my own education. So I dropped out
> and pursued my dancing on my own. Looking back, I have no regrets.
> *—Krista, class of 1984*

Others say that their experience with making sound decisions influenced their choice of a college that was suitable for them. A significant number of graduates have gone on to alternative colleges like Evergreen State in Olympia, Washington, and Prescott College in Arizona.

> I had so much practice at making decisions that I knew how to
> research colleges and get the information I needed to make a good
> choice. I had learned how to be my own advocate, so I felt confident
> in the decision-making process. I wanted something that fit my

learning style and a place where I could have a lot of freedom to design my own program.

—Bill, class of 1982

Many graduates refer to their feeling of responsibility and ownership regarding their education. One admissions officer told me, "Your students always seem to know what they want and what they need. It's impressive how they can take over their own program! Other students are just not like that."

The battle to get into colleges without grades and credits continues, but the road is smoother. More than nine out of ten of the respondents have gone to college. Many of them have broken through by being accepted at schools that had once refused to look at Open School transcripts, which is a sign that colleges are now looking for more from their applicants.

When I recently walked into the admissions department with some questions, one administrator asked, "Are you Abby?" When I said "Yes," he said, "We've all read your transcript. You're famous! It's an amazing document!"

—Abby, class of 2002

Also, once a track record is established at a school, admissions counselors are eager to accept more Open Schoolers, who often prove to be school leaders and superb scholars. Many have graduated with honors, and more than a quarter have received graduate degrees—a great testimonial to a school without grade point averages.

Finally, the wide variety of colleges and universities attended by alumni indicates an extensive range of interests as well as a willingness to experience different educational settings. They have gone to progressive schools, state universities, and prestigious private colleges such as Harvard and Yale. (See appendix D for a list of colleges, universities, and professional schools attended by alums.)

Also, one might expect a high concentration of alumni in certain fields of study, such as education or the humanities. Many have followed a humanities path, but some have chosen dual majors with disciplines that, at first glance, appear disparate, but on second look make sense.

I saw no problems with studying philosophy and science. My experience taught me to see the connections among different disciplines. For example, when I did my Logical Inquiry study, I began to relate it to the creative process I used for my Creativity Passage. Finally, when I had to write my transcripts, I was prompted to tie

everything together and make sense of it all. I continued to see those connections in college, so my choice of study areas reflected that.
    –Dan, class of 1993

A breakdown of college majors reveals a wide variety of fields of interest, including business and the hard sciences like mathematics and biology. The fact that nearly 25 percent of the alumni have studied in the arts and education reflects the school's focus on the joys of creativity and the love of learning. (See appendix E for a graph of alumni fields of study and types of degrees earned).

How Do They Do in College?

It has been more than seventy years since anyone followed the college progress of students from a public, nongraded, alternative school. The Eight-Year Study, published in the 1930s, tracked 1,475 matched pairs of graduates from public experimental high schools and public conventional high schools for eight years after graduation. The study found that the students from the nongraded schools earned higher grade-point averages, "possessed higher degrees of intellectual curiosity and desire, demonstrated more resourcefulness, and had better orientations toward vocational choices."[12] In fact, those students from the most "wide open" kinds of schools, such as the Ohio State Lab School, were "strikingly more successful" in college than their matches.

Eva (class of 2001) graduates magna cum laude from Beloit College, 2005

Unfortunately, most of the powerful conclusions of the Eight-Year Study were muffled by the Cold War period, especially the loud cries for a back-to-basics approach to education after Sputnik sparked renewed competition with the Soviet Union in 1958. It seems ironic now that the "experimental" students were in many ways the most competent and effective learners in the educational race with the Russians.

Like their progressive 1930s counterparts, most Open School graduates who go on to college are quite successful. The average undergraduate grade-point average reported by alumni is a hefty 3.44. More astounding is the college completion rate: 85 percent of those graduates who went to college have completed degrees as compared with a paltry 45 percent nationwide. Additionally, a robust 25 percent have earned graduate degrees.

The Open School Influence on the College Experience

The influence of the Open School on performance in college was rated highly by the alumni. Their responses acknowledge skills and attitudes that helped them to maximize their college experience.

Freedom and Responsibility: Students Who Can Handle Both in the College Environment

Many alumni say that they felt better prepared for the overall college experience than their conventional school peers. They observe that other students were not accustomed to all the choices and freedom—and consequent responsibility—that are involved in campus life.

> I noticed a dramatic contrast between myself and other freshman students in the dorms. This was the very first taste of freedom for so many students, and they seemed to literally not know what to do with themselves. This was no novelty for me, and though I was *far* from being any sort of goody two shoes, I was ready to get to work, not just to party as much as possible. Many of my peers felt later that their freshman year had been largely wasted; I had no regrets.
> *—Anne, class of 1990*

> Many of the kids from conventional schools were there to fulfill parental expectations or delay their own entry into the "real" world. Not many of them were interested in the learning process. I watched many kids party themselves into oblivion or at least academic probation.
> *—Lisa, class of 1979*

Other alumni refer to the sense of ownership of their education as being a key factor in adjusting to the college environment. They understood that they were ultimately responsible for their education and that they would have to deal with the consequences of not going to classes or skipping their exams. Open School is college-like in that way—there's no required attendance at study hall and no one calls home about missing assignments or poor grades. Students either study or they don't.

Social Skills and College Life: Students Who Know How to Get Along with Different Kinds of People

Alumni say they had the maturity and social skills to cope with the wide diversity associated with the college social scene. Open Schoolers are accustomed to being members of advisory groups, classes, and trip groups with students of different ages and socioeconomic backgrounds. They have a great deal of experience in group situations where they have to get along with others to make their group function and achieve its goals, and they have learned how to put the group's effectiveness and larger concerns ahead of individual differences or social cliques. Stacy (class of 1990) reflects the sentiments of many alumni:

My peers from conventional schools were much more concerned
with class, age, and superficial classifications. The dorms felt like
middle school compared to the Open School. Cliques and boy-girl
B.S. did not go on much at Open. I felt so much more mature than
my freshman peers! As a result, I had many more friends and a
wider diversity of them.

Self-Direction:
Students Who Know Where They're Going with Their Own Education

Most alumni say that their skill in self-directed learning played a major part in
their college experience. They became adept at directing their own education by
setting goals, managing their time, and setting up support groups. In college, these
skills were invaluable.

Part of self-direction is learning how to make good choices. Open School
students have learned how to pick their own classes and make a Mutually
Agreed-upon Program (MAP) with their advisors. These self-direction skills
became critical when designing a college schedule on their own. As one alumna
put it, "Choices abounded at college and I was accustomed to making them on
my own."

Many alumni report that the school helped them to be self-reliant and
determined in their college pursuits.

> The Open School encouraged me to become introspective, which
> helped me to determine what was actually of interest to me on a
> personal level. The school also instilled in me a disciplined work
> ethic by forcing me to become self-directed and self-reliant in
> the establishment and achievement of my personal goals. The
> combination of these traits significantly contributed to the ultimate
> selection of my major course of study and my ensuing academic
> achievements; I graduated with high honors.
> *–Brady, class of 1986*

Numerous alumni note that their experience with self-assessment gave them
a valuable skill that comes in handy in college. They say that they were frequently
asked to evaluate their own work in college classes. Whereas students from
conventional schools might either balk or casually dismiss the self-assessment,
Open School alumni took the process seriously. After all, self-reflection was a
daily practice at the school.

However, some alumni reported that they had trouble with the "grading game"
they encountered at college. They were so accustomed to assessing themselves
and demonstrating their competence in real-world settings that seemingly artificial

measures of assessment felt unfair to them.

> How could a letter grade sum up my performance? I was irate!
> I had to learn how to play the game, and it was very difficult for
> me. I learned that I had to pay some dues and play by their rules. I
> resented the Open School for a while because I thought it was not
> realistic enough. But it's funny; once I got out of college and out
> into the real world, I found myself right back where the Open School
> taught me to be. I had to evaluate myself, and I had to demonstrate
> competence every day! There was no one there to give me a grade
> on everything I did.
>
> *—Terry, class of 1984*

Many of the classes, trips, and experiences offered at the school are
interdisciplinary, encompassing several areas of study with a broad approach to a
topic or region, as opposed to the conventional, more narrowly focused courses.
As a result, college requirements often include specific classes that students
have not taken. Sometimes it takes a big-picture attitude to crawl through the
bureaucratic hoops.

> What the Open School had done was instill the fact that I simply
> couldn't be in school just to get through. Silly requirements were
> *very* hard for me to get through. But once I did get through them
> and the space cleared a bit to focus on what I loved, I couldn't get
> enough and I couldn't have been happier. School was finally, again,
> truly a joy.
>
> *—Matt, class of 1990*

Academic Preparedness: Students Who Know How to Learn and Who Demonstrate Competence in Their College Work

Most alumni feel that, despite the lack of required classes and specifically focused
academic instruction, they were prepared for the academic rigors of college. Many
cite their experience with writing for their Passages, evaluations, book reports,
personal journals, and final transcripts as providing a solid foundation for all of
the written work required at the college level.

> My experience with writing was one of the big advantages I had
> over many of the other freshmen in college. For instance: I took a
> medieval women's history class at college in my sophomore year.
> It was an upper-level class, so there were several seniors. For the
> final, we were to write a twelve-page book review on any book that

we chose. I remember talking to a couple of the seniors before class one day, and one of them made a shocking remark, "Twelve pages! I don't think I've ever written a twelve-page paper in my life. This is going to be so hard!" The other senior was nodding in complete agreement. I remember looking at them dumbfounded, thinking to myself that my high school transcripts were forty pages long and these *seniors* are afraid of a mere twelve pages? That's crazy! Nonetheless, it was true.

–John, class of 1986

Other alumni felt they had a distinct advantage over their peers because they had experience doing research. Most freshmen had little or no knowledge of how to use the scientific method, formulate a hypothesis, and test it in the real world.

I found that my Logical Inquiry Passage was a valuable experience for me. I knew how to do an original piece of research. I felt quite competent using the scientific method in other areas of study. The entire inquiry process seemed unfamiliar to my peers from conventional schools.

–Robin, class of 1997

The ability to find and utilize resources was also noted as a valuable skill.

From doing all of my Passages, I was forced to find different kinds of resources and use them wisely. Most of my peers at college had never had to do this. They had always been force-fed their education in the form of memorizing content. They didn't know how to learn new things, so they didn't have the passion and motivation that I had. They simply lacked confidence to find even basic information on their own.

–Rod, class of 1977

Many alumni said they were so accustomed to having to demonstrate competence in their Passage work that they felt comfortable with the rigors of college academics. Sometimes it helped to take the exams and objective kinds of evaluations with a grain of salt.

At first I was really hung up on grades and getting the right answers, but I soon realized that it was just a game. When I relied on my good old Open School instincts about pushing myself toward competence, it all disappeared. I could play the game, but I knew what was

important. I made sure that my professors really got to know me too.
That helped show them how serious I was about learning.
                                      –Lynn, class of 1983

Another alumnus, who is now a math and computer science professor in
Cambridge, England, says that his interest in math and science was sparked at
the Open School, and that it flowered into competence and expertise later, in
college. The idea of having the opportunity to become an expert at something
was something he learned from the Open School. Although he never took a single
math class at the school, he knew what it was like to strive for excellence.

I took this attitude of striving for competence more seriously
after having opportunities to explore and follow my dreams. I
loved working on old cars; that's how I got turned on to math and
science, by working on old VWs with a retired NASA scientist
who was really enthusiastic about those areas. The achievement
of competence came later when I went for my Ph.D. In my case,
competence was driven by passion.
                                      –Byron, class of 1990

Attitudes Toward Learning: Students Who Love to Learn
Many people today are questioning whether the Scholastic Aptitude Tests
(SATs) and other standardized measures of achievement are valid predictors of
student success in college. Many research studies say no. Some findings indicate
that the number-one predictor of college success is the number and quality of
extracurricular activities in high school. It's revealing that what is considered
extracurricular in most conventional schools is part and parcel of the Open
School's everyday practice. Trips, experiential learning, and social activities
(in or out of school) are all considered integral parts of student learning. Really,
anything and everything that is relevant to a student's personal growth is deemed
important in her education. Most alumni say this integrated approach makes for a
fuller college experience.

When I went to the university I knew that all of my activities and
interests could and should be part of my education. I knew that
my learning did not just take place in the classroom. I could not
separate my personal and educational lives; this helped to give me
a big-picture focus in college that allowed me more academic and
personal freedom.
                                      –Don, class of 1999

Sometimes just the attitude toward learning in general is a chief asset at the college level. Alumni speak of their excitement about learning—their almost zealous desire to learn new things. Perseverance and confidence follow. "I learned to believe in myself and persevere because I knew that others believed in me at the Open School" (Brooke, class of 1991). Some refer to this determined attitude as a toughness that they build up when they know it's all right to make mistakes and learn from them.

Another alumnus spoke of the advantages of being allowed to pursue his interests in high school. This student had done his Career Exploration Passage on guitar performance and the music business. He had also created a CD of original music for his Creativity Passage.

> I had more direction than other students. I already had a good idea of what my passions were, so when I got to college I had a head start. My professors appreciated my dedication and my curiosity about learning.
> *–Patrick, class of 2003*

Other alumni speak of their ability to stay motivated on the road of lifelong learning.

> I was so certain of my motivation in pursuing my goals that I knew I could do whatever I wanted with my education. College was not the end of my education but only another beginning.
> *–Nick, class of 1994*

Developing a true love of learning in high school helps students move on to college with a joyous, open attitude. This attitude guides their studies and enables them to keep the big picture in mind. Colleges appreciate students who like to learn for learning's sake and who are not afraid to think outside of the box. And students who have learned to live without grades or credits have a deep appreciation of the learning process itself. They have had to rely on their own sense of what it means to be engaged.

Relationships with Professors: Students Who Are Not Intimidated by Adults

One of the most powerful advantages that alumni have over their conventional school counterparts is their attitude toward teachers and adults in general. The relationships between staff and students at the school are collegial in the true sense of the word. In a genuine community of learners, everyone is a learner, first and foremost, and everyone is considered a valued human resource. Moreover, the advisor-advisee relationship implicitly stresses the trust and mutual respect that promote collaboration and a sense of equality. This engenders confidence in students that serves them well in a college atmosphere.

> I noticed other students having a hard time figuring out how to relate to the professors because they were used to a much more formal way of interacting with their teachers at conventional schools. As for me, I was never intimidated by them. On the contrary, I wanted to get to know them on a deeper level and share my ideas with them. I always felt free to approach them and confident when doing so.
> *—John, class of 1980*

Another alumna put it this way:

> I saw my professors as human resources to help me in my studies. I took immediate advantage of the professors' office hours. Other students seemed almost afraid to approach them outside of class.
> *—Tamara, class of 1995*

Critical Thinking: Students Who Ask Questions

Another area overlooked at conventional schools is the development of critical-thinking skills. The proliferation of high-stakes testing and the continual standardization of the curriculum make it hard to focus on problem solving and the necessity to check out the so-called facts for validation. Open School students, on the other hand, are consistently encouraged to look at information critically. They are not afraid to question and probe. In doing so, they can be a professor's best dream or worst nightmare, depending on the teacher in question. Some alumni say that they sometimes stand out in their classes.

> I was in one class with some fellow Open School alumni. It was interesting because we were the only ones to ask questions and start discussions. Most of the other students only raised their hands to ask, "Is this going to be on the test?"
> *—Matt, class of 1994*

College professors respond similarly.

> I know, almost immediately, if a student in my class is from the Open School. They are voracious learners who are not afraid to challenge ideas and theories. They are also quite articulate in their analyses as they probe and examine the unknown. In short, they are used to learning for learning's sake, not just for grades.
> *—Professor of political science*

Taking Risks: Students Who Are Not Afraid

A lot of the impetus for thinking critically comes from the confidence that students gain from being encouraged to take chances in a supportive environment.

> I think the critical thinking skills I acquired at the Open School gave me the confidence to participate in college classes and intellectual discussions. At Yale, these skills made for a much richer and more valuable experience.
>
> *—Heidi, class of 1978*

> I learned how to question and how to be willing to take risks and check out new things. That really served me well in law school and as a practicing attorney.
>
> *—Joy, class of 1990*

A good university education asks for sophisticated critical thinking skills from its students. Schools that give their students opportunities to practice these skills also encourage risk taking. The idea that it is not only acceptable to question things turns into the realization that it is vitally necessary to do so. Providing a safe, supportive environment from preschool through high school helps students prepare for the college experience.

The Flip Side

While most of the alumni felt they could fill in the gaps in areas of academic instruction and adapt to college, there are some who felt they were unprepared for college. A few alumni say they resented the lack of basics at the Open School.

> I did not feel I had the necessary foundation established in areas such as history, biology, political science, and math that is needed when a student enters college. I succeeded only through determination, and experienced a lot of anxiety and a sense of failure as I constantly met new academic challenges. Other students were building on prior knowledge. I was establishing initial knowledge, which meant I was doing double the work. I always made it clear while attending the Open School that I was bound for college. In addition, I was a self-motivated learner. I was completely unprepared for what I faced upon entering college.
>
> *—Tina, class of 1990*

Although the school has had a basic self-paced math lab for over twenty years, some alumni mentioned a lack of instruction in mathematics as a major problem with their preparation for college.

I found that I had to scramble to catch up with my peers in basic
math. I felt that the Open School failed to provide me with even the
most basic mathematical skills. I think they can do a better job.
                                    —Mary, class of 1991

On the other hand, students who feel strongly that they are college bound
often take advantage of the opportunity to take classes at other high schools for
subjects that are not offered at the Open School or are just not available at the time.
Sometimes, they will take college-level classes at the community college as well.

My advisor kept me abreast of my options outside of the school.
My senior year, I took a class in calculus at another high school and
a music theory class at the local community college. I played the
grades-and-credit game and I got A's in both classes. When I applied
to colleges, there were at least some letter grades and credits that
they could relate to.
                                    —Nat, class of 1989

There are also some alumni who, although they appreciated the social and
personal aspects of the school, thought that it could have been more balanced in
its approach. It is interesting that those students who expressed the most stringent
complaints were usually the ones who performed more than adequately at the
college level. Perhaps they somehow used the adaptive strategies they learned
at the Open School on the fly as they progressed through school, or they simply
knew how to learn and had mastered the process of learning itself.

Another factor to consider when looking at academic preparedness is the
process versus content debate in education today. The Open School continues to
focus on the process skills of learning: how to find and use resources, how to set
individual goals, how to assess oneself, etc. Most conventional high schools and,
to some extent, many colleges, concentrate on content: what it is we need to know.
This can result in cognitive dissonance for students at the college level because
colleges require process skills to succeed.

Profile of Success
JUST ANOTHER STEP ON THE PATH
Andrea Keyser, Class of 1984

An account of Andrea's life and adventures is not your conventional success story.
Andrea writes poetry, studies spider monkeys, and runs a household in a small

village in Panama. She says she never set out to make a lot of money, only to follow her heart.

Andrea came to the Open School from a conventional middle school. She describes herself as a "loner" and an "outsider" as a teenager. Her mother remembers that Andrea grew up "while nobody was looking." Andrea refused to go to the large conventional high school in her area (Columbine) and said she would drop out if there were no other options.

So Andrea and her mother sought out alternatives and discovered the Open School, at that time located in Evergreen. Andrea began to blossom. For the first time, she was able to develop a meaningful relationship with an adult male, who was her advisor at the school. Forming a close, trusting relationship with an adult was exactly what she needed.

> At the Open School I learned that I had the ability to cultivate meaningful relationships, and that these relationships were necessary for me to learn the things I needed to learn and become the person I wanted to be. I had to seek out people to fill the gaps in my soul.

> Now, as an adult, I see that meaningful relationships, like good books, allow me to experience the world more fully. I am able to step outside of myself and experience empathy. For me, relationships will always be inextricably tied with education, mentoring, and creativity.

Almost immediately, she began to see that in order to lead a fuller, happier life, she needed to address some of her issues with her father. Her advisor encouraged her to confront the situation, which she did. To this day, she cherishes the advice and support she received from her advisor on this important personal issue.

> When I lost my dad ten years ago, I was so glad that my advisor had encouraged me to deal with my problems with him. When he died, I felt at peace with him and I was able to let him go. At the Open School, there was a lot more than just academics to an education.

Andrea knew that her intellectual skills were already highly developed. What she needed was some attention in the personal and social realms of her life. She began to take classes in art and poetry and signed up for trips with students and staff members she didn't know. She began to expand her world.

> I found that the key to happiness was not how smart you were; it was the quality and depth of your relationships that really mattered.

Pursuing her goals through work and giving back to others was also a factor in leading a fulfilling life. Andrea's advisor helped her arrange a position in a work-study program for underprivileged children. She also began an internship at the Denver Museum of Natural History in the zoology department. Andrea also worked in the greenhouse at the school, a program that developed her botanical skills. For Andrea, work itself became an essential part of feeling successful about her life.

Work is prayer. Work is honorable. Work saved my life during emotionally hard times.

When Andrea applied to college, admissions departments were having a hard time accepting students without grades or credits. Like so many alumni, she saw her official transcripts received with something on the order of suspicion and disbelief.

I was admitted to the university conditionally because I didn't submit a traditional high school transcript with grades. I was told at orientation that I was deficient in U.S. history and would have to successfully complete two semesters of it before I was formally admitted. So I took the classes, and I loved them! I really liked my professors, and I got to know them well. So that "deficiency" turned out to be an advantageous thing for me. I got A's both semesters. At the end of the year, I had to meet again with the admissions officer about my formal acceptance. He sat down and read my entire Open School transcript, and said he wished that all of his freshman students were as articulate and well-prepared for a college education as I was. I never had any more trouble with the admissions office.

Coming from the intimacy of the Open School, Andrea wanted to experience a large university, its diversity, and its various opportunities.

My study habits were terrific because I knew that I was the only one responsible for my grades and credits. I didn't go to school to party, and I never thought there would be a big reward (like a high-paying job) when I graduated. I signed up for classes that interested me, and I dropped the ones that didn't meet my needs.

Before graduating from the Open School, Andrea attended a seminar on how to deal with the real world after graduation, conducted by the principal. His advice was to take chances, make friends, have fun, and join the Glee Club. That little talk had a great influence on her.

I signed up for beginning fencing my first semester, and I was the
kid who never felt athletic! In fact, I had refused to go to Columbine
High School because it was considered a jock school. But fencing
became a passion—I even became the president of the university
fencing club and represented the school twice at the national finals.
I continued to fence for the next fifteen years, and my coach became
a lifelong friend and mentor. I had learned how to have fun at the
Open School and make sure it was always part of my education: to
enjoy what I was doing.

Later she signed up for home gardening, Chaucer, Russian humanities,
German humanities, and honors English. She pursued her central interests through
coursework in Spanish, Latin American culture, archeology, and creative writing,
and took two summer sessions at a language school in Guadalajara. She also
took as many experiential kinds of classes as she could. She spent two semesters
working with the Tucson Garbage Project, an archeological and sociological
study. She was also the youngest student to work at the excavation site at the
Homolovi Ruins (now an Arizona State Culture Park).

Upon graduating college with a dual degree in archeology and creative
writing, Andrea was admitted into an MFA program, with a graduate teaching
assistantship in creative writing. Her master's degree then led to an ongoing career
as a prolific and accomplished poet.

The creative and scientific sides of Andrea merged again when she took a job
as an archeologist. For eighteen years, Andrea traveled throughout the southwest
U.S. working on digs and "forging extraordinary relationships, handling sacred
and lovely objects and bones, and learning how to— accept life." After working
as an archeologist for many years, she decided that she had had enough with this
career and was ready for a change.

I had taken two years off to live with my boyfriend in Panama.
When it was time for me to return to work, I balked. I just couldn't
go back to it. The world had changed for me after September 11th;
my view had shifted. I started to think about the important things in
my life: my peace of mind and my relationships. I'd had a wonderful
career, but it was time to do something else.

In the past decade, Andrea has gone through many changes. In Panama, she
fell in love with the beauty and serenity of the natural environment. Then, she
met someone from a small village and fell further in love. She got married and
began to help raise her stepson. She has also continued to pursue some of her
interests, such as studying wildlife (documenting the behavior of spider monkeys)

and making films (making a video comparing the Quinceañera celebration of an American Latina girl with that of a disabled Panamanian teenager). She has lived off some grant money for her studies and some funds she has saved up from her years of working a steady job.

Her life contains the typical challenges of parenting and maintaining good relationships, but most importantly, she says her life is peaceful and fulfilling. She is living the life she wants to live. For Andrea, success in life means trusting and chasing your dreams and living life to the fullest.

> At the Open School I was forced to confront some chaos and
> confusion in life. With lots of support, I was able to sort things out.
> As a result, I later found that I could keep my work in perspective.
> I didn't set out to make a lot of money or create an impressive
> resume, but I was a successful archeologist when I was younger,
> working on interesting digs in the southwestern United States. I
> was also a serious and prolific poet, but I let it all go when I went
> to Panama. I simply followed my heart by falling in love with the
> monkeys, the area, and eventually, a man. I feel strongly that the
> work I am now doing is equally demanding and valuable. I still

Andrea (class of 1984) with a white-faced capuchin in Panama, 2006

write poetry, I run a household with a stepchild, and I return home from time to time to care for my aging mother. I have a great life, and I'm happy. Certainly, I consider myself a success. I'm doing what I love and I'm responsible to those I love. The Open School profoundly affected my ideas about success by showing me that anyone who pursued their passions was a valued human being.

Putting Things into Perspective

So, it seems they do go to college. Almost 90 percent of the respondents rated the Open School experience as a positive influence in their continued education. Most agreed with John, currently an attorney in the Bay area, when he said, "College was a natural extension of my Open School experience in that I carried with me an overall enthusiasm for and interest in learning."

This commitment to lifelong learning is reflected in the high completion rate. The sad fact that only 18 percent of ninth graders in the United States go on to finish college degree programs amplifies the follow-through rate of the Open School alumni.

The general feeling of alumni is that, despite some problems with learning to live with grades, the skills that were useful at the college level were the process skills and attitudes they had already developed at the Open School. The feeling that they were responsible for their own educations helped instill a commitment to higher education. The skills associated with self-directed learning gave them the tools to deal with unsupervised study and inquiry. Experience with self-assessment came in handy, especially when college demanded more reliance on internal motivation. Many alumni felt that their deep respect for learning as a joyous, lifelong affair served them well at college. This inherent love of learning for learning's sake impressed college professors and contributed to higher performance.

Also cited as prominent in alumni success at college was the relationship with their teachers. Their open, uninhibited view of relationships with adults served them well in the adult atmosphere of university and college life. Further, the social skills needed to navigate the dorms and the diverse population of students at the college level were already quite developed by alumni. They said they felt more comfortable than their conventional-school counterparts seemed to be.

Finally, the ability to take risks and the ability to think critically were cited as invaluable skills in the more mature university atmosphere of inquiry and independence. In fact, some alumni reported that many of their peers who had been straight-A students at their high schools experienced a lot of trouble with the freedom and independence of college life.

> I just knew how to live independently. I also knew how to get along with different kinds of people, and I knew how to motivate myself. Some other kids who were really smart actually flunked out because they were so used to being told exactly what to do.
>
> *—Alison, class of 1989*

Some say they have felt out of place in conventional college settings because these environments seemed too other-directed and stale. One graduate student put it this way:

> I began graduate school at CSU. Let's just say that I feel aberrant in that environment. I find myself around people who have spent their entire adult lives being manipulated by the dominant culture's standards for success, people who are willing to be molded into workers to serve the culture's dominant interests. I guess I have finally realized that a lot of people pursuing Ph.D.s are some of the most brainwashed people in our society. The lack of openness is very limiting to me, and I feel profoundly frustrated. I question whether I should be here at all!
>
> I find that I really miss the individual attention, the understanding, the options, and the *people* of the Open School. I truly want to continue with my education at the highest levels, and I think that I can do it here without allowing myself to be marginalized. I'm just not sure how healthy the stress and pressure are for anyone in this stifling kind of atmosphere. What I really want is Open School Graduate School!
>
> *—James, class of 1993*

Tina (class of 2002) said that despite it being rather easy to accomplish good grades at a conventional college, she was dissatisfied. She also quickly learned how to play the game, but it made her uneasy. She said that even though the Open School instilled in her a great work ethic and even a sense of academic obligation, she found herself feeling like she was cheating on assignments because she quickly learned what the professors wanted and just gave it to them. Now she says she has an increased awareness of what the school was all about.

Now I understand the importance of the omission of grades at the Open School. Real lifelong learners are not motivated by outside rewards. I now plan on transferring to a more alternative college that can meet my needs as a self-directed learner.

—Tina, class of 2002

When I came to the school as a teacher, I was already in my thirties. I think that if I had had some of the support and encouragement that this school has to offer earlier in my life, I might have had the confidence to go for my dreams and shape my own education. Instead, like so many others, I was content to run out the clock and stumble into adulthood. Looking back now, I understand that I wasted lots of time finding myself.

A place like the Open School might have allowed me to find my way in my college years. Many alumni say that the school helped them prepare for college by giving them the chance to start shaping their own lives. This seems so much more valuable than any advanced trigonometry class could ever hope to be. For most alumni, college was just another stepping stone on the joyous path of lifelong learning.

While most of the recent talk about high schools and college preparation has to do with grades and test scores, it's fair to ask the question: what can schools do to prepare students for the psychological and emotional challenges of college? What attitudes about learning and life can we promote? Schools that build a strong foundation in these areas can help students get the most out of their college experience.

Work and Life in the Real World

● ● ●Eighty-nine percent of alumni say they are happy with their jobs. Less than 50% of Americans say they are even "somewhat satisfied" with their work (2004 Gallup poll)

● ● ●Eighty-four percent of alumni say that the Open School experience has had a positive influence on their work lives.

Blessed is he who has found his work; let him ask no further blessedness.

—Thomas Carlyle

How can a school without grades, standardized tests, and competition even hope to prepare students for the real world? In some ways, this is a question that penetrates to the heart of the perceived chasm between this school and its conventional counterparts.

Perhaps, in order to answer this question, a brief examination of the real world is in order. In most situations, this world is the realm of work and the subsequent act of juggling family, personal, and professional lives. For some, it may include a search for the meaning of what a full, satisfying life comprises. Most workplace settings require a modicum of self-responsibility, dedication, and communication skills. Rarely does a boss come around and grade one's performance. Surely there are times when external evaluation is necessary, but usually it is not the only assessment tool. Especially in these days of flooded information systems, knowing how to learn, relearn, and unlearn has become almost essential. Big business has even bandied about the term *self-directed learning* as a prerequisite for the modern age. They say they are looking for people who are intrinsically motivated and self-sufficient. In fact, companies are now more likely to list *collaboration skills* than *competitive nature* as necessary tools in the workplace.

Of course, some of the old standbys for employers remain: experience in the workforce, perhaps some leadership skills, and the ace of spades—problem-solving abilities. No one suggests that dividing knowledge up into discrete chunks like Algebra 101 and Language Arts 107 reflects the way we use knowledge in our lives. Most adults know that in the work world one must act in a more interdisciplinary manner, incorporating a variety of skills and knowledge in a number of different ways. Learning skills in isolation or out of context will just not cut it. In fact, some of the more progressive employers would love to see more merging of the realms of life and work—a deeper connection with the meaning of work in the lives of workers.

Whatever one's chosen career, a full, meaningful life requires a deep examination of the place of work in one's life and which particular skills, talents, and enthusiasms one can bring to it. Young people who are accustomed to external direction and evaluation are less apt to engage in such an appraisal.

Some educators and observers have asserted that we are graduating lots of straight-A students who know nothing more than how to prepare for and take standardized tests. These high school graduates are lost in the workplace, not because of their deficits in trigonometry or advanced grammar, but due to their lack of self-motivation and self-direction. They simply do not know how to get started on their own. Some employers say they that they appear to be waiting around for someone to tell them what to do!

I know that feeling, because I was in the same boat. For years, after I graduated from college, I had had no idea what it meant to be self-directed. Indeed, at one point I headed out to San Francisco to go to law school because it was what my father had always wanted me to do. It took me two weeks of feeling uncomfortable to realize that a law career was not for me and that it was not connected with my real strengths or interests.

While living in Colorado, I went through a lengthy exploration process. By working as a school bus driver and a school custodian, I found that I liked being around kids. So, after not having taken a single education class as an undergraduate, I worked my way through a teacher licensure program and began my teaching career. But after twelve years of teaching, I felt that I was beginning to burn out. It was then that I transferred to the Open School.

When I came to the school, I struggled to find out just what was expected of me as a teacher and advisor. I was in an environment where I was encouraged to ask questions and examine my life as a teacher—something that I was not accustomed to doing. It took a period of trial and error for me to discover the new possibilities and deeper meaning in my work and to see how my work and my life could be more than just compatible and become truly synergistic.

Initially, I balked at what I perceived as an invasion of my private life by The Job. What I learned from the Open School is that work and life could mingle quite amicably in a full and joyous way. I began to see my workplace as an integral part of my community, not something I just went to and came home from. Like most Americans, I had little experience with genuine communities. It was something of a shock to realize that along with community came responsibility and commitment.

I learned much of this just by watching the kids grow and evolve in the school environment. I was amazed to see how quickly they discovered and developed their passions—at twenty years younger than I did! Feedback from the alumni often mirrors my personal story. Those who came from conventional schools speak of the revelations that came from the transition from an externally directed world to an inner-directed one. In their lives as adults, almost all of them attribute their attitudes toward work to the journey of self-discovery and self-direction they engaged in at the Open School. One alumnus, now a teacher, put it this way:

> The Open School struggle to find my goals prepared me for the workforce more than college did. I say this because the school was a real place, while college was just a contrived atmosphere. Work is not like taking a test and reciting what I have read and getting an A without any thought or preparation. Work is like the Open School: flying by the seat of your pants. Work is solving problems and communicating with people you may or may not like, not for the sake of a paycheck, but for your own sake. Work, for me, is always striving to do better, not just to get by.
> *–John, class of 1991*

Alumni have a deep respect for the struggle to find their way in the world. They tend to see this process as the continuation of their education and as personal growth. They aren't desperate to fit into other people's ideas about the world of work. They take their time and keep their faith—faith in themselves and in their place in the world. As a result, the vast majority report that they have satisfying careers and that they are happy with their working lives. Alumni say that there are seven distinct outcomes of their education—particularly related to the real-world experiences offered in the curriculum—that help them achieve satisfaction in their professional lives. They

• have authentic on-the job experience via internships, apprenticeships, and community work

- choose work that reflects their passions, due to self-assessment and experiential learning
- are self-starters who know what it's like to have responsibility and follow through on work
- have people skills—they know how to collaborate and work with others through group work
- have problem-solving skills acquired from trips, Passages, and community experiences
- have leadership skills—they know how to be assertive and take the initiative due to being given leadership responsibilities
- have creative abilities nurtured through the emphasis on the creative process

Real-Life Experience: Students Who've Had Practice

All students get a head start on the world of work by doing a Career Exploration Passage. This project entails an in-depth examination of a career field, including all of its good, bad, and ugly aspects. The student has to complete a self-aptitude test called a personal profile that examines the student's strengths and challenges as they relate to any career. This process occurs after the student has had extensive experiences and advisor contacts have prepared her to honestly reflect on her personal qualities. Students begin their Career Exploration Passage after having spent some time exploring their interests.

Once the student decides what career field she will explore, along with her advisor she arranges for a hands-on experience, such as an internship or an apprenticeship, plus a job shadow, in which she follows someone performing her job for a period of one or more days. The student must also conduct interviews with different workers in the field. Information about the skills, characteristics, and attitudes that might be suitable for the job is gathered from various sources. The student examines related career fields and outlines the necessary qualifications.

Then, the student attempts to match the career profile to her own. It is not a matter of deciding what to do for the rest one's life. In fact, the Career Exploration Passage frequently results in a revelation about the field the student is exploring.

> What I found out from doing my Career Exploration was that I definitely did not want to go into architecture. I am so grateful that I got the opportunity to get some real experience in the field. I saved a lot of time. Today, I thank the Open School because I have a career that really fits my life and passions. I see so many people out there who end up doing something they don't like for their jobs.
>
> *Wendy, class of 1984, commercial artist*

Other alumni find that it's okay to continue the search. Time, patience, and confidence make for a more relaxed yet focused approach to finding one's way.

> The school taught me not to sweat it if I wasn't on the prescribed path for people my age. When I graduated from college, I wasn't ready for a career, and my experiences at Open made me feel like it was okay not to know. I explored and traveled for a couple of years, and now I couldn't be happier with going back to school to become an elementary school teacher.
>
> *—Willow, class of 1997, graduate student in education*

Some alumni, however, say they found in their Career Exploration Passages a perfect match. Alethia (class of 1991) always wanted to be a pilot, but she had other interests as well. So her career exploration took her not only to commercial aviation but also to baking. She simply loved to bake and see her customers satisfied. Soon after high school, this experience turned out to be useful.

> I give the Open School the highest ratings on its influence on my work. I actually put myself through flight school by being a baker! I am now a pilot for a major airline. Talk about the practicality of the Career Passage! I'm a living testament.

Alethia (class of 1991), baker turned pilot, 2008

Other alumni say that the practical experience of teaching and mentoring younger children that they gained at the school contributed directly to their choice of career fields.

> I learned that I loved the little kids by doing an apprenticeship in the early childhood area. I learned so much about teaching and about myself and how I relate to kids. I am now a preschool teacher, and I think constantly about the importance of that opportunity to see what it was actually like to work with young children.
>
> *—Patty, class of 1994*

Students also have the opportunity to teach classes to their peers, with advisor and staff support—experience that is highly prized in many career fields. Some alumni say that their teaching experience at the school guided them in the pursuit of their passions. Lia (class of 1995), now a Harvard University researcher, reports:

> It was very formative to have the opportunity to teach piano and creative movement at the Open School. It gave me an introduction to considering the career path more holistically. I began to look at the different parts of my life, consider my talents, and decide what I get energy from. As a result, I was able to look more clearly at what the world needs and how those things converge in my life. I still go through this process every three or four years. I think it's healthy.

Schools that offer opportunities to practice work skills help students prepare for the world of work. Apprenticeships, internships, and in-school options for teaching and organizing all contribute to on-the-job readiness. Time spent on these options along with ongoing personalized assessment and evaluation is time well spent. The modern work force requires it.

Being Allowed to Chase Their Dreams: Students Who Know How to Go for It

A large percentage of alumni point to the confidence to do what they love as a prime factor in choosing their work as adults. Alumni say they are grateful for the chance to have become themselves at the school. They are comfortable in their own skins, and they often jump directly into the challenge of life after high school. When Nick (class of 1994) left the school, he had a fairly good idea of where he was going. He had been allowed to develop and pursue his deep love for Mother Earth. Indeed, Nick's travels had served to open him up to the earth's beauty and mystery. He went on archeological trips, the Boundary Waters canoe trips, and other challenging outdoor experiences. Through it all, he gained a profound respect for the environment.

> It's pretty simple. The Open School cultivated my desire to seek a life that I really believed in. I was able to find a love for the planet and a gratitude for life itself. I had a strong desire to help other people discover their own truths in the way I was allowed to at the school. I began to see my role as helping others explore and learn from the wilderness. It was my niche, my path.

During college, he became an outdoor-course director, introducing students to the wilderness as a classroom. After school, Nick began working at Outward Bound, leading trips and sharing his wonder about and love of the wilds with others. He is now a staff trainer and a well-respected leader in the organization.

> I am exploring the beauty of the world through simple means. Less is more. I fit everything I have into a small backpack. I walk through the wilderness to preserve my own wild spirit, and with that I go to work helping people realize that life is all about following dreams in order to find your very own truth.

> The Open School philosophy had a huge effect on me. Money is not my main priority, yet I still feel rich because I know some important secrets. I have learned about my place on the planet, and I feel that I am constantly on a journey of self-discovery. My work is through my education. Overall, the school got me going on the right track. I walked away from it feeling excited for life, ready to explore, and filled with passion!

Josie (class of 1997) took full advantage of her opportunities at the school. She took many trips, developed a strong relationship with her advisor, and became an important school leader. She was also well known as a wonderfully creative writer. Another love was biology and the other sciences. In fact, Josie did her Career and Adventure Passages on human anatomy and physiology. Part of her Passage work included taking some classes at the local community college. When she graduated, she knew she was college bound, but her horizons were endless. She majored in English and creative writing in college. When she graduated, Josie worked as a freelance writer. She also wrote for the local newspaper, but she felt she was in rut. A crossroads in her life loomed large.

> I just started feeling like I was lost. Things didn't seem right. I sat down and thought, "Here I am with my whole life in front of me, and I can choose anything I want. Why can't I be one of those people who loves her life and her job?" I knew this feeling came from the Open School!

The school stresses the importance of self-assessment because living a life of engagement demands the consistent reappraisal of goals, strategies, and priorities. Students learn to constantly look at where they are and where they are going. All of the Passages include a reflective approach to experiential learning. Students are encouraged to evaluate themselves just as they will have to in real life. Josie says:

> The Open School gave me the tools I needed to stop everything and reassess my life. Who wants to wander through life not asking questions, not asking yourself, "Am I living up to my fullest potential? Am I really happy?"

After this reassessment, Josie decided to change direction and go to medical school. She had a personal vision in mind—mixing conventional Western and alternative medicine. It was a bold new move in her young life.

> When I started to have fears about not being able to get into medical school and not being able to pay for it, I remembered my advisor at the Open School encouraging me and assuaging my fears about going to college. I had lots of practice making decisions, so one thing I knew was that if I wanted something badly enough, I could get it.

As an English major with practically no science credits under her belt, Josie signed up for the summer session of Foundations of General Chemistry. For the next couple of years, she plugged away at general biology, trigonometry, and physics. She went to school during the day and waited tables at night. She still managed to earn a 4.0 grade point average. There was one more checkpoint before Josie took the plunge into the world of traditional medicine.

> I learned while doing my Career Passage that I needed to get some real experience in the field before I could make that long-term commitment to medical school. I worked as a medical biller for a small private practice for almost a year. When it was slow, I was allowed to work with patients and take their vitals. This gave me a good taste of what it would be like to be a family practice doctor. The doctor there quickly became a close mentor and I had a lot of respect for her. But I realized something about the profession. I saw the doctor spend most of her days prescribing drugs and dealing with poor health after it occurred. I wanted to be involved in preventative medicine, helping people lead a healthier life, not a "drug doctor" doling out medication.
>
> I also noticed the anxiety of this reactive kind of medical practice. I was even stressed out just taking the vital signs and dealing with the patients.
>
> Once again, I felt the need to reassess my life. Was I being true to myself? Would I be happy on this path? Would I have any kind of life if I went to medical school for six to eight years?

Josie came to her next crossroads. She decided to pursue Chinese medicine and acupuncture so she could help people without the constant use of drugs and so she could have some kind of life of her own.

> Without the Open School, I might have decided to just grit my teeth and keep my head down all the way through medical school, a long residency, and a career in medicine because it was something that was expected of me or because I might be perceived as giving up. Fortunately, the Open School gave me the courage to stop going down a path if it doesn't feel right and the wisdom to know that it doesn't mean failure. My school and my advisor helped me to see that life's potential includes a full spectrum of living in the personal, social, intellectual, and even spiritual realms.

Intrinsic Motivation: Students Who Are Self-Starters

Alumni say that they are more motivated to learn new things on the job because they are confident in their abilities to self-direct.

> As a medical researcher, I had to be assertive and take the initiative where other workers might not. For example, our project called for a database for data we had collected. I taught myself the new program in a short period of time. I was motivated to learn new things and challenge myself through my experience of supported risk taking at the Open School. I created invaluable niches for myself as my employers recognized I was not waiting for someone to pat me on the back. I actually enjoyed learning for learning's sake.
>
> *—Aaron, class of 1996*

A self-directed program stresses that each person's standards for success have to ultimately come from within. This leads to a work ethic in the school environment that says: I am responsible for my own education. This translates in the work world as: I am responsible for my own work. Brad (class of 1988) owns and operates his own business producing fusion splicing for optical fiber. He says the school gave him confidence to chart his own course.

> I always knew that I would be working with my hands and that the classroom was not the best place for me to learn. So I started out at the Open School doing field work, internships with carpenters, and even working on building houses. I never got graded for these things, but I got recognition for working hard and being responsible.

I was allowed to go at my own pace, so I was more relaxed, knowing that I could achieve my goals in time. This gave me confidence that I carried to the work world, where I built homes and became an expert technician in a new technology. I now have my own fusion-splicing company, and I am completely responsible for my success or failure.

The idea of being motivated just by money or extrinsic rewards is often foreign to alumni. David (class of 1991), a psychologist with a Ph.D., says, "I learned from the Open School to dedicate myself to my work out of a sense of loyalty and integrity, not just out of convenience or the need for comfort or extrinsic reward." A project manager for a major entertainment company puts it this way:

Because of the school, I am much less influenced by the need to conform. I'm not afraid to take risks either, because I know that in the end, it will be up to me to be my own judge. I also feel that I am much better at taking responsibility than my coworkers. I see some of them playing games with their bosses, trying to be the "good student" and then turning around and creating the old student-teacher dynamic of the conventional school. I view everyone at work as basically equal, only with different jobs. I drive myself.
—Adelle, class of 1986

The wide variety of career fields and jobs represented by alumni is a testament to the school's commitment to helping all kinds of students achieve success in life, not just those who do well on standardized tests. (See appendix F for a list of alumni professions.)

Alumni Careers	
Education or related work	25%
The sciences or related fields	17%
The arts	15%
Business-related fields	13%
Social work, psychology or related fields	12%
Involved in languages or cultural studies	9%

The breakdown of the types of work that alumni are involved in illustrates a broad distribution of interests, with particular emphases in some fields. Nearly one-fourth of alumni work as teachers or in related fields of endeavor,

Chris (class of 1978), with prayer wheels

and one out of ten are in the human service fields, such as social work and psychology. Many alumni are in the sciences and research fields; the idea of continuous, focused inquiry is integral to the school's philosophy. The concentration of alumni in arts professions would be expected with the importance placed on creativity and freedom of expression in the school's Passage curriculum.

In addition, there is a large group of business people, mostly entrepreneurial types. As David (class of 1979) said, "I learned at the Open School that with hard work and focus, anything was possible. I also found that I had the creative, self-directed spirit needed to complete difficult projects while organizing and working with coworkers to get the job done."

These days, employers are looking for workers who are motivated from within. Schools that encourage such personal initiative put a high premium on self-assessment and experiential learning. It is that inner drive that counts.

People Skills: Students Who Know How to Get Along with Coworkers

Daniel Goleman, author of *Emotional Intelligence*, says that "I.Q. and academic skills might predict what kind of job you can get and hold, but once you're on the job, those capacities disappear as predictors for whether you will be a star performer or a leader."[13] Social intelligence, he continues, is the key to success as a team member and as a leader. The work of many creative geniuses, such as the Wright brothers and George Bernard Shaw, was shaped and advanced far more by social skills than by academic training.

In this light, it is no surprise that most alumni refer to their sophisticated social skills as major assets on their jobs and in their workplaces. Graduates' strong commitment to building positive relationships takes them far in the real world. Some alumni say that if there was only one thing they could take away with them from the school, it would be those all-important social skills.

The school's trips, groups, and experiential projects are designed to involve students in group work where one must rely on others to get the job done. Trip planning and living away from home for long periods of time in closely knit groups takes lots of patience, tolerance, and collaboration. Many alumni remember those experiences.

> I remember the colonial trip like it was yesterday. Twenty-seven kids packed into three vans traveling across the country through twenty-seven states! I learned a lot about dealing with different kinds of people. When you are with the same group for four and a half weeks, you have to learn how to be patient and how to share with others. I learned a lot about American history, but I learned even more about life itself. Even though I didn't graduate from the school (I got my GED), I still carry these group skills with me today on the job and in all areas of my life.
> *—Todd, class of 1978*

Alumni frequently discuss the "people parts" of their jobs. One private businessperson says that she learned to deal with people "with whom I didn't necessarily get along" from her school experience with groups and advising. Respect for others comes up as a key factor in communications skills and overall efficacy on the job. One exchange student from Italy, now a director of a world relief organization, put it this way:

> The Open School had a great influence on my work. I learned to always put the person at the center of my work. I once worked with American companies in the fields of cost reduction and productivity improvement. I made sure that I consistently considered the human element of any strategy or restructuring technique. I learned that people come first, even in the private sector, and if you show respect for others, it will make your work more productive.
> *—Antonella, class of 1982*

Students are constantly asked to collaborate with others, often in challenging circumstances. Brooke, now a sales supervisor, found these experiences useful in the private sector.

> Confrontation and active-listening skills are the most important things on my job. As a supervisor, I have had to work with people under stressful conditions. Needless to say, I have faced some tough challenges. I am the one who has to take people aside and confront them with professional and, sometimes, even personal issues.
>
> From the Open School, I learned to do this in a nonthreatening, growth-producing way. My employees have always felt free to

come to me with their problems and concerns because they know
that I value and respect their personal growth. I'm so glad that I had
practice with these skills at the school.
—Brooke, class of 1993

Other social skills, such as speaking in public and dealing with conflicts, have
influenced alumni from lawyers to plumbers. Practice in a supportive environment
is the key. As an advisor, I learned to take some chances with expressing myself.
I changed from a rather shy introvert to a confident public speaker because I felt
that I had a safe place in which to practice. This opportunity to gain confidence
in self-expression and learn how to embrace constructive criticism changed many
lives. Mark, a master plumber, states:

> In my job, I have to communicate clearly with clients and
> coworkers every day. I learned to express myself without fear in my
> experiences with school governance and advising. I also knew that
> criticism was not a bad thing if it could help you grow and change.
> *—Mark, class of 1997*

However, one alumna, now a computer programmer, said she had difficulties
translating the skills and attitudes she learned at the school to her work setting.
When she first entered the work world, she found some things "shocking." She
had a difficult time adjusting to the way people acted on the job. She says the
school set her up for disappointment.

> Relating to my coworkers and bosses was also a very large
> adjustment, and in this, my experience at the Open School made
> things more difficult. Relationships in the school were very relaxed
> and comfortable, and I seldom felt I was being judged or pressured
> to conform. Work relationships are entirely the opposite, and it is
> critical to maintain a good impression and a professional attitude
> with all colleagues, supervisors, and customers.

> This was no surprise to me, and I began work knowing that this was
> the case, but I found it very hard to strike a balance between being
> myself and maintaining a professional attitude. In most cases I felt I
> had to suppress things that came naturally to me—hugging people,
> expressing honest opinions about things, being spontaneous in my
> actions—and I often went too far toward being stiff and formal in
> my work relationships. That formality has furthered my success
> in business, but has often left me feeling isolated and friendless at

work. I think that conventional schools are more formal to begin
with, and people who have attended them are better able to reconcile
the need to be businesslike with the need to be social.

–Jean Anne, class of 1979

Schools that focus on personal and social skills tend to develop students who
are flexible and cooperative in the work place. Employers are looking for workers
with the people skills to succeed on the job. Schools can do their jobs by making
these skills part of their standards and curricula.

Problem Solving: Students Who Can Get the Job Done

The school puts its members in situations where real problems need to be solved.
School trips often involve a multitude of issues that need to be resolved on the run.

I remember well one of my first trips with the school, to the Copper Canyon
in Mexico. We had to decide how to get our vans through the canyon on the
railroad. We had to put the school vans, loaded with food, supplies, and even
students, on a flatbed railroad car on the Chihuahua Pacifico train. When we
missed the ferry in Topalabampa, we had to decide what to do. The next boat
left in three days.

The whole group discussed our options and came to the consensus that we
should head up the coast. This led to more adventures and more problems to be
solved. We had to find a place to stay, decide how to budget our money for the
extra days of travel, and make some adjustments in the remainder of our itinerary,
which included the focus of our trip—several days of whale-watching in the Baja.
Meanwhile, we had a medical emergency on our hands when one of the students
cut his hand on a pop bottle. Everything turned out all right. Students scouted
places to stay and we ended up under the awning of a generous Mexican family.
We also a found a medical clinic in a small town and took care of the student's
hand. The point is, we were all in it together and we couldn't rely on one person
to make a unilateral decision.

Later, however, when we discovered that a number of students had been
drinking on the sly, we had to make another decision. We decided to send the
students home by plane, at their parents' expense. This eventually became a
precedent by which offenders of the Big Three—no drugs, sex, or alcohol on
school trips—were treated.

On another trip, a sailing adventure in the Bahamas, our group project was to
rescue a sea turtle that had somehow become trapped in a lagoon. Before we left,
we decided to set up nets and observation systems to track and catch the turtle. It
became a lesson in problem solving that was at once exciting and meaningful.

School governance is another forum for problem solving. While many
conventional-school student governments are elected bodies of elite students,

Open School leadership classes are open to anyone who wants to join. And where a student council might vote on the school colors or a date for the homecoming dance, Open School governance takes on important problems. Critical decisions—like what to do about a theft in the school community, how to hire a new principal, or what classes to offer in the next schedule—are presented for discussion and resolution.

In fact, there have been times throughout the history of the school when everything is dropped for an emergency governance session that lasts for several days. Students and staff alike realize that the big picture is more important than the daily routine. At times like these everyone has the opportunity to pitch in and solve problems.

Many alumni remember specific instances when they learned the value of directly facing and solving problems rather than just ignoring them and going on with the routine. Pam (class of 1992) is a business manager who, as one of the few women in a position of power at her company, must assert herself at work. She recalls a school trip to Cortez when she witnessed her advisor constructively confront a student who had broken one of the school rules. Pam then watched as her advisor relied on the group to collaboratively deal with the problem. Pam says she "took a little piece" of that experience and has used it more than once as inspiration and direction for positive problem solving on her job.

Pam also reports that her colleagues at work were, at first, reluctant to embrace her collaborative approach to problem solving:

> I remember the shock factor that raised some eyebrows at work. I
> realized very quickly that some members of the good ol' boys network
> did not appreciate collaborative, honest problem solving. In fact,
> group discussions were strongly discouraged, as was any other form of
> "emotional talk." I learned how to stop and listen to what others had to
> say. Now that I own my own business, I have a deep respect for those
> who work with me. I value what they have to say, so when I need to
> solve a problem, I know I can rely on them. Being open and honest is a
> way of life at the Open School. I use it in my work every day.

Many professions demand a facility in problem solving. Students who are now high-profile executive chefs worked in the school's Munchie food program—a self-directed, healthy lunch program run totally by the staff and students. They say that they learned how to solve problems through on-the-job training and preparing and serving food to the entire school on a daily basis.

> The food service industry is very fast paced and demanding, with
> crazy hours and even crazier coworkers. I think that being an Open

School student gave me a different way to cope with all the stressful things that happen in a kitchen. I really think the ability to look at a problem and come up with different ways to solve it was a skill I learned there. Also, perhaps more importantly, the ability to impart that knowledge to my colleagues without offending them is invaluable.

–Melissa, class of 1996

Leadership Skills: Students Who Take the Lead

The opportunity to lead does not readily present itself at conventional schools. Usually, only the most popular or the most ambitious students are the ones who become school leaders. At the Open School, however, leadership is an open invitation. Whether in the small groups of advising or the larger arena of governance, all students have the opportunity to step forward as leaders. Most take the plunge knowing that leadership is really a community-shared responsibility. Almost all of the alumni remember running governance meetings or taking a leadership class.

As a teacher, my own growth as a leader was substantial. At first, as a conventional-school refugee, I dreaded staff meetings; I was used to them being occasions where many staff members dozed off listening to the principal's dull litany of announcements. I changed slowly from one who was reluctant to share anything to one who was eager to participate. I began to thrive. Like the students who flowered at the Open School after transferring from conventional school settings, I started to gain the confidence to contribute. I learned how to trust my expertise, experience, and, most importantly, my instincts as a veteran teacher.

Many alumni point to leadership skills as key factors in their development on the job. In fact, there is a sense of empowerment associated with self-directed learning. Some alumni say they had the confidence to crash the boardroom. This is probably not what Big Business has in mind when they clamor for self-directed workers. Corrine (class of 1997) simply insisted that her skills, experience, and participation be taken seriously by the board of directors with whom she worked.

Does it sound snobbish to say that I wish there were more grown-ups in the workforce? I'm grateful that I learned a lot about healthy work politics at the Open School.

When I went to work for a nationwide service organization, I was quickly introduced into the politics of a rather conservative board of directors. They did not seem eager for my participation or input as a worker.

I did, however, have a huge advantage in dealing with a skeptical board. I had experienced what it was like to be part of a genuine community at the school. I had attended staff and budget meetings, been on hiring committees, and even spoken at district school board meetings. I was not about to be denied as an equal participant in my work as an adult. I had learned that I had to be involved in the decision-making process.

Many alumni who had never seen themselves as leaders emerged as effective leaders when given the chance to do so. Some developed slowly as they benefited from the practice and experience offered at the school. Aaron, a social activist and a Ph.D. candidate, says:

> I did not really blossom as a leader until I went to college. The Open School showed me that I could excel as a leader if I just took the chance. I became the president of the university student government. I organized and led several social justice activist groups. I had cultivated a belief in myself as a leader and now there is no looking back.
>
> *—Aaron, class of 1997*

This kind of confidence is contagious. The most effective leaders are those who can inspire others to lead and who empower others to take responsibility for their own lives. Heidi (class of 1978), an environmental manager who works in Mexico, says that her leadership qualities have inspired confidence in both her colleagues and supervisors: "People enjoy working with me; they trust and respect my decisions. They also feel that I inspire confidence in them as coworkers."

Words like *hardworking, reliable, resourceful*, and *self-starter* are commonly used by employers and coworkers to describe alumni. These are wonderful descriptors that run across the professions, from plumbers and carpenters to businesspeople and attorneys.

> I have been really impressed by the students from the Open School who have worked for me. It's not just that they seem to be so committed and diligent; it's that they take the lead in training and setting good examples for other workers.
>
> *—Restaurant manager, 1992*

Opportunities for leadership are sorely lacking at most schools these days. They're simply not part of the standardized curriculum. In contrast, the work force is crying for leaders—workers who aren't afraid to step up and make decisions. Today's schools should provide leadership options for all students and make it clear that everyone has something to contribute. Our future depends on it.

Creativity: Students Who Are Confident in Using the Creative Process on the Job

Creativity is a highly valued commodity at the school. The Creativity Passage is considered an important step in gaining confidence in self-expression. Students

Astrid (class of 1988), professional skydiver

also learn that embracing new ways of looking at things is inherent to both the creative process and problem solving. Plus, the connection between creativity and the other areas of life is emphasized as the student weaves together all his Passages when he writes his final transcript.

Many alumni say that confidence in their creative powers has helped them to become more innovative and daring workers.

I'm a businessman who is constantly forced to use creative ways to approach problems and issues of growth and competition. At the Open School I was always encouraged to be creative and take risks with new ideas. This attitude toward the process is something I don't think would have been encouraged at a conventional school.

–John, class of 1980

Byron (class of 1990) made his way as a professor of mathematics. Recently, he came up with a new theory in his field. He credits the school for allowing him the freedom to create and take some chances with his academic inquiries.

I definitely gained the confidence in my creative abilities at the school. It was even nurtured and expected to develop. Now, I'm the one who takes chances in my field; I trust and cherish my creativity. It's a life force for me, and my colleagues respect me for it.

Developing creativity in our schools should be one of the most important standards. Employers today bemoan the lack of creativity and innovation of students coming out of high school. Schools can set kids free to come up with their own creative solutions to the growingly complex problems of today's world.

Job Satisfaction: Students Who Like Their Work

The idea of being happy with one's job is foreign to many Americans. Many feel trapped in jobs that they perceive as deadening and futile. They often wonder how they ended up in their professions. They see little or no connection between their working and personal lives.

Theories of self-directed learning state that curiosity and a drive to learn are natural human instincts. The ideal is that people who have been encouraged to go after their dreams at an early age will carry that process with them as they become adults; they won't settle for anything less than a fully engaging life.

Guy (1992) teaching in Japan, 2007

Alumni feedback confirms a high level of job satisfaction among these former students. Much of this contentment involves their knack for finding a career that fits with their personal worldview or philosophy of life. Mark (class of 1979), a solar resource manager, had a clear vision for the kind of work he wanted to do.

Feeling like the school taught him that he could do anything he was committed and passionate about, Mark decided he wanted to do something "transformative." His work with solar energy easily fit the bill.

Some alumni began their job journey with one career and then shifted to another that seemed more suitable. In this respect, Joanne's story (class of 1978) is not unusual. After high school she worked for a petroleum information office before going on to college. During college she worked at a sandwich shop and cleaned homes and offices. When she went to law school, Joanne worked at a food cooperative and interned at the Vermont Supreme Court. During this time, she realized she had a need to be involved in community groups and collaboration.

> While studying for the bar exam, I worked as a legal consultant for a large pharmaceutical firm that was involved in antitrust litigation. I realized that this was not in line with my spirit, so I returned to working at another food co-op, did some legal work on the side, and returned home to start a family.

Returning home, Joanne found her heart was more in the nonprofit sector. She decided to wrap her interests in family and community together into a more cohesive, meaningful whole.

> Now I am "home" where I work, at an organization called Parent-to-Parent. It is a nonprofit that serves families with children who have disabilities or special needs. I love the people I work with, and I often equate my situation with the Open School because there are so many like-minded people around me. I appreciate the camaraderie and the feeling of being with kindred spirits. At the school, my eyes were opened to what was possible as far as integrating what you loved with your life's work, and once I found it in my life, I never looked back.

The idea that one can achieve some kind of balance and integration between work and life is essential to job satisfaction. Open Schoolers have to contend with lots of ambiguity—there are not a lot of hard and fast rules and structures to hang on to. Students get much practice making critical decisions about how to mix their work with their ideals and lifestyles. Some have to battle their own demons. Becky, a music teacher, says that she learned how to find that balance by becoming aware of her personal hang-ups at the school.

> When I first started working, I found myself reverting to my perfectionism and the feeling that I had to be a huge success at every aspect of my job. I think that, without the skills that I learned at school, I would have gone on like this forever. As I've grown into the working world, however, I have been able to apply the things I learned about balancing my life and letting the little things go. Now I'm much happier.
>
> *–Becky, class of 1997*

Another alumna says that her decisions regarding jobs involved values that were nurtured in her education. She had learned that interests were more important than money when it came to work and its place in a healthy lifestyle. In fact, for many alumni, job satisfaction is commensurate with happiness. Without the passion, it just doesn't seem right.

> After I had accepted a job as a teacher at one school, I was offered
> an interview at a well-known school in a more affluent school
> district. I declined the interview even though I hadn't signed a
> contract. My friends thought I was crazy, but it was more important
> for me to work in a good environment and at a place where I agreed
> with the philosophy of learning. Money and job security meant less
> to me than being in tune with my spirit.
> *—Rebecca, class of 1996*

Many alumni say that they are satisfied with their work because they had a good look at the work-a-day world in their Career Exploration Passage. All of the interviews, job shadows, apprenticeships, and internships helped students become more aware of the good, the bad, and the ugly of a job field.

> I feel like I got a head start at the Open School. I learned early
> on what I *didn't* want to do from doing my Career Passage as a
> scientist. I think it helped me to see that I needed to be in a job
> where I wasn't so isolated. I found that I was happiest when I was
> working with other people. I ended up in teaching. Working with
> other teachers and students gives meaning to my life, and I'm
> happy.
> *—John, class of 1995*

Profile of Success
EVERYTHING WAS POSSIBLE
Russell Bowman, Class of 1978

When Russ Bowman came to the Open School, it was like coming home. He had started out at the Open Living grade school and now, after what he calls two "insipid" years at a conventional middle school, he was returning to help start the new Mountain Open High School program. Russ remembers going to a district school board meeting to argue for the need for an open school that could graduate students with a district diploma. The Mountain Open High School was accepted by the board that night.

> That meeting was the beginning of my Open School education. I
> was actually in on the ground floor, the initial planning and hiring
> for a new kind of education. I was learning how to be responsible for
> my own education without even thinking about it.

Once the school got started there was so much to do that Russ and the other new high school students were busy every day, talking philosophy, creating classes and participating in every facet of building a school from scratch. It was a wonderful, exciting, and nerve-wracking job. It was hard work, but, at the same time, a joyful and meaningful experience.

> We had a huge retreat before the school year and we talked and
> argued into the night. I began to understand that the possibilities
> were endless, that I could set out to do anything that interested me,
> and that the support would be there from staff and students alike.

Russ had always been interested in the sciences, experimentation, and photography. One of his first learning experiences at the school came from an unlikely source—the school bus driver. With the support of a program that supported all of its members, custodians and secretaries alike, to be teachers and learners, the bus driver taught a class on photography and the development of film. He let the students use his own equipment as he shared his excitement about photography. Russ found that his interests began to expand and connect as he worked with chemicals in the developing process. His curiosity for learning about science was ignited, and he was on his way.

Immediately, Russ was introduced to the idea that schools could be places where passions are shared without the hierarchy of formal instructors and professors. The idea that everyone was included in this community of learners helped Russ realize that if he had the spirit, he could fully engage his drive to learn. And if learning could be so much fun, why couldn't work?

With the help of his advisor and the principal, Russ began to prepare for an internship at a lab at the University of Denver. Russ picked up the coursework he needed, and in his last year at the school, worked in the labs at the university several days a week. At the same time, he arranged an internship in photography and earned certification as an emergency medical technician. To top it off, Russ spent three months in Oxford, England, working for a scientific film company, and finally, was able to fit in an internship at the immunology laboratory of a major hospital. All of this in high school? Russ explains:

> I was able to do so much because of the strong support I received from my advisors and fellow students. I started to think about careers early on because my advisor had a way of getting me to consider what I wanted to do and how I could make it happen.

From all of these experiences with "real life" work in high school, Russ decided that his interests lay in medicine. He proceeded accordingly, going off to an alternative college to study science and medicine. After a brief departure in the Peace Corps, he took his family medicine residency and a master's degree at Marshall University in West Virginia.

Russ's odyssey continued with three years in private practice and eleven years in the Coast Guard. He then went back for another degree in Health Administration and is presently the medical director for a major clinic in Alaska.

Dr. Russ Bowman (class of 1978) on the job in Alaska

For Russell, work is life and life is work. His early experience with work was a positive one in which his enthusiasm for learning, growing, and healing could be included. The support he received from the school to explore the world of careers at an early age worked in his favor. Further, the responsibilities of starting a school from scratch gave him the confidence to pursue a position as a manager and director in his field.

Putting Things into Perspective

The overwhelming majority of respondents say that their school experience had a profound effect on their attitude and skills in their work. The real (often on-the-job) experiences of the Career Passage provided a meaningful base from which to explore the world of work.

The everyday life of the school, including the development of self-directed learning skills and attitudes such as intrinsic motivation, helped students see that they could, in fact, pursue their interests without fear. Also, the alumni emphasize the importance of the critical thinking and group work involved in the Passages and trips. Most feel that their social skills and problem-solving skills are tangible assets in their jobs. Many think of themselves as dynamic leaders who have the confidence and fortitude both to personally take initiative and to empower their coworkers.

Most alumni report high levels of job satisfaction because they feel that they have happily married their work to their personal lives without losing their ideals. Some talked about a balance that they had learned how to achieve from navigating the sometimes ambiguous waters of the school. There were no absolutes, no one telling you what to do all the time. Students had to find their own ways, the paths that felt the most suitable for them. Sometimes finding a happy blend of work and life takes courage and the confidence that alumni speak of when they have to make hard decisions about what direction to take.

The UNICEF Report on Child Well-Being discloses that the United States rates seventeenth (out of twenty-one First World countries) in transitioning young people into the work force. The report goes on to say that schools must take the blame for neglecting the skills and attitudes that are needed to become happy, productive workers. Many kids lack experience with the world of work and come to see work as just a means to an end, not having anything to do with their regular lives.

Conversely, work is more than just a job to most Open School alumni. Most feel that their work is part of the fabric of their lives as adults, places where they can be themselves and continue their journeys of personal growth. One alumna describes work as "a place to learn and grow." The idea that your work is another way of giving yourself to the world is also at play. Mark (class of 1989), who works for the Dalai Lama and has helped establish a self-sustaining community in the Himalayas, puts it aptly:

> My work is like an ever-evolving Passage. I aspire to create the
> perfect life for myself and for others. How much more Open School-
> ish can it get?

Employers are screaming for young workers who are job-ready. Internships, apprenticeships, and active career explorations can and should be a part of any worthy school program. If schools take the time to develop the whole child, they will set priorities for work experiences that help students begin earlier to develop the positive attitudes and necessary skills for the work place. The key is to get students to see that work and life are interrelated.

Lighting the Fire of Learning

● ● ●Ninety-seven percent of alumni say that the continual joy of learning is important to their lives as adults.

● ● ●Ninety-nine percent of the alumni report that the school has had a positive effect on their sense of the joy of learning.

Education is not filling a bucket, but lighting a fire!

–William Butler Yeats

Before I came to the Open School, I was bored, frustrated, and angry. It didn't take long before I realized that I had an inherent love of learning that had been repressed by a system that didn't even value such things.

–John, class of 1980

It makes sense that rediscovering the joy of learning is the first of the five school goals. As Joseph Campbell, the Jungian scholar, said, "The only life worth living is the passionate life, the journey of the joyous, lifelong learner." The exhilarating, blue-sky feeling that the world is right in front of you, just waiting to be discovered, is a wonderful thing to experience. Many theorists believe that this curiosity and eagerness to learn is part of natural human development.[14] So what happens to the bright-eyed, fearless learner of early childhood? Too often, the conventional school system saps children's natural curiosity to explore and discover through controlling their attention and forcing them to regurgitate what someone thinks they should know.

And these days, a terrible storm has moved in. The ideas of educating the whole person and developing a genuine love of learning have been clouded over by high-stakes testing and standardized curricula. The entire meaning of what it means to be educated is being reduced to a single test score or someone's idea of what every ninth grader should know. The true essence of learning is lost in the fog, adrift in a sea of predetermined outcomes and extraneous measurements of achievement.

At the Open School, however, it is the appreciation of pure learning that drives the staff in its quest to develop joyful, lifelong learners. One alumnus, who transferred to the school from Columbine High School soon after the tragic killings there, put it this way:

> At Columbine, many of my teachers did recognize that I had a love
> for learning, but they were frustrated by their inability to reward
> me for it. At parent conferences they would tell my folks that I was
> a good student but that my grades were poor. It was too bad, but
> the grades were all that mattered. We were all confused and a little
> angry.
>
> It wasn't long after I transferred to Open that I began to be
> recognized as someone who really loved the learning process. I
> immediately began to loosen up and feel more secure about myself
> and my idea of what it meant to be a good student.
> *–Dean, class of 2002*

As I became part of the school community, my own experience with rediscovering the joy of learning took some interesting twists. For nearly eight years after finishing my master's degree, I was uncertain if I wanted to pursue further graduate studies. And if I did decide to pursue further studies, I was uncertain what direction to take. I eventually decided to return to school and get my doctorate in education, and I did my dissertation on the Walkabout curriculum of the Open School, receiving my Ph.D. in 1989. I never would have even considered completing this degree without the influence of the school. I finally had something I felt passionate about, an idea I believed in.

Other activities in my life started to come alive as part and parcel of who I was and what I had to offer others. My love for music now became a way to share and learn about American history and literature, and how passions can affect personal growth.

I also learned to challenge myself, which was something that I had tried hard to avoid, as do so many people. I ran marathons, went on some tough outdoors trips, and even reexamined my personal relationships with friends and family. Finally, I felt the confidence to confront some personal issues that I never would have dreamed of approaching before, like quitting smoking and learning how to relax and let go a bit with life's inevitable challenges.

My view of life was changing. What once were immense frustrations and disappointments now became learning experiences and opportunities for growth. Like so many of the alumni you have heard from in this book, I adopted a framework for learning and living that was more positive and synergistic.

Everything at the school begins with those seeds of interest and curiosity that already exist somewhere within each child. A personal advisor helps to nourish the seeds by encouraging each student to develop his or her personal plan. The guidance and coaching from advisors helps kids grow into themselves because it allows them to identify and then pursue their particular goals.

Kids who were once bored stiff in conventional settings found that they were set free by the Open School model.

> I was so unchallenged and bored in conventional schools. Also, I could have painted myself purple and enclosed myself in a clear plastic gerbil ball and no one would have even noticed. When I came to Open, my advisor and other staff modeled a love for learning and knowledge that was amazing. Their enthusiasm rubbed off on me. I realized that all of the passions that I had (which were many) had been marginalized. They weren't considered part of the curriculum.
> *—Tom, class of 1983*

Students Who Discover What Gives Them Joy

The advising process involves students in an exploration of themselves; a genuine self-assessment has to take place for students to begin their self-directed journey. Without grades to artificially hold students back, they are free to shoot for the stars. The reward is the pleasure of learning for its own sake, not meeting someone else's standards of achievement. Some alumni talk about discovering their "inner learner."

> Before the Open School, learning was something that you did in drills, something one memorized but never applied. It was what others told you was important to learn. How could anyone find joy in that?
>
> Thankfully, the Open School and my advisor helped me discover my "inner learner" by letting me pursue my own interests. In the

process, I found out how to search for my own truth by constantly
questioning the status quo. Learning became the most important
thing in my life! I don't know what would have happened to me if I
hadn't discovered the school.
—Aaron, class of 1996

Everything is evaluated. Students are responsible for documenting and
assessing personal, social, and intellectual growth for every class, trip, and
experience. Whether in or out of school, everything is considered part of one's
education. One alumnus who joined the Army attributes his aspiration to constantly
learn to his well-developed self-assessment skills.

Because of the self-evaluation that took place at the Open School, I
am driven to learn new things, and I constantly evaluate what I learn
from experiences. Now, as an adult, I actually look for opportunities
to gain new perspectives and knowledge. Without this ability to
self-assess, I would be limited to the success-or-failure concept of
learning.
—Brian, class of 1992

It is, in fact, this self-assessment process, guided by an advisor, that allows
students to identify just what it is that turns them on. Schools that encourage this
kind of self-evaluation help students realize that this is what they need to do for
the rest of their lives—ultimately they have to rely on their own feedback. How
they feel about themselves is the most important measure of a successful life.

Middle school science trip to Utah

Students Who Are Free to Explore

Because of the freedom to explore that students enjoy, many alumni say that they were able to develop their interests in a relaxed, natural way. Benjamin (class of 2001) was able to focus on his love of music and different cultures, and this made it possible for him to examine his own family heritage and thereby combine these two loves.

> While at the Open School, I was able to specialize and focus my
> on my passion for music and my fascination with Swedish culture.
> Early on, I learned how to play the nyckelharpa, a rare Swedish folk
> instrument. This became the starting point of finding my way on my
> educational path, using my passions as a guide.

Benjamin was able to place his love for Swedish folk music at the heart of all of his Passages. This led to an exploration of his identity and his search for self.

Benjamin (class of 2001) with his nyckelharpa

> I saw that all of my goals were related, and that I could make
> my dreams come true. My plan was to attend the Swedish Royal
> Academy and learn about my heritage and myself.

Benjamin did indeed spend two years in Sweden studying with the Swedish Royal Academy. He is now fluent in Swedish and is known globally as one of the few masters of a rare instrument. He says he learned what it was like to feel good from his experience at the Open School. He has recently been accepted with a full scholarship to Brown University in their ethnology of music doctoral program. Benjamin describes himself as a happy, successful student of life.

Another budding musician tells how the discovery of his love for music was nurtured. David (class of 1997) says that he never felt as if the school sloughed off his desire to be a musician as just a passing fancy or a hobby. Instead, the school allowed him to make music the central part of his curriculum. This helped him to discover a "sense of creative play" that otherwise might have been stifled. David just received his master's degree in music from a major conservatory. He contends that the value he places on the joy of learning has served him well in a program that can sometimes feel rigid and structure-bound.

Similar stories are prevalent among alumni. One who had once described herself as a "humanities junkie" found that by having the freedom to choose her own classes and build her own curriculum, she was able to discover a wider array of interests than she had previously thought she had.

> I give the school credit for expanding my horizons by making all learning mysterious and wonderful. Learning for me became a process of exciting discovery. It simply made me feel good. I found that my interests changed and became less narrow. I found that I loved the sciences! When I went to college I decided to do a double major in biology and philosophy because, in high school, I had been able to find the connections in my passions.
>
> *—Ann, class of 1991*

Other alumni say they remember that very first spark, that time when everything started to come together.

> I remember the first time I realized how much I enjoyed learning. I was in a science class and I had written a report about DNA. The teacher called on me to read it to the class. I was scared, but I trusted the teacher, and it was one of my personal goals to break through this fear of speaking in front of groups, so I took a chance. My report was really well received by the class. I was elated! From this experience, I decided then and there that I wanted to regain that feeling from every piece of my schoolwork. I never looked back. Learning has been a joy for me ever since.
>
> *—Brooke, class of 1995*

Trips are also noted as valuable vehicles for recognizing and then relishing one's sources of inspiration.

> The Boundary Waters trip was pivotal for me. I did my trip project on raptors, and I had the chance to observe and study their behavior. When I shared my report with the group, it was the first time that learning felt good to me. I realized that what I learned could be valuable to me and to people around me. I often think that this experience helped inspire me to become a teacher, which I am today.
> *–Eric, class of 1984*

A school that nurtures the glow associated with finding one's bliss can change lives dramatically. Learning feels natural and free, not artificial and dull.

No Fear: Students Who Know the Fun of Facing a Good Challenge

Many alumni say that their school experience has continued to motivate them to seek out challenging learning situations. Part of the fun of learning is the feeling of overcoming obstacles. Trips and experiential learning are mentioned frequently as prime sources for this robust approach to learning.

> The trips really instilled in us a sense of adventure. I went on ten different trips with the school, and each of those trips gave me something valuable.
>
> Now, I think I am more willing to take risks because of the challenges I had to face on trips. For example, on the Hurricane Island trip we had to face harsh weather conditions and exhausting days of physical and emotional stress.
>
> I really feel that I am more willing to take on and face challenges than my conventional school counterparts because I learned to tear down my boundaries of fear. On trips, we constantly had to face real-life challenges. Now, I look at these challenges as opportunities for growth in everything I do.
> *–Heather, class of 1999*

Other alumni who were once fearful of certain aspects of life and learning felt that the trips showed them how to break through their fears. Derek (class of 1995) challenged himself to combine things he liked with things that were difficult for him. On the New England bike trip he was able to mix physical fitness, exploring colleges, marine biology, and literature.

These seemingly disparate topics were carefully and elegantly combined into one experience. Along with the things I already loved to do, I was able to learn to enjoy the backpacking and camping part as well. Now, as an adult, I am not afraid of the outdoors and I actually look forward to experiencing nature. Further, I am able to transfer this feeling of joy to other challenging situations in my life. Thus, I feel like I can live a fuller, more meaningful life.

Along with trip challenges, Derek had to contend with what he describes as a math phobia. His math skills were low, but he kept trying. Without grades to penalize him and make him feel badly about himself, he was able to take a Survey of Calculus class three times. This was a critical point for Derek as he struggled to discover his passions. As it turned out, he was on the right track, because he ended up majoring in math and engineering in college.

We keep talking about creating a more rigorous curriculum for our students in the public schools. What can be more demanding than helping kids to look at challenge as a positive thing, something that contributes to their personal growth, not just a score on a tough test or a grade on a paper that has nothing to do with their interests or their lives? Schools can challenge kids in meaningful ways by allowing them to go after what inspires them.

Personal Power: Students Who Feel Good About Themselves

Many alumni feel that empowerment follows from the freedom to pursue their interests. They begin to trust their instincts and skills as learners. Although the starting point for some students is zero, the reward eventually comes, though gradually. It often takes time to build—or rebuild—one's confidence and personal power.

When Jack came to me as an advisee, he was a solid mess. His self-image was as low as it gets. His history of failure at conventional schools was extensive. His physical delays in maturation and body growth only made matters worse. Considering what he had gone through, his personal and social skills were predictably poor.

We had to start somewhere, and it needed to be at a basic level. Jack and I decided to explore his strengths and interests. He had a vast appreciation and knowledge of fantasy literature and computers. We began with these as we tried to build a one-to-one relationship.

Slowly but surely, Jack began to trust me. After some predictable ups and downs, Jack began to realize that I would not give up on him. A turning point came after a much-dreaded parent conference in which Jack kept his cool.

Trust began to blossom. Soon, it was time to challenge Jack to take some small steps in a new direction. Jack began to branch out. Finally, the time came for a serious confrontation with fear. We decided that, after an aborted, ugly trip to New Orleans during which Jack had played out some of his most antisocial behaviors, it was time for another try. Since Jack was interested in literature and sorely needed some physical exercise to improve his body image, he chose a more appropriate experience: a bike trip in New England. The combination of interest and challenge (reading Hawthorne and riding many miles) seemed just right.

Reluctantly, Jack accepted the challenge. When he returned, he was a different person! Jack had overcome many fears on the trip. His physical fitness and social skills were tested dearly. Meanwhile, it certainly helped that some of his strong intellectual skills were recognized for what they were—a contribution to the group's knowledge and even pleasure. From this improved sense of personal power, Jack began to renew the joy that he had always, privately, experienced in his learning. Now, he could be proud of it.

Many alumni report that rediscovering the joy of learning led to a sense of confidence and personal power. Some even say that they depend on their love of learning when things get tough.

> Before I came to Open, I looked at school as something to get through. After coming to the school, I came to understand that education is a blessing and a privilege to enjoy.

> When I had my daughter, I was very young. The Open School gave me a love of learning that provided me with the wherewithal to finish college. As an adult, I have had the personal strength to work my way up in my job. I have a deep well of power to draw from.
> *—Jen, class of 1992*

Another alumna says that when she went through a very hard time in college, her boyfriend said it was burnout. She wasn't used to being so disengaged from her life and learning. Reconnecting with her dreams enabled her to reclaim her sense of purpose and direction.

> I had never experienced anything like it! For the first time in my life, I didn't want to learn. I think it is truly amazing that the Open School was able to keep these feelings at bay throughout my entire education. I finally realized that it was through engaging what I love that I would be able to find a purpose in the class I was struggling with. I was able to see the big picture. This helped me pull out of the slump I had fallen into.
> *—Eva, class of 2001*

Kelli (class of 1991) said that she found the strength to stay in high school when she felt like dropping out. In conventional schools, she had lost all of her joy in learning, and she didn't think she had any talent at anything. Things felt desperate and hopeless until a counselor recommended the Open School as a last resort. Almost immediately after her transfer, things began to change.

> Finally, I felt that I was actually learning something. I felt engaged and good about myself. I found that I had some real aptitude for languages. I learned Spanish by going on school trips to Mexico. I truly discovered this inner power, this happiness, in what I learned.

> Today I teach Spanish in community colleges, after-school programs, and even abroad at times. I found what gives me joy and it keeps me connected.

Confidence, trust, and joy in the process of learning provide an excellent foundation for living a full, *productive* life. Empowerment and joy together promote an embrace of lifelong learning. Can a school really cultivate this feeling? Jen (class of 2000) says yes:

> Each goal I set for myself at the school was ultimately achieved. With the support of peers and advisors, I became confident and passionate about my ability to learn and grow.

> I became addicted to learning and sharing what I have learned with others. Since third grade at the Open School, I have been taught that I have the power to find answers on my own. Since I was encouraged to find my own truth, I became self-reliant. It truly brings me joy and confidence to expand my mind.

Students can learn to feel good about themselves in school. Supportive programs give kids the message that it's okay to be who they are, to have their own particular interests, and to look deeply into their well of passions. All schools should aspire to building a sense of confidence in their students, which then enables kids to empower each other.

Passing It On: Students Who Want to Share Their Joy

Apparently, the joy of learning is contagious. Alumni say that they can't wait to share this sense of excitement with others. This sharing takes many forms. Some say that their own joy in learning enhances their child-rearing capabilities.

> I take an active role in my children's education. I have learned skills
> and attitudes at the Open School that I am able to pass on to them.
> Now, they in turn enjoy learning as a never-ending process.
> *—Jess, class of 1992*

Alumni who teach are especially grateful for this attitude toward learning. Many report that they seek to model the joy of learning for their students. They see themselves as constantly encouraging their students to see school as a fun and stimulating place to be.

> Being a teacher allows me to explore my passions alongside young
> learners, which is a true joy! In addition, the general activity of my
> life centers around joyful pursuits: art, playing music, reading, etc.
>
> At the Open School, equal attention was paid to all curiosity and
> interests as long as they inspired learning. Art, basketball, and
> math were all viewed as important. This view is certainly helpful
> in dealing with all kinds of students. I think it makes me a better
> teacher.
> *—John, class of 1996*

Mike (class of 1983) lives on a working dairy farm. He helps raise three children, along with doing the hard work on the land that is required of him. He credits the school with his holistic and hands-on approach to learning, which he now shares with his kids.

> I enjoy learning new things with my kids and helping them
> understand how things work. The Open School taught me how to
> get my own children involved in and exposed to new learning. I get
> them to touch things, observe, and understand how things relate to
> the world around us.
> *—Mike, class of 1983*

We need to move our schools in the direction of making it paramount to support the joy of learning, to share inspirations, and to respect those of others. It can be done if schools change their priorities.

Lifelong Learning: Students Who Will Never Stop Growing

Because alumni embrace the joy of learning, they see themselves as lifelong learners. They do not perceive graduation as an end point, but rather a transition or milestone, as one part of a continuous process.

One recent college graduate says that she "freaked out" when she first arrived at a large, impersonal university. She was not prepared to look at her education as a series of tests and assignments. It all seemed so other-directed and meaningless. At first she was angry and even a little bitter at the Open School for not preparing her for the large-college experience. However, just recalling the joy and engagement she had experienced at the school helped her to adjust, and she reconnected with the idea that learning and living were part of the same process.

> I started to use my self-directed skills. I asked for help. I went to see my professors during their office hours. I actually got to know them. In return they got to know me and my interests. My poor grades turned into A's and B's and I ended up graduating summa cum laude. But that wasn't the point. What really saved me was returning to that feeling that learning was a joy and that I was a lifelong learner. I am eternally grateful for that solid foundation of love and connection that I was able to develop at the Open School.
> *—Rosia, class of 2000*

Another alumnus tells a story about how his attitude toward learning became a curiosity to others in a conventional school setting.

> I am a stained glass artist and I was never interested in going to college. Of course, that didn't mean that I was not interested in intellectual things.
>
> I remember I once went with my sister to one of her college classes. I was so interested in the subject that I began taking notes and asking questions. The other students were either half asleep or restless for the class to be over, and here I was totally engaged.
>
> The whole thing made me realize that I am a well-rounded lifelong learner. I don't learn for grades or credits. I learn because I want to learn. That's all.
> *—Matt, class of 1989*

An alumnus who is a master plumber says that he learned to love writing and reading poetry at the school. He wasn't restricted to a vocational track like he might have been in a conventional school program.

> I'm not just a plumber, although I love what I do. There is more to me than just one thing. My advisor at the Open School encouraged

me to expand my horizons. I felt free to do just that. Now, I continue
to read and write in my spare time. I'll have these things forever.
                                                    —Mark, class of 1997

Heni (class of 1989), a teacher, says that she is constantly "seeking out
learning situations inside and outside of schools." Like many professionals, she is
required to update her education. This, she says, comes naturally to her because
her greatest joy is to "continue my learning and my personal and professional
growth." She tells her students that learning never stops, that, in fact, it continues
always and in all parts of one's life.

A graduate who has a Ph.D. says that the school taught him that there is no
such thing as a terminal degree. By seeing living as learning, he knows how to
keep a good thing going.

Sure, I have completed my formal education, but I still maintain a
well-defined course of study that ensures my continual personal and
professional development. This insulates me from the likelihood
of burnout or intellectual and emotional fatigue. The Open School
placed me firmly on this course by allowing me to see that learning
is a continuous process.
                                                    —Dave, class of 1994

Claude, who entered the Marine
Corps after graduation, talks about having
to change, modify, and adapt to different
life situations. He says that his embrace
of learning and the challenge of change is
something he will always carry with him.

The Open School is the main reason
that I am a lifelong learner. Many
people do not understand that life
is a matter of learning and adapting
to the world in which we live. A lot
of people think they have to either
succeed or fail in dealing with the
world.

Claude, class of 1992, organic farmer

I learned early on that the key is to enjoy the process, and to see life
itself as learning. There is no winning or losing, just changing.
                                                    —Claude, class of 1995

Lifelong learners usually know how to weave their many interests together. At the Open School, students and staff are constantly trying to find the themes or threads from which their dreams are shaped. Adult alumni say that this helps to fill out their lives. Plumbers are also poets, mathematicians are also artists, and professors are engaged parents.

> I learned at the school that life has many facets. I am not restricted to one role in my life. Everything is related. This makes me feel more whole as a person. Plus, I know that my learning will go on until the day I die. This gives me something to hold onto.
> *—Ralph, class of 1979*

Schools must encourage kids to look at their lives as a never-ending adventure, one in which learning is always evolving, changing, and growing. This is the committed life that the philosophers speak so eloquently about. Schools are not an end unto themselves, but merely vehicles that students use to direct their lives toward whatever inspires them.

Are They Developing Their Passions?
Are They Still Doing Their Passages?

Ninety-five percent of the responding alumni say that they are still doing something related to the Passage work that they started at the Open School.

The Passages are designed for exploration, experimentation, and skill building. Students are consistently asked to design, modify, and evaluate the learning that takes place. They are encouraged to go for it with the support and help of the learning community.

Most alumni feel that they had a head start on the rest of the crowd in that they had a fairly well-formed idea of their direction in life. By making life skills and the love of learning part of their school curriculum, most alumni felt that the school made it easier for them to transition to adulthood.

For some alumni, the continual pursuit of inspiration was shaped by a belief that anything related to their interests was valid and important, something to be taken seriously. Thus, Matt was not afraid to do his stained glass work; Abby could really become a professional musician. Every dream could come true. All it took was drive, a commitment to lifelong learning, and the belief that anything was possible.

Ian, whom I talked about earlier, is a classic example of a graduate who has avidly continued to engage the interests he discovered at the school in his adult life. Bound to a wheelchair from birth, Ian had never been anywhere on his own before he came to the school, so he certainly didn't see travel and adventure in his future. Yet, with the support of the school community, he participated in the wilderness trip (overcoming both his mother's anxiety and his own fears) and later went on to take challenging trips to San Francisco, New Orleans, the Mississippi Delta, and, eventually, Mexico and England. He was like a bird set free.

> After the first couple of trips, I knew that I had support from my community to try whatever I wanted. I felt free to take some chances. I planned and prepared for one of the school trips to Mexico. I took Spanish and studied Latino culture and history. My first trip to Teacapan [a small fishing village south of Mazatlan] was amazing. I was able to negotiate the lack of accessibility with help from other students and my newfound confidence.

> I fell in love with everything Latino! I ended up designing some of my Passages around Mexico and Latin American issues. I also continued to challenge myself with traveling to difficult places. I went to England and confronted my fears and insecurities around inaccessibility.

> These experiences ignited a love for teaching and a commitment to social justice. At the Open School, the real teacher within me was born. I also became more political as I was able to see more clearly the issues of social justice in Mexico and even in this country, in places like Mississippi.

These passions found further expression in Ian's Passage work, which included educating others about disabilities, examining cultural relations between Mexicans and Americans, and investigating some of the bioethical issues involved with underweight babies. Subsequently, he explored careers in the fields of communications and law.

Ian emphatically says that he has continued to develop the interests and skills he explored in his Passages in his adult life.

> It's wonderful because I now educate others about disabilities for a living, working at the Association for Retarded Citizens. From my Global Awareness Passage, I use the process of exploring and discussing pertinent issues having to do with disabilities. My Career Exploration inspired me to seek a career as an attorney and disabilities-rights advocate.

> My interest in Mexico has blossomed exponentially. I have developed fluency in Spanish, and part of my focus at college was

around Latin American issues of social justice.

> Because of my Adventure Passage, I felt competent enough to
> go to college out of state in the southern United States, where I
> had learned to appreciate southern culture from all of my trips to
> Mississippi.

> And finally, from my Adventure Passage and all of the other
> confidence-building experiences at the Open School, I have found
> the strength to travel alone to England and Mexico a number of
> times.

Ian emphasizes that the school did not actually create all of these inspired pursuits; it simply helped cultivate them.

> These passions were within me, but I was allowed to investigate,
> reflect, and act on them. I feel I was provided with the environment
> and tools that define my life to this very day.

Corrine (class of 1997) started a school newspaper as part of her Career Exploration Passage. She went on to complete her master's degree at the London School of Journalism. She has spent time all over the world covering important issues. Her Passage work in journalism and documentary filmmaking continues today as she creates video blogs for a major newspaper and develops promotional documentaries for civil rights groups.

Meredith (class of 1992) did her Global Awareness Passage on the North American Fair Trade Agreement. She traveled extensively with the school to Latin America, and even went to Colombia in 1991. After graduating, she spent time teaching English in Mexico and working with women's groups in a small village. Her focus changed to immigration and women's issues in the Third World. Today, these issues are still important to her. She travels the world as an adventurer and lifelong learner.

For his Creativity Passage, Matt (class of 1986) designed and created a piece of stained glass. His extensive internships with various stained glass artists helped prepare him for the project. Now, as a renowned stained glass artist, Matt says that he realized, even back then, one of the most important keys to the creative process.

> The Passages taught me that the process is more important than the
> product. My work and, really, everything I do, is more enjoyable
> because I learned to appreciate the creative process for what it really

is—a joyful experience in and of itself. Now, I do my Passages over and over again as part of my life.

Many alumni talk about everything they do in their adult lives as fitting into a Passage category.

I find myself doing new Passages all the time. I recently completed another Adventure Passage when I backpacked alone throughout Europe. I will never stop using the premises of the Passage process; it's how I live my life.

–Brooke, class of 1995

Heather (class of 1999) did some of her Passages around biology and studying birds. She tracked birds on several extended school trips, examined water purity on the Mississippi River trip, and studied wildlife in Mexico. After receiving a college degree in biology, she took an internship with a conservation organization working with sea birds on Farallon Island.

My days were spent netting, bonding, banding, and re-siting birds such as the Common Murre, the Rhinoceros Auklet, and the Tufted Puffin. I was in heaven, working with thousands of seabirds all around me. After that, I went to Puerto Rico to study the Smooth-Billed Ani, a small black bird that is part of the Cuckoo family.

Now I am working for a company in California studying the Northern Spotted Owl. I am part of a team effort to protect these birds. It's rewarding, because for every owl I find, I am able to preserve a habitat in an area that would otherwise be logged. In addition, I get to spend the days outdoors in one of the most beautiful places in the country! The Open School and my Passages taught me that I could make my dreams come true. I couldn't be happier.

Other alumni say that their Passages almost magically blended into their lives as adults. Aaron (class of 1996), who is a researcher and philosopher in Oregon, recalls his Logical Inquiry and Global Awareness Passages:

My Logical Inquiry Passage had to do with the big questions of biology and meaning, which I am now pursuing as I study the evolution of religious behavior and ritual. Also, my Global Awareness Passage was a paper on "The Necessity of Intuition," which really reflects my quest to balance the logical and the emotional, something I pursue now as I try to synthesize science and art.

Tim, from the class of 1988, just completed his master's degree in education. He calls it his "latest Logical Inquiry Passage." Meanwhile, Tom (class of 1983) says that he thinks about his Open School projects all the time. Indeed, they blend in smoothly with his adult life.

I did most of my Passages around art, music, and writing. I am currently the executive director of a well-known art museum in New York City. I also write for a local magazine, and I am the leader of a popular blues band. I became interested in the harmonica on a school trip as part of one of my Passages. It's also interesting that my Career Passage was on solar architecture, because it relates to a new building project I am working on at the museum.

Students who have had opportunities to discover and nurture enthusiastic pursuits in a project-based curriculum find that their familiarity with the experiential process serves them well as adults. They look at their lives as a series of never ending projects and adventures. As a result, many former students have had the courage to take the road less traveled.

Profile of Success
LET YOUR VISION BE YOUR GUIDE
Joey Slowik, Class of 1994

Joey is a genius. *Webster's Dictionary* describes geniuses as having "natural ability and great mental capacity" along with "an original creative ability." At conventional school, however, Joey was just another underachieving kid. No one recognized his vast potential, his voracious curiosity, and his startling capacity for invention and design. Sadly, he was just another kid lost in the system. He felt lost and lonely.

So Joey came to the Open School as a self-described "refugee" from a conventional junior high school. He felt that he did all of his real learning on his own, so he was curious about a school that supported self-directed learning and, purportedly, enabled students to pursue their interests both inside and outside the classroom. He soon found that he could take off with his many and various passions.

For his first Passage, he researched how to apply advanced mathematical techniques and studied the background astronomy and physics related to his inquiry about gravitation. His advisor and his consultants were amazed with the depth and inventiveness he displayed in his work. His passions were, at last, being validated.

> For the first time, I got some recognition for the stuff I had previously done in private. I started to feel good about being recognized for just being myself.

However, after some initial feelings of success, Joey became restless. He thought about dropping out and getting his GED. He complained that the school was too structured for him and that he could explore what he wanted on his own. In retrospect, he salutes his advisor for sticking with him and persuading him to stay in school.

> I didn't realize, at the time, that I really needed the social and personal skills to go with my intellectual abilities. I needed practice with getting along with different types of people and being patient with ones who were different than me. I began to appreciate that different kids had different talents, and that they all cared about learning in their own way.

Long argumentative governance sessions, Joey says, were among the experiences that helped him become more patient, understanding, and attuned to the world around him. He easily might have become absorbed in, even obsessed with his own world. The school, with all of its group activities and interdependent projects, had a softening effect on Joey. He began to see that having a good life included getting along with people and developing deeper relationships.

After high school, Joey felt the expectations and pressures to go to college. He majored in botany (he

Joey (class of 1994) hunting spiders in Ecuador

had a lot of experience identifying species in science classes at the Open School) and took lots of chemistry and biology. He really didn't think he needed this kind of return to conventional education, but he dealt with it. He worked his way through school by hanging gutters and graduated five years later. Joey says that he paid his dues.

> Sometimes you just have to grit your way through things like getting a formal degree. I guess it's part of having a well-rounded kind of life.

Afterwards, Joey wanted no further part of the academic world. When he heard there were some Forest Service openings in Alaska, he applied. He ended up in a small remote Alaskan village of 800 people, mostly Native Americans.

> I mostly cleaned toilets and did the grunt work, but I loved it. I was in a beautiful natural setting, and I had time to read and explore on my own.

Joey also appreciated the feeling of community in the small town atmosphere. If you had car problems, you could borrow someone else's truck for a few days, or if you needed money, you could get a personal loan any time, no questions asked. He says, "I recognized that this was similar to the Open School community, with the same kind of support and respect."

It was there that Joey met his girlfriend, a local whose parents taught at the small community school. Joey and his new partner then got jobs counting fish on Prince of Wales Island off the coast of Alaska for the National Forest Service for its ecological updates. Life became ideal for Joey's tastes and values.

> We had it all! We worked the summers and took time off to relax, read, and explore. We lived in a little, rustic cabin. We had to redesign our fresh water system, so I learned all about that and other survival kinds of skills. It was an ideal kind of life because it was real and natural. There were no egos involved; there was no "getting ahead" or mindless materialism. It reminded me of what my core values were.

One day, Joey got an email from an old friend. It was the scientist he had worked with during an internship at the Denver Museum of Nature and Science. She had a three-year grant to study and identify spiders; she wanted Joey to be her assistant. He took the job.

Spiders were fascinating to me. I also liked the idea of challenging
myself in the scientific community again. It would be a change of
lifestyle for us, but it would only be temporary.

Joey is now in the last year of his grant as the territorial assistant to the chief
arachnologist at the Denver Museum of Nature and Science. He has written at
least five monographs on rare spiders and classification techniques. Joey is one
of a select group of about five hundred spider experts in North America, but he
doesn't have any egotistical attachment to what he has done.

I don't have a big head about it at all! I enjoy doing the research, and
what I like about the spider community is that no one is arrogant or
conceited about what they do.

Joey says that the Open School helped him to be at ease with himself and relish
the pure love of learning and exploring. He says that the school, by allowing him
to just be himself, has enabled him to be confident in pursuing what really interests
him and not worry about things like status and material rewards.

The school, Joey observes, helped him to appreciate that success involves
cultivating diverse skills, interests, and relationships. He has found that, in his
interactions with other scientists, he guards against overspecialization and a
rigidly narrow focus, which is a danger in the scientific community. He says he
learned at the school that success means not only diving deep into a particular area
of study, but remaining receptive to the amazing experiences and possibilities that
surround us all the time, if only we are open to them.

Now, when I go on spider searches with my colleagues, I caution
them to slow down and explore the whole environment. I also
encourage them to have fun and keep the joy of discovery alive, not
just to focus on this exact species of spider and that's it.

This statement reminded me of Joey's initial wilderness trip, on which I
was the leader. I remember Joey and some other curious kids new to the Open
High School going off and exploring a strawberry patch, deeply appreciating the
beauty of the mountains. Now, I see the adult Joey has become, and it doesn't
surprise me.

Joey now looks forward to the end of the grant and his return to the good
life in Alaska.

Success for me doesn't mean making a name for myself or
accumulating possessions. I learned at the Open School that the real

feeling of success has to come from within; it can't be external like grades or credits. I am successful because I have been able to adapt and create my own lifestyle. Happiness is the only measure that counts, and that comes from within. Success and happiness are both derived from learning and experiencing new things.

Putting Things into Perspective

My own experience at the school reflects the stories of the alumni in many ways. It didn't take long for me to become more aware of the many passions I already had, such as music, cooking, running, literature, baseball, politics, and education. I began to see myself less as a dilettante and more as a serious learner. I changed the way I looked at my work and its relationship to my life. Suddenly, I was a lifelong learner who just happened to be a teacher.

Many of the alumni report similar changes in their lives. The fire that is lit by this kind of education can never be extinguished, because the students carry the flame wherever they go. Most say that, because of the focused attention on self-assessment, they were able to discover what gave them joy. And they were encouraged to take seriously and dig deeply into the topics they loved. Other alumni say that they came to appreciate the challenging aspects of learning as well, including the personal power they experienced from overcoming obstacles and dealing with the frustrations of learning new things. Finally, alums say they are eager to pass on this love of learning to their own children and to others in their lives as adults. Almost all of the alumni say they are still following what inspires them as adults. They have learned that they will always be doing their Passages.

Our public schools should be places where the fire of passion is lit and kindled. Progressive educators have been arguing about making schools relevant for over a hundred years, yet the basic approach to curriculum hasn't changed. Drop out rates are going through the roof, alienation and even violence leave their marks on our students, and yet we continue to feature content-based, not student-centered programs. The Open School presents an example of what is possible if we get to know students well enough to understand what drives them. As the alumni say so well: a school can and should be the keeper of the flame, a home to which students return to remind themselves what life and learning are all about.

What's It All About? Engage in the Search for Meaning in Your Life

● ● ●Ninety-five percent of the alumni say that the search for meaning is important to their lives as adults.

Always keep a diamond in your mind.
–Tom Waits

I pretty much didn't care about anything, including myself, before I came to the Open School. Now I see that the school opened my eyes to the fact that I had a lot to live for and that it would be a waste of time if I didn't try to find some kind of meaning in my life.
–Nadia, class of 1999

It would be highly unusual, to say the least, to find "search for meaning in your life" as one of the goals or mission statements of a conventional school. In fact, it might be downright controversial. Many Americans think that this kind of personal search should be left to the family, churches, and synagogues. This is a values-laden subject that typically remains far outside the purview of our schools.

Does finding one's values and what gives one's life meaning have anything to do with education anyway? At most schools, it's a moot point; the exclusive focus is measurable academic achievement. Students are seldom asked to look at their lives as journeys of self-reflection or to give any attention to subjects that don't appear on standardized tests. High-stakes testing is further eroding students' opportunities to explore subjects such as philosophy, psychology, or art; these courses are cut back to make room for the coursework that "really matters."

This focus on the so-called fundamentals has made for a rigid curriculum, one that sometimes dismisses the importance of personal growth and that creates additional distance between what is being taught and the learner herself. Too often, students in conventional schools say that what they are being taught is not relevant to their lives, especially at a time when they are trying to find themselves. They feel disconnected and bored.

> I think that what we should be learning is how to examine ourselves
> and create meaning in the lives we are leading. We should be
> talking about the important things, not studying details and facts,
> but looking at the big picture of life. We never get a chance to
> personalize anything. We never talk about life and living as it relates
> to school.
>
> *–Senior at a conventional high school in California, 2000*

When I began to teach at the Open School, I was already comfortable with the concept of ILPs (Individual Learning Plans) from my days as a special education teacher. However, I immediately saw the value of the school's more encompassing, holistic learning program as compared with the restrictive, narrow program that is typical in special education. While the special education ILP was overly prescriptive (e.g., "The student will read at the 8.3 grade level."), the Open School educational plan was relevant to the student (e.g., "John will come up with strategies for controlling his anger."). And, as every student has an individualized plan, everyone is in the "special" category!

All the members of the learning community are encouraged to be seekers, people trying to make sense of their lives. Viewing life as a journey of self-discovery is something the school explicitly supports. Most alumni absorbed the idea of the search for meaning into their adult lives.

> Suffice it to say that the Open School emphasized this search, and
> I feel like I am still on the path. It's a meaningful, lifelong journey,
> fundamental to the human experience. How far we each delve into it
> is a personal decision, but the school put us on the road.
>
> *–John, class of 1980*

This kind of education makes each student think about life and her own particular path. Isn't that what we really want from our schools? It is commonplace for the alumni to say that the school is not a factory—a place that turns out students that conform to some predetermined mold. It is a school of life, a place that really helps in the search for self.

Priorities: The Search Is Important to These Students

Most alumni rated the search for meaning in their lives as highly important. Almost 50 percent said that the priority placed on living a meaningful life and its pervasive role in the school's curriculum affected how they lived their adult lives.

> We talked about it all the time in advising, on trips, and in classes: how was our learning related to making some kind of sense of our lives? It became a mantra that we carry with us in our adult lives.
> *—Mark, class of 1989*

Many former students said that, because the school environment recognized different approaches and different paths, they were able to investigate and integrate multiple perspectives and disciplines in their personal searches for meaning. The bottom line was finding your own path.

> There was so much room for personal points of view to be heard at the school that I felt safe exploring ideas outside standard convention. I felt encouraged to question and learn from many disciplines, to see the interconnections of things. This has been a huge part of the way I live my life—questioning, looking for meaning and connection.
> *—Sue, class of 1976*

For most schools, however, the search for meaning is not a priority. There simply isn't enough time, and it might interfere with academic preparation. Or, it might be a matter for the counseling staff, certainly not for the classroom teacher. Thus, many schools are ill equipped to engage serious issues when they inevitably arise.

Gregg, a student teacher at the Open School whose first teaching job was at a conventional middle school, said that three students at his former school had committed suicide during the year. After these tragedies took place, the obvious issues of alienation and social acceptance were never addressed. Instead, the main topic of conversation at staff meetings was gum chewing in class and how to prevent it. The subject that had traumatized the entire school was, it seemed, taboo.

For Open Schoolers, dealing with important issues is a central part of their education. One alumnus reflected, "We always took time to deal with a crisis; it definitely was more important than an algebra class."

In September of 1987, a drunk driver killed a popular Open School student, riding as a passenger in a car driven by another Open School student. Everything stopped cold as the school experienced its first grieving of a tragic death in the community. The funeral became a process during which the entire school could mourn, share, and commiserate. Speeches were made, embraces were offered, and tears were shared. Everyone felt part of the grieving process, as if the school had always been one big family.

Soon thereafter, the school organized a march against drunk driving, one of the first of its kind in Colorado. Everyone participated. This grieving process became the curriculum for the school for that period. It was important. Looking back on that time, some alumni see that they experienced an acceleration of personal growth. They were becoming adults, many of them dealing with personal tragedy and loss for the first time. Plus, they had a community in which to process and discuss their emotions.

Ero (class of 1988) was the driver of the car that was hit on that fateful night. He was a typical teenager trying to find himself and his path in life. Suddenly, life came cruelly crashing down on him. He couldn't help feeling guilty for what had happened, even as it was obvious there was nothing he could have done to prevent the tragedy. He remembers how the community saved his life.

> I was feeling suicidal, when one of the staff members interceded. She recommended that I leave on a trip of self-discovery, to get away from the situation and engross myself in something I was interested in.
>
> So with money provided by the school, I was able to go to Norway and study a different culture and language. I spent six weeks as an exchange student, busily connecting with a whole different life. In the process, I was able to cleanse myself and get a fresh start on life. My own school helped me survive a tragedy. I learned that having a community that valued real learning experiences was something rare and wonderful! I have never forgotten this.
>
> *–Ero, class of 1988*

Obviously, Ero's curriculum had changed. His studies now included a search for meaning in a world where a random accident could have profound consequences and where terrible things could happen to decent people. Fortunately, he had the guidance of a staff member who knew him well enough to help him through a difficult time when nothing made sense.

School Trips and the Search for Meaning

School trips also helped to create a collective consciousness about searching for meaning from experiences. Mike (class of 1978) says that he appreciated the fact that the trips and Passages were designed to encourage one to see what the world had to offer and "to force one to interpret experiences in terms of the Open School philosophy."

Meredith (class of 1992) on the mountain in Norway, 2008

With as many trips as the school has offered over the years, it is inevitable that some problems with students have arisen that trip groups and the larger school community have had to address. I recall a time when a student broke one of the Big Three Rules (no drugs, alcohol, or sex) on an overseas school trip. We had to process the whole thing when we returned; instead of getting ugly, the trip group talked calmly about the affair in governance (the all-school meeting). We also discussed the roles other students played, either knowingly or unwittingly, in this breach of trust. And, we talked about the fact that the school's reputation was always at stake. Because the school was a place we loved and cherished, we could not allow this potentially tarnishing event to pass without the community's input. Everyone in the community had a chance to contribute and contemplate the larger meaning of the incident. One student said that he learned some basic truths from a difficult situation.

> I learned that there was something bigger than just myself and my own needs. The school meant so much to us that we realized there were some sacrifices we had to make for the greater good. I think it taught me that any school worth protecting was a big idea. It was really a moral dilemma that I have thought about as I approached similar situations in my life as an adult.
> *—Robert, class of 1992*

Making Time for Learning as Part of the Search

Time also stops for less serious but still important learning opportunities. When we had an artist-in-residence dance program, all classes and trips were suspended. Everyone participated and learned from the experience. We were not confined to a predetermined curriculum.

The message is loud and clear: learning takes place everywhere. The important things in life are often unplanned, and difficult times can present wonderful opportunities. Valuable learning can happen at any moment if we are attentive and responsive to what's important.

Every student is continually asked: What did this experience mean for your personal growth? Evaluate what you learned in the three domains. Alumni say that they are apt to ask the same kinds of questions as adults. One alumnus from 1977 puts it this way:

> Constant evaluation! Being open to change and understanding the process of life has made it easier to deal with the ever-changing meaning in my life as an adult. The school instilled in me a priority for the quest for meaning that has touched every aspect of my life. I think we are different from our conventional counterparts. We are used to always looking for a meaning in things because everything at the school had to be evaluated in this light. Now I search for meaning in my work, my relationships, and all areas of my adult life.
> *—Brian, class of 1977*

As Mark (class of 1988) put it so succinctly: "Personal growth became a matter of focused intent, rather than just a side effect of growing up." Many alumni refer to a "sense of purpose" that was engendered by the school community's emphasis on finding meaning in one's education.

Making Sense of It All: Students Who Know How to Put It Together

Many alumni say that the process of putting all the parts of their lives together in an integrated whole was a cornerstone of their school experience. Many point to the Passages and final transcripts as examples. In each they were forced to web, or synthesize, the different forms of learning that took place. Some alumni refer to the process as finding their own voice. They say that they became aware early on that their education at the school was not extraneous to the search for meaning and purpose in their lives, and that integrating all facets of their learning was the key.

Their Passages led students easily into the search for meaning. They had to dig deep and defend their ideas in terms of their relevance and connection to all the different parts of their personal-growth plans. One student worked on several Passages dealing with anger and frustration. At her meetings, she had to discuss why this was an issue for her. In fact, it pervaded all of her Passages, even the ones on ecology and the preservation of wildlife. She had to see the connections and share them with her Passage committee. Now, Heather (class of 1997) says that she realizes how the insights she gained then affect everything she does in her adult life.

Most former students say that writing their final transcripts was the vehicle for seeing the connections among the different parts of their lives. They learned to recognize the themes or strands that were most prominent in their lives and determined how to weave them together in a summary document. Most say that having grappled with connecting themes such as self-image, confidence, and family relationships has led to fuller, more complete lives. Ryan (class of 1982) contends that recognizing the inter-relationships among parts of his life makes it easier "to figure things out when life gets confusing and hard."

> I had to show how each of my Passages, trips, and experiences related to the themes of artistic self-image, confidence, tolerance for frustration, and family relationships. It was hard, but it was worth it.

Kelli (class of 1994) came to the school with a severe drug problem. She worked closely with her advisor and me (as a special education teacher) to confront her issues. In her final transcript, she had to write a personal statement—an account of the important themes in her life. Kelli wrote from the heart:

> My life has been a rough road with lots of traffic. In the past year I have grown, matured, and changed so much. For the first time in my life, I have enjoyed going to school. I have been consistent in my attendance. This has made me feel good about myself and given me the chance to get to know other people.

I never thought I would go back to school. I never had enough faith
in myself until this year. I now know that I can trust myself to have
goals and successfully complete them.

I realize now that I have grown up way too fast, and I wish I could
be a few years younger. But I cannot go on thinking about the past; I
can only try to make better decisions for myself in the future.

Kelli goes on to say that she worked on basic academic skills such as reading
and writing as well as her computer skills. She also discusses other important
issues in her life, like completing the goals and projects she began and developing
her artistic abilities. She continues with the theme of dealing with her tough family
situation. Nothing, however, would have been actualized without her confronting
her drug abuse.

I never would have even been aware of these issues if I hadn't come
out from the fog of drug use. With the support of the school, I was
able to see more clearly, and I was able to make choices that were
actually good for me.

Kelli even incorporated her drug issue into her curriculum. She spoke to
advisory groups about her battle with drugs. She did research papers on drugs
and their effects. She shared her new-found knowledge by giving back to the
school community. It felt good to give back to a place that had been so supportive.
And, by putting it all together in a personal statement, Kelli was able to glean the
real meaning of her education. Time and again, she credits the Open School for
facilitating such a personal search for meaning.

Julia (class of 2000) offers another example of the power of writing one's
own final transcripts. She took the idea to the next level by personalizing her
education in the most meaningful of ways. In her personal statement she wrote:

My education resides in healthy relationships and learning to treat
others with respect and decency. For me, education means observing
an object so thoroughly that it almost becomes a part of you. Real
learning is not easily contained. My personal education stretches
far beyond the four walls of one building; it encompasses all the
moments of my life.

Julia divided her final transcript into what she identified as the central themes
in her learning experience: being a part of a community of learners, creating
the world, the creative mind, the global perspective, the evolution of logic, the

power of language, and the "creation of myself." Putting the pieces of her self-crafted education together, Julia added the specific components that comprised each theme, and proceeded to integrate and give shape to her education.

For instance, in her section on acquiring a global perspective, Julia elaborated on classes, trips, and participation in various groups and organizations that had expanded her vision and helped her embrace a sense of global citizenship. Among the formative experiences Julia included were: classes on the Holocaust, world religions, and twentieth-century history. She also noted her participation in the Teacapan trip, in which she explored another culture in depth, as well as trips to Europe and the Boundary Waters. Julia added other experiences that broadened her horizons and gave meaning to her life as a young woman transitioning to adulthood, such as teaching classes to new immigrants at an inner-city elementary school and tutoring refugees at a bilingual center.

The Boundary Waters canoe trip

Julia's transcript is a work of art in its own right. It courageously addresses the real issues in her life. She creates meaning for herself on every page by tying her growth themes together into a dynamic web of meaning.

The Three Domains and the Five Goals:
Students Who Have a Compass for Their Lives

All of the alumni were raised in the three domains: social, personal, and intellectual. Alumni are readily able to recite the litany of these three pillars of learning at a moment's notice. Most feel that this framework, along with the five goals—rediscover the joy of learning, engage in the search for meaning in your life, adapt to the world that is, prepare for the world that might be, and create the world that ought to be—serve as guideposts in their lives. Many say they learned to see everything in these terms. Because every single experience, class, and project had to be evaluated in terms of the three domains, alums learned to accept this as a way of living. Many former students say that the three domains and the five goals function as a compass or map that shows them the way when they have to make life decisions.

> Recently, when I had to make a decision about a graduate program
> versus a job, I asked myself what it meant to me in the three
> domains. My values are still based on the Open School philosophy
> about meaning and passion.
> *—Joe, class of 1990*

I recently went to Haiti on a medical service trip to start a clinic in a small village with a church group that was quite religious. I soon found that I was the first nonbeliever to have ever gone on the mission trip. I was scrutinized. What did I believe in? Why was I there? After sharing my Open School experience and the five goals of the school, one of the doctors said, "I see that you are a passionate believer! You have excellent values, and you have a strong framework for living a full life." Many alumni concur:

> I have many friends who are, like me, Open School alumni. We
> often talk about how we use the five goals of the school and the
> three domains in our lives. It's a way of living according to some
> basic principles. It adds to and gives meaning to your life. I always
> ask myself about the joy of learning, dealing with the world, helping
> others, and the meaning of the whole thing.
> *—Nick, class of 1995*

Students Who Continue to Ask Questions on Their Search

Others say that the critical-thinking skills they developed helped them search for their own meaning. They were taught to question everything, to continually explore and examine. Some credit their Logical Inquiry Passage as a particularly formative experience.

> Doing my Logical Inquiry Passage really helped me see that I
> had to think critically. Using the scientific method—formulating
> hypotheses and testing them out—is a way of searching for the truth.
> As an adult, I never take anything at face value.
> *—Larry, class of 1989*

One alumna has found it interesting that the fellow alumni she knows have all turned out so differently: "Some joined the military, others marched for peace." She realizes that everyone is searching for his or her own truth, not some prescribed version of it. Her fellow former students, she observes, all have a sense of healthy skepticism that helps to inform their decision-making processes. She sees that, like herself, alumni continue to ask questions and examine the consequences of their decisions for themselves and for others in their communities.

> I often find myself asking: How do my decisions affect others? Am I contributing in a positive way? What are my core values, and am I living in accordance with them?
>
> For instance, I am a nurse, and I feel that I am helping to better the emotional, physical, and even spiritual lives of my patients. But I also choose to live in a small town where I don't have to drive too much. I also hang my clothes instead of using a dryer, and eat organic food. It all comes from this constant questioning of whether my life is in sync with my values.
>
> *–Emi, class of 1995*

Being a critical thinker and persistently asking questions does not come without its pitfalls, however. One alumna, who lives overseas, tells this story.

> "The unexamined life is not worth living!" This describes the Open School philosophy in a nutshell. If there was one thing that the school was good at, it was teaching all of us to question everything: the world, the government, the social structure, and even ourselves. The school taught us to attempt to make improvements in all aspects of our lives on an ongoing basis.
>
> It is, however, a double-edged sword. I met a woman, years ago, who was from a very religious, strict upbringing. This woman had married at a young age and had devoted her life to raising her children and keeping the house for her husband. She believed that her husband was the head of the household, and she followed his decisions on everything. She knew, from the time she was young, exactly what was expected of her and what her role in life would be, and there was never any doubt in her mind that this was the correct path for her to follow.

I, on the other hand, have never been that certain of anything. I have chosen to be independent, to make my own decisions, and to earn my own way in the world. I have had successes and I have made mistakes, and sometimes I couldn't tell the difference between the two. I have questioned my life over and over, and have struggled to find my place in the world.

Many, many times I have remembered that woman and her secure, structured life, and I have envied her. There is no doubt in my mind that she is the happier one. If I could do it over, however, I would never choose to live her life over the one I have led. I am glad that I have been taught to question, to examine, and to struggle to improve. It may not, in all cases, have made me a happier person, but it has made me a better one.

−Jean Anne, class of 1979

Courage: Students Who Are Not Afraid to Keep Searching

Many alumni say that their advisors were the first to give them the courage and confidence to try new things and to look for their own truths. Graduation itself was an excellent testing ground.

Graduating from the Open School was one of the hardest things I have ever done. My advisor helped as a kind of self-concept coach. She believed in me, so I began to believe in myself. This sense of self-worth led me to a feeling of real accomplishment when I finished my last Passage and wrote my transcripts. I have carried this forward in my life as a social activist and a scholar. My search for meaning is fueled by the feeling that I can actually do it on my own and keep on doing it the rest of my life.

−Aaron, class of 1996

Corrine (class of 1997) reiterated the idea that one needs confidence and self-esteem to embark on the search for meaning in one's life. She notes that a person who "constantly questions her self-worth" is not in a place where she can even begin to pursue a deeper meaning. In her years at the Open School, Corrine struggled to find her voice. It took lots of time and patience and many heart-to-heart talks with her advisors to develop a sense of self-worth, but this gave her the confidence and inner strength to get started on the journey of self-discovery.

I needed to have my desires validated before I could proceed on the fumbling journey to figure out what meaning is and what it means to go looking for it. In the end, the confidence and sense of identity that the school fostered in me were enormous components in my search for meaning and continue to give me strength as I make important decisions as an adult.

—Corrine, class of 1997

Schools can offer the backbone for students to become lifelong searchers and learners. The advisory system and personalized projects at the Open School help students experience and process the search itself while they are in their formative years, and provide a support system for them as they begin to deal with life's challenges and triumphs.

For some alumni, the search has taken on some dramatic twists and turns.

Profile of Success
A SEEKER CONNECTS WITH LIFE
Johannes Wirth, Class of 1993

Born into the rigid social system of East Germany, Johannes felt that he just didn't fit in, and his early adolescence was painful. His desire to break out of the pressurized uniformity was seen as anti-social. His father was as disapproving of him as the establishment was. His relationships with the men in his life were stressful. No one seemed to care about how Johannes was feeling. He sees now that he was invisible to his teachers. He felt physically ill because his love of learning was being stamped out by an autocratic system.

On November 9, 1989, things changed dramatically. As the Berlin Wall tumbled, Johannes saw a ray of hope. His curiosity about the outside world was piquing. At the tender age of thirteen, he began to make his plan. He spent the next three years applying to and preparing for an international student exchange program. His parents, however, were not supportive.

> I had to do all the work, fill out all the papers, and go through all
> the bureaucracy. I was determined to see the world and explore the
> possibilities.

One day a letter arrived. Johannes had gotten into an American high school in Denver, Colorado. His host family lived in Golden. Johannes seized the opportunity to begin his adventure. Unfortunately, when he arrived in the U.S., the exchange organization informed him that they had made a mistake. Golden High School was full. Johannes had already settled in with his host family. Their kids went to a different kind of school, and they recommended that he give it a try. Johannes had this to say about his first impression:

> The first time I came to the Open School, they were having a swim day at an outside pool. There were kids of all ages there just having fun and talking. It was incredibly free and natural. Could this really be a school? I was immediately taken in and made to feel at home.

There was a distinct lack of pressure in the air and a sense of openness about school and learning. He now says that it was like coming out of "an oppressive fog" into the daylight. Johannes was definitely in the ecstasy stage. He was free at last, and loving every minute of it.

> I began to blossom like a flower that had not been nurtured enough. I wanted to do everything! I decided to take every possible trip, every class, all of the experiences that were available. I was like a thirsty man who had come to an oasis. I wanted to drink until the water was running down my neck!

Looking back, Johannes sees that this initial recognition of his joy for learning led to the idea that success was somehow related to a zest for life. This was the starting point for self-discovery: a validation of his approach to life and learning.

> I started to see that successful people were those who were passionate and free. No experience was too much for them. They saw it all as a grand adventure.

Johannes took eight extended trips during that year. He went to Mexico to teach English in a small fishing village; he went on the Archeology trip to Arizona, on the desert sea trip to California, and even to the Missouri River to help with flood relief. He learned how to make snow caves on a winter camping trip and how to canoe on the Boundary Waters of Minnesota.

> I really connected to the idea of initiation and belonging to a real community. For the first time in my life, I felt acknowledged for who I was and who I was becoming. The kids and teachers spent quality time with each other. They really cared. It was like a balm on my heart, a healing medicine.

For the first time, Johannes had the chance to become actively involved in his own education. He took advantage of this opportunity and began to contribute to his newfound community. He worked in the cafeteria; he played with the little kids. He even took on a leadership role by educating others about the Open School.

Quickly, Johannes became part of the school mythology. Stories about him eating hot chilies in Mexico and building snow caves in the San Juan Mountains spread throughout the school. He was the tall gangly kid from East Germany who had really taken off at the school.

In many ways, coming from his restrictive social and political environment, Johannes was not unlike the students arriving from strict, rigid conventional schools. All of a sudden, he was in an environment that required self-direction, not blind conformity. He couldn't wait for someone to tell him what to do; he had to take the initiative. He began to realize that success did not come without the sometimes difficult step of setting out on the journey of self-discovery. Sometimes it meant being willing to take risks.

> I think that being unafraid to take the first step was really big for me. Once I had the confidence (built from many Open School experiences), I really got to like taking chances.

Relationships with adults helped with developing courage. Johannes connected closely with several male staff members, the first such positive relationships he had ever experienced. These were important parts of his growth in becoming an adult.

When the year was over, Johannes felt the dread of going back to Germany. His parents persuaded him to come back right away to finish his studies. His return was not without problems. He had to deal with some difficult challenges in his homeland.

> My principal referred to my year abroad at "that garden school."
> He thought I had been a farmer for the whole time. He also took the attitude that I was probably very behind in my skills and credits.

Of course, Johannes proved him wrong. His grades actually improved, and his attitude was obviously changed. He said that he didn't feel the pressure as acutely after relishing the joy and freedom he had experienced. He had learned how to relax, and it made a difference in his ability to learn. He even improved in math, previously his weakest subject area. To support his well-being in his return to a straight-jacketed curriculum, he took tai chi, karate, and piano lessons. He rode his bicycle whenever he could to stay in shape. In short, he continued the well-rounded approach to life he had learned was best for him.

His confidence in his own abilities led him to present educational seminars about the Open School model to German principals around the country. He also talked about finding his German roots and exploring his own culture in more depth. He was still searching.

> I was just taking "seeking meaning in my life" to another level. I desperately wanted to share my joy and passion for learning with others. At the same time, I began to search my roots to see what I could relate to in my new awareness. I found that German culture had lots of influences in environmental and even holistic approaches to education. I began to see the connections and it made me feel more rooted and confident.

Because of his sense of empowerment, he even came to terms with his father, another big step in becoming a man and in his personal education. Then, through good fortune and a lot of searching, Johannes found a new educational home. It was a unique college in Germany that resonated with the Open School philosophy—a training program for holistic health practitioners. The three-year program's motto was: "Heal yourself first in order to help others do the same."

> The school was a godsend for me. I already knew what was possible from my time at the Open School. Now I was back in a supportive environment where people were encouraged to feel passionate about life!

Johannes (class of 1993) in Tanzania with an Aborigine elder of the Yalanji

Johannes has pursued a career as a holistic counselor, in which he works with people who need help and guidance, in much the same way as his advisor did with him. The goals are similar: to help people find out who they are and where their passions lie. Johannes has continued, in various forms, the service work he experienced at the school. He has helped to create the world that ought to be, knowing that a successful life depends on giving back to others.

Johannes says after working for some time as a counselor, he felt an urge to explore what he calls "functional communities" in different countries. This led to a trip around the world, looking into some of the various forms of support networks and communities that people in different regions have established. He says, "I know that communities like the Open School are not only feasible, but probably part of our hope for the future: sustainable, nurturing kinds of places that most people never dreamed could exist."

So the search continues. Johannes returns to the Open School every couple of years or so to volunteer by teaching classes and leading trips. He sees it as giving back to a place he loves and admires. He cherishes his experience at the school and how it has enabled him to help others who are struggling to free themselves from feeling trapped in a "rigid, other-directed world" as he himself once was.

> I find I can help kids adjust to a unique environment wherein they will be valued for their gifts, not demeaned for their deficits. My connection to the school will last a lifetime. After all, it's the place where I became myself!

Johannes's plans for the future include marriage and the establishment of a community in Germany based on Open School ideals. Johannes describes his life as "very successful." He says he has found ways to help people find their own gifts and follow their own paths. He has also developed meaningful relationships with his friends and family.

> I learned at Open School that being successful is all about having good relationships. It's such an important part of being happy with your life. It also takes hard work to keep relationships going.

Freedom, discovery, and happiness are central to the meaning of success for Johannes. As he continues his quest for the ideal community, he keeps the Open School goals in mind. Feeling successful in life depends on it. His story is a great example of how encouraging personal growth can make a passive student into a vigorous, hopeful adventurer.

Putting Things into Perspective

It is evident that alumni are seekers and searchers. Much of this curiosity and drive to find the meaning of things comes from the high priority they place on the constant examination of life itself. Obviously, they are not afraid to ask questions and confront the status quo. They are also well-practiced in the art of putting the different arenas of life together into a meaningful whole. Alumni say that they use the guideposts of the three domains and the five goals of the school for support. They observe that the nurturing environment of the school community helped them gain the confidence and inner strength to begin the never-ending search for meaning in their lives. Most say the journey, despite its many ups and downs, is well worthwhile.

The idea that the journey of self-discovery and meaning is the crux of an authentic education goes back to the dawn of time. The school's alumni realize that, without personal meaning, learning and living are pointless. Further, without this focus on meaning, education can seem useless, even absurd.

But, when the search for meaning is emphasized, and even revered, it makes education synonymous with living. Suddenly, the roads and paths of the journey are brightly illuminated and our life choices feel vibrant and exciting. All schools can assist in this search by providing a strong base from which to reach out. We should be demanding the development of these important life skills from our education system. The Open School alumni show us that when we do, the journey never ends and that the possibilities are infinite.

The Real World:
Adapting to the World that Is

Be careful out there! Somebody's gonna get hurt.
–Ruth Posner (my mom), 1914–1997

The Open School helped me to get over the shoulda-coulda-wouldas and cope with the world that is. Sure, there are some things you just can't change, but if you don't try to change the things you can for the better, all you're doing is taking up good oxygen.
–Jeni, class of 1990

Adapting to the world that exists—the third of the five Open School goals—is an objective that some conventional schools like to think that they do better at addressing than the Open School does. Some mainstream educators criticize the school for being "too idealistic," "not competitive enough," and "failing in the basic academics." Some of these sentiments, I think, can be attributed to plain old jealousy. I have heard several teachers and parents admit, "School was hell for me, why should it be fun for them?" and "I had to do it the hard way, why not you?" For whatever reason, the school is frequently looked upon—particularly by those who have taken only a cursory look at its curriculum and track record—as unrealistic, a fantasyland where everyone does whatever he wants without ever compromising, accommodating, or adjusting to the real world.

I also had some concerns about the school when I first arrived. Initially,

I had to fight my own conservative demons about what I had been taught to believe about education and life. How could students be motivated without grades? How would they turn out with an education that didn't give them enough structure and rigor in their academic pursuits? Would they gain the skills and the drive people need to succeed in the real world?

These worries, I soon found out, were actually the result of my own anxieties. When I looked deeper at my own life and questioned what motivated me, I realized that, in fact, I was not beholden to grades or driven by competition—unless I was competing with myself, striving to better my own accomplishments. In grappling with these issues, I went through the same kind of self-examination as any student new to the school.

In addition, when I first arrived, all I saw around me were staunch individualists. After a short time, however, I began to see how the school community came together and cooperated in ways that the conventional world only gave lip service to. Concepts like "shared leadership," "collective struggle," and real "democracy" started to come alive for me as I led staff meetings, engaged in debates in governance meetings, and took part in all-school activities and community service projects. Gradually, I began to see that the kids were going through a necessary process of finding themselves and discovering how they personally could best contribute to the larger community—something all teens need to grapple with, but are usually discouraged from doing in the context of school.

As I began to see the fruits of my labor (my first graduates) and the students' obvious maturity, self-awareness, and personal responsibility, I started to see the light. Students had experience in making important decisions, in choosing their own schedules and goals, and even in hiring staff and administrators. I began to understand that these kids went out into the real world all the time. Indeed, there was little separation between school and the outside world. As one alumnus put it, "The real world was always coming in and out of the Open School; you couldn't avoid it even if you wanted to!"

When I reflected on my years teaching in conventional schools, I realized that I never saw the real inclusion of kids in the decisions that shaped their education or their lives. In fact, their voices were intentionally marginalized because they were "just kids." Thus, students in these settings were seldom allowed to make decisions or given any real power over their lives. What part of the real world were they being sheltered from? It was probably the important part.

Many alumni describe their ability to engage with the real world as unfolding in stages. First comes the development of some self-awareness or sense of one's place in the world, followed by an increased confidence in one's ability to adapt to and confront the realities that exist. Next comes a growing awareness of the world and its challenges and possibilities—the development of a world view. As a result of this process, an attitude develops; it's a feeling that one can shape one's life within a context outside of school. This attitude allows students to develop a set of skills that are honed through trial and error in the outside world, backed up by the supportive environment of the school. Former students report that it is through this process that they have found ways to achieve real-world goals without compromising their personal values.

Learning to deal with the world that is begins with self-awareness and confidence and then broadens into inquiry and interaction with the world at large. The idea that schools can be fertile ground for building confidence and promoting personal growth is not some pie-in-the-sky idea. It all starts with a personalized plan of action.

Self-Knowledge: Students Who Face the World Knowing Themselves and Their Possibilities

Each student has to create an Individualized Learning Plan (ILP), with his advisor and support groups, that includes an understanding of his strengths and challenges when it comes to dealing with the real world. Taking a hard, honest look at oneself is the starting point for self-knowledge.

Christian (class of 1998) addressed in his ILP his difficulties with completion and endurance in all three domains of personal growth: social (maintaining relationships), personal (following through with commitments), and intellectual (closure on assignments). Consequently, he set running a marathon as one of his goals. The training and preparation involved all of his issues in all three domains. The completion came right before graduation. In his final support group, he felt like he had confronted real-life issues directly. He spoke, as do so many alumni, of wrestling with issues of commitment, planning, and closure. Looking back, he says that "it was as real as it gets" and that walking out of high school he was ready to take the real world head on.

Other students talk about becoming more aware of their limits by challenging themselves in real-life situations.

> When I deal with things that are tough, I remember my Adventure Passage, which was climbing some fourteeners [mountains over fourteen thousand feet]. I look at these situations as opportunities for problem solving and learning more about myself and my limits in the real world.
>
> *–Brian, class of 1981*

Alumni like Christian and Brian say that that they gained a sense of who they are, which gave them confidence about facing the real world. With the help of their advisors and peers, Open Schoolers tend to find their place in the world by continuously exploring and processing their experiences in and out of the school setting. In fact, if they choose to, students can do most of their work outside of the building. Jeff came from a conventional school as a junior in 1981. With his advisor, he realized that the things he was enthusiastic about would take him out of the school building, that he was an active, experiential learner who needed the real world as his classroom. He took advantage of his newfound freedom to design his own program.

Jeff did as many internships, apprenticeships, and trips as the school offered. He now sees that the Open School was like a guidance center for him, a place where he could return to share his learning and progress in dealing with the real world. He observes that, in many ways, conventional school does not prepare one for the real world.

> The real world isn't like conventional school. I've never called a boss "Ms." or "Mr." And true fulfillment in life isn't something you're pushed into.

> The Open School never pushed me into anything; it just helped me to know myself. This helped me find the goals to reach for and a whole lot of experiences on which to build. I soon discovered that I had the strength and passion to make my way in the world without all of that hierarchical nonsense of the conventional school.

In today's world, one frequently hears stories about what heavy baggage many kids take to school: dealing with dysfunctional families, drugs, gangs, or poverty. Many teachers are frustrated by their students' lack of confidence; their angry, negative view of themselves; and their fears about dealing with the world at large.

Students who come to the Open School are no different. They often come into the building with a giant chip on their shoulders. It takes some time for them to adjust. They think, "A school that is welcoming and cherishes personal freedom? You must be putting me on!" Gradually these newcomers begin to catch on, but they usually go through an ecstatic stage (I can do anything I want to!) where they try to push the limits of their freedom by skipping classes or being uninvolved.

This is typically followed by a crisis stage, when they tend to hit an existential wall. Now that I have all of this freedom, what do I do with it? This is usually the time when they have to begin dealing with the real world, particularly the responsibility and self-control that comes with their newfound freedom. The nice part is that the school provides a safety net under all the inevitable trial and error that is bound to occur.

Many students came from families and backgrounds where there was no sense of trust or foundation upon which to build confidence in oneself. They were starting from rock bottom. Derek (class of 1995) recalls that he was an angry person who had plenty of personal and family baggage when he first arrived. He pushed the limits of the school and made some people quite upset, but now he feels like he had to learn from his mistakes. With strong support, Derek began to confront his issues and along with them the real world.

> I learned to trust for the first time. As a result, I grew confident in
> trying new things, putting my neck on the line with social stuff,
> and dealing with the world that is. I got the opportunity to grow up,
> really. I began to get to know myself, my strengths, my challenges.

> Now that I am an adult, I have the confidence to make my own way
> in a world that often seems negative and out-of-whack.

Awareness of the World that Is: Students Who Know the Score

All of the trips and experiences outside the classroom help students develop an awareness of the world around them. One alumnus described this as "an expansion beyond an egocentric view of the world that plagues many teenagers." Getting outside themselves can be healthy for adolescents. Some alumni look back on their first trips with school as awakening a new consciousness.

> The wilderness trip opened my eyes to a respect for nature that I
> didn't even think about before. Now, as an adult, I have pursued a
> career as an outdoor educator, and I help others become more aware
> of the world around them.
> *–Nick, class of 1995*

The school trips I led to the Delta area of Mississippi were like going to a Third World country. Some students were jolted by the experience.

> I saw a lot of things that white suburban kids just don't see. I saw
> poverty and desperation in our own country. Also, I felt what it was
> like to be a minority as a white person in what seemed to be an all
> African-American community. It was hard not to become more
> aware of the world around me.
> *–Joey, class of 1996*

In the early nineties, after the Missouri River floods, waves of Open School students went to the riverbanks to help the victims. Students gained an understanding of the effects of a natural disaster; this gave rise to a newfound awareness of the world, its tragedies, and the resilience of its people.

> The Missouri River trip changed the way I saw the world. It took some personal courage to even go there and think I could help and make a difference. I became aware of what can happen to anyone in the world and how I could help others as they struggled to save their lives.
>
> *–Beth, class of 1995*

In 1989, after the Berlin Wall came down, I asked if kids wanted to go see for themselves what was really going on in the world, and to "make history instead of take history" by going with me to Berlin. We ended up taking seventeen students to Berlin, staying with German families, and exploring history, culture, and politics. We were there for almost three weeks. Meanwhile, a conventional high school in Jefferson County, near the Open School, captured the local education section headlines by taking three of its student council students to Germany for one weekend!

The Berlin trip had lasting effects. We raised our consciousness. For some, this experience led to a lifetime of geopolitical awareness.

> The Berlin trip changed my life. I didn't know anything about communism or European history until we took the pretrip classes. My trip project was conducting video interviews with East Berliners

The Berlin wall

on the day of the first (and last) democratic election in East Berlin!
NBC couldn't have gotten better coverage. I fell in love with the
German people and their new freedom. As a result, I have lived and
studied in Germany as an adult. I'm able to adapt and fit into the
world that is.
—Mike, class of 1990

Another trip that had a huge impact on students was the Middle East trip of
2000, where students stayed with Israeli and Palestinian families and youth groups
on both sides of the Green Line, including the Gaza Strip. We visited refugee
camps where the teenagers handed us flowers for their loved ones who were killed
in the first Palestinian uprising. It was a powerful experience, seeing the grief and
mourning on the part of a people that many of us had recently considered as the
enemy in the Israeli-Palestinian conflict.

On the other side of the line, in Israel, we met Israelis who served as soldiers
in the Six Day War. We also spent some time at a kibbutz and talked with Israeli
teenagers about their views of the conflict. Outside of Ramallah, we stayed in a
youth hostel that had only recently been an Israeli jail for Palestinian political
prisoners. We actually slept in the cells! The trip had a powerful impact on the
kids' worldviews; they learned how perspectives and interpretations are shaped by
history and culture and that people's lives were much like their own. All they really
wanted was what we all want—to be happy and live healthy, fulfilling lives.

On the Middle East trip, I learned that teenagers are very much alike
all over the world. The Israeli and Palestinian kids listened to the same
music, watched the same movies, and even ate the same food as us.
We had so much in common, yet the killing continues. I wish everyone
could realize how alike they really are. This trip changed me forever;
I know the road to peace is a rough one, but I think we can get there if
we just focus on what we have in common.
—Lynn, class of 2002

Obviously, these exposures to real-world situations helped students develop
an understanding of the world that couldn't be realized in a classroom. Firsthand
experience with the world is something the students have plentiful opportunities
to get. Sometimes kids get an early glimpse of the injustices of the world, the
poverty, and the grinding struggle of the lives of the majority of the people in
the world.

When I went to Colombia on a school trip, I had my eyes opened
to the way of life for most people of the world. I met people who

were still in the feudal mindset, people working the rich plantation
owner's land. It was amazing to see something that must have been
like a pre-Civil War situation in the U.S. in the modern world.
This experience gave me a real and somewhat harsh taste of the
real world. Since then, I have traveled through Latin America and
continued my education about the world that really exists beyond the
textbooks and lectures of the comfortable and privileged First World.

–Nicolas, class of 1995

Just learning not to take our comforts and luxuries for granted makes a
difference in our worldviews. Meeting real people—in Latin America, the Middle
East, Europe, or even in rural Mississippi—and listening to their stories and
sharing their meals: this is what real-world education is all about. The community
service component that is part of most trips also serves to deepen this awareness.
This is experiential learning at its best.

After trips and school activities, students spend time trying to make sense of
and interpret their experiences. This process adds to their understanding of the
world that is.

I learned to put things together in a comprehensive way after mind-
boggling experiences like the Lakota Sioux trip to the Pine Ridge
Reservation. We learned to look at our experiences in a shared way,
with each of us contributing his or her point of view. After a trip like
that, no one ever looked at the world the same way.

–John, class of 1999

Two school trips to Cuba at the time of the Elian Gonzalez affair (2001)
opened plenty of eyes too. Traveling on an educational license, the Open School
hooked up with a performing arts school outside of Havana. After going to baseball
games, dancing with Cuban students and teachers, and just hanging out playing
stick ball on the streets of Havana, students were amazed to discover a world that
had always been taboo for Americanos.

I saw an entirely new way of living in Cuba. Here was a poor Third
World country with excellent health care and highly educated
citizens! There was no animosity either. We got along just fine with
the Cuban people.

–Logan, class of 2002

The political realities of the world are rarely explored on an experiential
basis in conventional schools. Open School students, however, are constantly

afforded opportunities to become aware of the political issues facing the world. Many alumni recall working for and even creating political action groups. One alumnus worked for the Governor's Council on Education while another created a new organization called the Student Empowerment Association, made up of high school students from all over the state.

> I learned so much about the political world through real-life
> organizing efforts that resulted in a statewide conference.
> There weren't too many high school kids who had the freedom
> and opportunities to do this sort of thing for their education. I
> learned that I liked to empower other people. As an adult, I have
> always felt that I had the confidence and the vision to make
> things happen, so I have stayed active in the political arena in
> many different areas. My worldview included being active and
> involved in issues that affected my local life as well as the
> larger world.
> *—David, class of 1990*

Open School trips around the world

All the trips and experiences have had their effect. Most alumni say that their increased awareness of other cultures and societies has resulted in a far less insular, self-centered view of the world. After working with Israeli and Palestinian teenagers on peace initiatives and picking chilies in the fields of Mexico, alumni say they can never see the world in quite the same way again. Now, as adults, they feel that they know something about the human condition; they know that we are all part of the same small planet, and they know that we need to depend on each other now more than ever. Students come to understand the interconnectedness of the world.

Antonella (class of 1982), now the leader of a major world development organization in Europe, says that what she learned at the school directly relates to her work throughout the world.

> I see that we all have a responsibility for each other's well-being in this world. The school also taught me how important it is to be different, to respect these differences, and not to be afraid of them. I now see diversity as a resource, as an asset in a globally connected world.

The school as part of a global village is a forwarding looking concept. If part of the mission of education is to prepare students for the real world it seems critical that schools allow for experiential learning on trips and exchanges, not just for the honor roll students but for everyone.

Along with this exposure to the real world come some problems and frustrations. Some students object to what they see as political bias or a rosy picture of an ideal world being promulgated by the school.

Other Points of View

Because globalization brings all of us directly or indirectly into increasing contact with diverse cultures, the understanding of and respect for differences often comes in handy. However, some alumni felt that the school went too far in promoting respect for cultural diversity.

> Sure, I learned patience and tolerance from our forays into the real world. But, while we learned to respect cultural diversity, I don't believe that we focused enough on the negative aspects of other cultures as much we should have. When we want to change the world, we need to know what is wrong with it, not just realizing our own [the United States'] mistakes, but the mistakes of others as well. We can't do that if we are so concerned with being politically correct that our vision is colored as much as that of people who commit acts of hatred. A balance has to be maintained.
>
> *–Joe, class of 1999*

Another alumnus, from the seventies, echoes this sentiment. He says the school limited its perspective of the world to a hippie viewpoint that excluded other, more traditional, points of view.

> *A Whale for the Killing* could have been an interesting counterpoint to *Moby Dick*, much as *Small Is Beautiful* could have been set against *Wealth of Nations*. What terrific fights those would have been! But we didn't get Herman Melville or Adam Smith. We got

the minor, newer, more liberal points of view instead of, rather than
in comparison to, the older, more mainstream American thought.
—Allan, class of 1976

Some alumni found it rather disheartening that the values and attitudes they
had learned to embrace were not always those shared in the mainstream world.
For some this led to a feeling of frustration and even anger.

While I found the Open School an oasis of love and caring, it
was a surprise for me to enter the world-that-is and find out that
not everyone is like that. I was completely taken aback by daily
transgressions like hit-and-run drivers, civil servants who are
dishonest, Presidents who try to cover up lies, and, in general,
people who fail to take responsibility for their own behavior. I still
don't know how to deal constructively with these problems.
—Ann, class of 1992

From all of the alumni responses, one particularly harsh characterization
of the school's influence came through to temper the abundance of positive
feedback.

I was in shock when I left the Open School because of my inability
to deal with the real world. I was not prepared. I had the idea that
everything was happy-go-lucky and would somehow magically
work out for me. This attitude got me into trouble. I had to readjust
to the real world, and I was actually quite depressed by the fact that
the school had painted a world for me that was not accurate at all.
—Meredith, class of 1992

Other students, however, said that they fully expected that the norms and
values of the existing culture would be at odds with the school's in some ways.
They say that that was why they chose to go the school in the first place. Further,
they expected to take what they learned there and use it to challenge and change
the limitations of the status quo.

Every person who chooses to deal with this culture rather than
confront it represents another link in the chain of conformity that leads
us to the precarious situation we are now faced with on this planet.

I came to the school to escape the world of robot teachers, prison-
warden principals, and high school security guards, and it provided

me with the opportunity to fall in love with life. It gave me the awareness of what was possible beyond merely dealing with what I am told is right or wrong. Now, looking back, I prefer to think that the Open School gave me the courage to reject and confront the world that is, rather than simply deal with it.
—Jamie, class of 1993

Another alumnus takes a somewhat different approach when managing his frustration with the mainstream culture. He says that his main tool for working with unpleasant realities is to refer to one of the graduation requirements of the school: to develop and maintain a sense of humor.

I remember humor being a big part of the Open School. It was emphasized as much as anything in the curriculum. Believe me, I rely on it frequently when I am dealing with difficult situations in the real world.
—Dave, class of 1990

Finally, a response that was common among alumni was that they learned that they were the ones responsible for dealing with the world that is.

I probably had more dealings with the real world than some of the other kids. I had been living on the streets, raped, cold, and hungry, while most of my peers just came to school and went home to a safe place. However, no one at the Open School ever tried to paint the world with a rosy brush. I came away from the school with a sense of knowing that whatever my world was to be, I was the one who was ultimately responsible for its creation.
—Kate, class of 1976

Life Skills: Students Who Know How to Deal with the World that Is

A majority of alumni say that the school gave them opportunities to develop effective life skills. Alumni report that they are grateful for the focus on setting goals and evaluating them on a continuous basis. One alumnus, who is a plumber, said that this kind of planning and evaluation was "what the school was all about." Passages, ILPs, and all of the evaluation writing helped this alumnus to use these skills in his adult life.

I have to go through a lot of bureaucracy in my work. I had to go through four sets of licensure: the Back Flow Technologist license, the Journeyman, the Certified Pool Director license, and finally the Master Plumber license. I used my planning skills from Open School to follow through and deal with these kinds of steps in my career.

—Mark, class of 1997

The following is a list of life skills that students learn at the school, cited by alumni as having served them well as adults facing the world:

• Doing what needs to be done in order to make things happen

• Taking responsibility for budgeting and planning

• Dealing with different types of people

• Adapting to constant change

• Setting goals and evaluating progress

• Dealing with challenging situations

• Dealing with bureaucracy

• Compromising

• Listening

• Decision making

• Being responsible for your own behavior

• Learning from one's mistakes

• Taking the initiative

• Multitasking

Nearly everything that a student needs to do in order to graduate requires some measure of these life skills. In fact, many of these are listed in the Graduation Expectations that are used as a framework to guide students through the school program. One alumnus refers to these kinds of skills as comprising an intellectual agility that develops as a result of all the experiential learning. One simply learns how to take care of oneself and to deal with the world that is.

When a school expects these kinds of life skills from its students, the curriculum changes from a focus on "let's get ready for the test" to "let's get ready for the real world." Teaching life skills should be part of every school's mission. As the next profile demonstrates, the transition from school to real world is smoothed by knowing how to deal with the world that is.

Profile of Success
THE WORLD IS READY TO EMBRACE YOU!
John Mattox, Class of 1981

School seemed easy but boring for John until his family broke apart in the mid-seventies. Then things began to crash. His life started to flood with truancies, arrests for drugs, and even some jail time. As he became even angrier and alienated he began to see school as a dead end. He even took to tripping on mushrooms to battle the boredom. School was something he "just wanted to end" so he could finally start his real life.

When he moved to a new area, his mother discovered the Open School. He thought he'd take one more chance with school. On his very first day at the Open School, John confronted his advisor with the news that he was "fucking bored." Her quick reply took him by surprise: "You are the one who is fucking boring!"

> Being called out like this really shook me up! I immediately realized
> that this school was different and that it was on me to make a move
> or just get into my old rut of looking at school as a prison yard.

After that, John began to look at his new school as a godsend. He rediscovered the interests that had been so effectively buried before. He now refers to this awakening as connecting with "what speaks to my heart."

John says he was influenced in subtle but powerful ways by his advisor and the rest of the staff to become more grounded in himself. Finally, he felt like he had found a place where he could push the envelope and go beyond the rote and repetition of his former education.

He soon went on a school trip to Alaska to study bears, culture, and the environment. In preparing for the trip by making calls and arrangements, John began to see that school could be related to the world that is. He didn't have to just wait for it to end to start his real life.

There were more changes in store for John when he chose to do his Adventure Passage by hiking the 250-mile Pacific Crest Trail from Mexico to Canada by himself. He had planned a refueling schedule as part of his Logical Inquiry but things didn't work out, and he got stranded in California. According to his advisor, John had to deal with disappointment of not completing the trip for a while before he could see it as a valuable experience: "He quickly and painfully discovered that he needed other people more than he thought." After some tough processing, John began to see the value of learning from challenging real life experiences. It was all part of becoming his fullest self.

When John applied to the state university where his parents had gone, he had to confront another real world barrier—he didn't have grades or credits. With help from the staff, he broke through the admissions process by providing the university with his detailed and revealing final transcripts.

While sitting in his Freshman Chemistry class, John remembers feeling a little resentful that the Open School had not prepared him along more conventional lines. But he recalls breaking through this resentment by relying on the positive attitude about learning and life that had been so carefully nurtured there.

John soon found his interests shifting and synthesizing. His growing love of the sciences and environmental issues soon combined with his passion for working with and empowering people. Law school seemed a natural option to put everything in play.

At first, during law school, John felt like a fish out of water.

> I found myself getting really immersed in the cases and going as far as I could with my studies. Meanwhile, the other students seemed to be just doing enough to get by. They were having a good time, and I was not. I decided I needed to lighten up a bit by focusing on the big picture. The Open School encouraged going deeply into things, but also taught me to relax and have fun with my learning.

John Mattox (class of 1981) at the Matterhorn

After law school, John searched for a position where he could continue to combine his love and respect for the environment and his desire to raise the consciousness of people. He eventually found his niche as the senior staff counsel for the California Department of Fish and Game. Now, he can educate, advocate, and empower.

John still loves to climb mountains, hike trails, and do all the things that he learned to love at the Open School. He is one of the authors of the California Endangered Species Act and acts as a consultant on large scale environmental projects in the northern part of the state.

He's had his ups and downs with relationships, but John feels he has learned how to lead a balanced life. He remembers another incident in which he got into trouble on a school trip. When he went to the staff member in charge to make amends, the teacher simply said: "You screwed up. Let's get some coffee." Such learning experiences inform John's world view.

> I learned that a school could be a place where you could practice being in the real world by getting out of your comfort zone. I began to see the world as a big, beautiful place that you need to love and respect.

Schools can do a lot to get students to embrace the world that is by allowing them to run, fall, and get up again.

Putting Things into Perspective

Alumni responses about the influence of the school on their ability to adapt to the world varied greatly. While most of the alumni (over 82 percent) said that the school's influence was positive, some felt that the school created an idyllic vision of the world that could be difficult to reconcile with the world that exists.

> The Open School was a bubble, and a nice one, but a bubble nonetheless. Coming from the school, I felt very comfortable with people and, generally, with the world that I thought was out there. However, when I left the school, my bubble popped. I suddenly found that the entire world was not as fortunate to have had the opportunities that I had had, and that not everyone was a person like me, who processed and reflected on every detail of my life. I was very confused. I felt that I had been protected at Open.
> *—Lauren, class of 2001*

Others stated that contending with the differences between the values and attitudes they learned at the school and those of the wider culture only made them more committed to questioning the status quo.

> As a nineteen-year-old, I was astonished. I felt nearly contemptuous
> of the world I found outside of Open School. My peers were vastly
> more concerned with scoring drugs and alcohol than focusing their
> energy on school, community service, travel, or their future. It has
> taken me a long time to realize that so many people just don't
> understand that there are better things than just getting by. So while
> I am able to deal with the world that is, I differ from most people
> in that world with regard to accepting the status quo, as I imagine
> many of my fellow Open School alumni also do.
> *—Stephanie, class of 1990*

Meanwhile, most of the alumni felt that they could adjust to the different kinds of expectations of the world outside the school with the creation of their own support groups. This strategy was cited by many as a key factor in acclimating to the outside world.

> I found that I could gather a sort of quasi support group of friends,
> family, and mentors together because I had the skills to do so. After
> all, I had to get all of those Passage committees together, and I had
> to plan and organize school trips and activities. I had lots of practice.
> *—Ryan, class of 1994*

Other alumni cited the use of mentors as a way to adjust.

> I had to find new mentors to replace my advisor at the Open School.
> I quickly found that I could not only find them rather easily, but that
> I myself was able to be a mentor for others. I knew how the system
> worked. After all, life is all about having and being a mentor or
> advisor.
> *—David, class of 1990*

In the early days of the school, the first principal, Arnie Langberg, used to have a series of talks with the matriculating seniors about the real world, its potential pitfalls, and its unexpected challenges. One alumna remembers his advice.

> Arnie said to carry your ideals with you and to stand up for what you
> believe in. He also said there would be times when you would have

to weigh the options, and perhaps compromise or adapt. I took his talk to heart and felt like I kept my values at the same time as I was adjusting to the real world.

–Andrea, class of 1984

So, does the school fail its graduates when it comes to understanding and dealing with world that is? For the most part, the alumni say no. While the outside world can be shocking with its irresponsibility, dog-eat-dog behavior, and downright treachery, the school prepares students for the plunge by steeping them in real-world experiences and skills.

Many alumni say that the school presented them with a model of an authentic community where people helped, nurtured, and supported each other. While dealing with the world that exists, they realized that it could be changed and even transformed into a more ideal place.

Most of the alumni are now busy adults trying to recreate the Open School ideals in their own lives and communities. They say they have the moxie and wherewithal to make their way in the world, even to carve out a life they value within the world that exists.

When all is said and done, most alumni feel quite knowledgeable and effective in understanding and dealing with a rapidly changing, complex world. The argument for experiential learning should be clear. These kids have had practice and real experience with the world well before they leave high school.

Any school can make dealing with the real world a priority. Everything from learning how to get along with people who are different, to gaining practice on internships can make a long-term difference. Our young people cannot afford to live in an isolated, academic world based on test scores and grades. We must encourage them to branch out and take some chances in the real world. We do that by trusting the process of experiential learning and by helping students understand and integrate what they learn. We can show them that the world is nothing to be afraid of. Instead, with love and respect, they can see that life in the real world is often wonderful and fulfilling.

Changes: Preparing for the World that Might Be

● ● ● Eighty percent of the alumni say that the school had a positive influence on their ability to prepare for a future that is uncertain.

There is no greater preparation for the world that might be than facing a fear, confronting a major obstacle, or making a drastic change in your life. That's what Passages were all about.

—Josh, class of 1999

The fourth goal of the school—preparing for the world that might be—is one that is always changing because the world itself is in constant and rapid flux. How can we prepare our children for a future that we, ourselves, are uncertain about? This is a question that has haunted educational systems throughout time. In today's climate, politicians, bureaucrats, and educators are telling us that we have to prepare by competing with other countries in areas such as mathematics and science. Focusing on academics has once again become popular.

But today's student is faced with a barrage of information, sent at light speed, affording little opportunity to digest or process it for relevance and meaning. And tomorrow's world will be faster and even more intense. Futurists such as Alfred Toffler have been warning us that we long ago moved out of a time when schools could simply dispense information and facts as their sole mission in society.[15] In this era of globalized media and broad access to information systems, students need to develop new skills. Instead of memorizing and regurgitating facts, they need to learn how to analyze, filter, and synthesize new information as it comes at them at video game speed.

The future also requires a certain degree of confidence, awareness, and imagination that tends to be sorely lacking in our high school graduates. What we need to know now is how to learn, relearn, and even unlearn. The challenges of an uncertain world are better faced by courageous, adaptive lifelong learners and adventurers than by students trained to memorize disconnected facts. As the psychiatrist James Hillman has asserted, we are becoming a nation of illiterates because we are stifling the imaginations of our children. Our use of standardized-response testing and rote memory have fooled kids into thinking that success in life depends on someone else's idea of how and what they should learn and that preparing for the future means getting the right answer now.[16]

Authentic assessment and accountability can be adopted by any school. The ability to reflect on one's progress and achievement through self-evaluation, modify behavior according to circumstance, and confront changes with confidence and creativity helps students prepare for the future.

The influences of the school on alumni's readiness for the world that might be can be divided into several categories: courage to deal with change, awareness of the possible trends of the future, the ability to imagine the world that might be, and the life skills to deal with a changing reality.

Students Who Are Not Afraid to Confront the Future

The challenge of a self-directed project provides a good example of how students have to confront uncertain situations with courage and dignity. One alumna chose to do her Passage on meeting and confronting her long-lost father. This quest for identity and reconciliation had to be carefully prepared for. What would she do if her father rejected her or cut her off? How would she react if their meeting went badly? She made contingency plans in much the same way that another student would have to do in designing an Adventure Passage of hiking a fourteen-thousand-foot mountain in mid-winter. Safety valves and unusual possibilities were planned for. "What ifs?" abounded. She prepared for the possibility of disappointment by meeting with a counselor and her advisor. Regardless of the outcome, she was sure to gain confidence.

As it turned out, her meeting with her father was a mixed bag of conflicting emotions, but her preparation paid off. She found that she was able to process and learn from her experience.

Another alumna decided to confront her issues with the world of advertising on the subject of being overweight. She researched the look that advertisers were after in their models and the effects that this had on a young woman's body image. For her, the Passage was scary and very risky. She knew that her self-image would be a part of her life forever. To deal with it as part of her education in high school was being remarkably proactive.

> My Adventure Passage was describing what it was like to be an
> overweight teenage girl to the entire school community. I did lots of
> preparation, and I was scared stiff. Afterwards, I felt that I could have
> overcome any difficulty or obstacle. It's a feeling that has helped me
> to feel confident as new challenges come up in my life. I can't predict
> the future, but I feel ready for anything that can be thrown at me.
> —*Lauren, class of 2001*

Sometimes facing the physical challenges of a project translates into the emotional readiness needed to deal with difficulty and uncertainty. One alumnus, who completed a tough winter camping trip, said that he learned to trust himself and his abilities to deal with challenge.

> I had to deal with snowstorms, freezing to death, and bad equipment.
> I came out of it a better, more confident person. I really learned that
> I could be strong just by being myself. Now, whenever a tough, new
> situation comes up, I have [this experience] to look back to.
> —*Scott, class of 1993*

David (class of 1990) said that he learned to anticipate the unexpected and look forward to it as a learning opportunity. Student confidence can grow from experiencing what is sometimes called peripheral learning on projects and school trips.

> Peripheral learning is the unexpected learning that takes place
> during an experience. In a personal-growth framework like the Open
> School, it is really what you didn't intend to learn. Often, it is the
> most important stuff, like learning about yourself—your strengths,
> your weaknesses, and your limits. In most cases, just being aware
> of it can help with adjusting to changes and the future. You just feel
> more agile and flexible in dealing with the unexpected.

Some alumni look back at their community service work on trips and passages as an experience of building the strength and inner resources to confront a changing world.

> We worked hard on helping people by building schools in Mexico,
> assisting victims of floods and natural disasters, and even promoting

peace by supporting youth centers in the Middle East. What we really learned was that we had the strength and the power to change the world. So, when we grew up, we carried that strength and confidence with us. I always felt ready and able to address the demands of a changing world in some way by helping others prepare for the future.

–Maggie, class of 1989

Awareness: Students Who Are Attuned to Change

Many alumni look at their travels with the school as the turning point for how they would perceive the world for the rest of their lives. Trips to the West Bank, Pine Ridge Reservation, and Latin America gave them a chance to see the real world outside of the middle-class American bubble. What they saw was the daily life of most of the planet—a constant struggle for survival and security. The needs of the world were revealed as basic and urgent. What students discovered stood in stark contrast to most middle-class white teenagers' obsessions with luxury items and instant gratification. They got a sense that the future would be more about these people and their needs than about what the next big teen movie might be.

In fact, as alumni began to understand more about the tensions and conflicts in the underdeveloped world, they came away with a sense of how the world really worked and what changes would be necessary for a just, socially responsible future. Some alumni say they carry this sensitivity to change in their everyday lives as adults. They became tuned into the needs of diverse people in a rapidly changing world.

The Open School impacted me early on by telling it like it is. My trips to Colombia and Pine Ridge Reservation opened my eyes. As an adult, I feel that this awareness has helped me to prepare for changes by keeping in mind how most of the world lives and how their needs are evolving. Now, as a teacher with many students from Third World origins, I try to adjust to those needs every day.

–Nicolas, class of 1995

Others say that they are attuned to change by being more aware of their personal relationships with the world and its people. They begin to see that change can start with their own personal power.

I see the priorities and power relationships of the world changing rapidly. I still view my place in this world in terms of the personal, social, and intellectual framework that I was exposed to at the school

through trips and experiential learning. Now, I ask myself every
day: How am I oppressed? How do I oppress others? The school
taught me to be prepared with a strong sense of social justice and
sensitivity to the needs of the world's people—the have-nots, if you
will.

—Jason, class of 1996

After experiencing the real world in a personal, firsthand way, most alumni
also feel that blind acceptance of the status quo is unacceptable. Accordingly,
they feel that change is not only inevitable, it is desperately necessary. They
know that life is constantly changing and that the powers that be do not want to
lose their grip. Through being acutely aware of the needs of the many and the
privileges of the few, alumni say they are poised for change. Moreover, from
their familiarity with a constantly changing, organic community at the school,
they realize that new paradigms are possible. One alumnus who is a dedicated
social activist says:

I saw the inequalities in the world. I developed a strong
revolutionary spirit at the school. Meanwhile, I saw a vision of what
was possible. I learned to challenge the power structure. I learned
how to be ready for change and prepared to act with a good firm
base of hopes and dreams to guide me.

—Aaron, class of 1993

Schools can also help to prepare for change through their language classes.
In the Open School's Spanish program classes come with a large dose of cultural,
political, and historical context, always grounded in real experience. Trips to
Teacapan, Mexico (a small fishing village south of Mazatlan) and other Latin
American countries always focus on real experiences, living with families,
interacting with everyday people, and teaching English to local students.

Spanish and all things Latino are a large part of the future of the United
States. The effects of the changing demographics of the country on politics, the
economy, and the culture have been far reaching. Immigration issues are the topic
of the day. Preparing for the future depends on skills, knowledge, and especially
awareness in relating to this immigrant culture. The influence of Latinos in this
country is increasing rapidly. Being attuned to change depends on awareness and
sensitivity.

In this light, many alumni applaud the school for all of the opportunities
to raise their consciousness about the language, economics, and culture of Latin
America. The influence of this heightened consciousness is evident in their lives
as adults.

So many options were there to explore in Latin American studies and language. I, as have many fellow alumni, made Latino culture the center of my life. I have worked with women's groups and taught school in Mexico. I have worked locally with Chicano families to help make their lives better. We knew, because of our experiences, that the time would come when immigration and Latin American culture would be a major influence [on us]. Thanks to the Open School, we already had the awareness that this would drastically change our world. We were and are ready for the change.

—Sara, class of 1996

Many alumni refer to their Global Awareness Passage as having sparked their interest in preparing for what might be. By taking an issue and exploring it and then doing something about it, students are able to anticipate changes and prepare to deal with them in effective, meaningful ways. Some felt that they were primed to deal with the possible consequences of change in their own lives.

I did my Global Passage on the reintroduction of wolves to Yellowstone National Park. I had to make hypotheses about what might happen and how to deal with the possible problems that could arise. I had to prepare effective strategies for dealing with the potential effects. As an adult, I use this kind of thinking all of the time to examine issues and even to make decisions in my personal life. It's a new way of looking at things that may or may not happen in the future.

—Brooke, class of 1995

Imagination: Students Who Creatively Anticipate the Future

Increased awareness of the important issues facing the world today leads to a deeper understanding of what could be done about them. One alumnus said that he could see the time "when oil production would peak and petroleum-based products would become prohibitively expensive." Others say that their experience with the real world and exposure to real issues led them to be more prepared for the possible effects of global warming and the AIDS epidemic.

One student did her Global Awareness passage on AIDS in Africa. As a part of her project, she worked in an AIDS orphanage in Kenya and organized a Day of Dialogue at the school to discuss the issues when she returned. She said she could imagine what Africa might look like with a hundred million orphans by the year 2030! By helping to raise the consciousness of others, she felt more prepared to face a future that might include the destruction of a large part of the world's population. At least she felt that she could do something and be ready to cope with an unpredictable future. Another alumna, who explored the phenomenon of global warming, said:

> I began to see how global warming might affect the world for years
> to come. I started to ask myself if this was a world that I wanted to
> raise children in. I decided that it was not futile, that I would have
> the awareness not to be paralyzed by inaction, that I could make a
> difference in a tough new world.
> —*Corry, class of 1996*

Jason (class of 1998) says that while preparing for his Adventure Passage, which involved working with an autistic student, he had to come up with myriad creative strategies to get the student's attention. He devised games with puppets that revolved around his interests to keep him focused. He also had to anticipate and deal with tantrums and frustration, and he came up with several cool-down methods, such as using a dark, quiet room to do deep, relaxed breathing. Some of his strategies worked, some didn't; but he felt that he was allowed to come up with his own creative ideas in anticipation of what might happen with a student who could be quite unpredictable.

Most alumni agree that they were encouraged to think creatively about how to approach the world that might be. There were no right and wrong ways of approaching a potential problem.

> I learned how to expect and embrace the complexities of planning
> for the future. One of my Passages was on dealing with the possible
> future of disabilities laws and the problems with physical access for
> the disabled. I learned to analyze problems and imagine solutions.
> I was allowed to be as creative as possible. Some of my strategies
> turned out to be unrealistic, but others tended to be right on. As a
> result, I felt balanced and prepared to face the future in my work as
> an advocate for the disabled.
> —*Ian, class of 1996*

Many alumni anticipate a time when self-sufficient communities will be required to sustain life on this planet. Several look back at their internships with organic gardeners and the greenhouse project at the school as good reference points for imagining what future communities might be like.

> I am not a survivalist nut, but I can see the time when we will need
> to grow our own food and form new communal living arrangements.

> I learned from real experience that these kinds of communities were
> not only possible, but practical as well.
>   *—Adam, class of 1995*

Some alumni use the model of the school as a standard for imagining what is possible in a rapidly changing world.

> I always find myself using the Open School community as a model
> when I deal with changes and uncertainties. You have to have
> something to strive for when you are planning for the future. For
> me, the question is always: how would the Open School deal with
> this? Or, is this solution in line with my values and beliefs that were
> fostered at the school?
>   *—John, class of 1987*

Life Skills: Students Who Have the Tools to Prepare for Change

> At the Open School, they arranged to give me high school credit
> for "life."
> *—Cateland, class of 1976*

Among the students' responses, a number of life skills developed at the school stand out as providing a strong foundation for preparing for the world that might be: improvisational skills, building support groups, using resources, focusing on process, questioning, quest orientation, decision making, people skills, multitasking, and dealing with ambiguity. I'll expand further on some of these in this section.

Not measured by the Colorado Statewide Assessment Program, improvisational skills are based on the confidence to trust one's instincts, strengths, and ability to respond in problematic or pressurized situations. Many alumni say that improvisation was the skill they valued most. One alumna even refers to it as "a spiritual process," an open way of looking at and dealing with the big questions of life. For one alumnus, it became an important part of his repertoire of skills.

> Much of my work at the school had to do with creative expression.
> In the theater, in literature classes, even in my music, I learned to
> appreciate the idea that one great way to cope with change is to
> improvise. I think many of us devised ways to be more resourceful,
> and to adapt to, not simply react to, change. I use this skill all the
> time, whether it is in repairing bicycles or working on my music.
>   *—Dean, class of 2002*

Over 90 percent of the alumni said that they have stayed prepared for the future by continuously forming their own support groups. They choose from their network of friends, family, and colleagues in such configurations.

> At the Open School, I had to gather friends, family, and mentors for Passage work and ongoing support groups as I made my way on the personal journey that was my education. Now, as an adult, I find that my whole life revolves around the changing groups I continue to assemble. I use them on my job, in my family life, and when I face any difficult, unexpected situation.
> *—Jason, class of 1995*

> I have constantly created and recreated support groups in my life, just like I learned to do at the Open School. They help to create the world that ought to be by being good forums for debating ideas, and they often lead to political action. Life can be a continual search for like-minded people who are able to help each other make changes in the world.
> *—Jen, class of 1979*

Most alumni also had experience in being resources for others, through planning and teaching classes at the school or counseling their peers in formal and informal settings.

> I taught classes to kids at the school, even to young ones in the elementary program. I had the experience of being a mentor to many people, including my own advisor, who also took my class. I focused my class on the world that might be, on environmental issues and global peace and justice topics. As an adult, I am now a teacher. I know what it's like to mentor, and I know how important it is to be more than just an instructor. As a mentor, I am more influential; I have their trust and confidence. I try to prepare my kids for an uncertain future by developing the same skills in them. I remind them to be flexible and adaptable and that change is inevitable.
> *Nick, class of 1993*

Others find that they act as advisors and mentors in many different roles in their lives. In their jobs as managers or counselors, in their communities as leaders, and as part of service projects, alumni say they enjoy mentoring others.

> In mentoring others, I find I am always open to change. I am usually helping others prepare for the future by modeling things like keeping

an open mind and focusing my energies on the process of learning
new ways of adapting to the "new world."

–Mat, class of 1988

Students say that in dealing with the unknown, focusing on problem-solving processes and learning creative methods to grasp the crux of an issue are far more useful than just delivering the expected result. This process-rather-than-product orientation is a portable way of dealing with the unexpected; it is a creative perspective that gets to the heart of the matter—particularly when the issues and challenges are always changing—that students take with them as they go through life.

John (class of 1987), an engineer, tells a story that illustrates that really learning and internalizing a problem-solving process is far more important than just getting the right answer. Twenty years ago when he was a senior at the Open School, John saw that a Calculus for Poets class would be offered on the schedule. He remembers thinking that the class, which met for only one hour a week, would have to be a quick and cursory introduction to calculus. He wasn't expecting much more.

So I showed up the first day, and the teacher gave the class a problem to solve. The problem was to plot out the graph of $Y=X^2$ at a bunch of points between $X=0$ and $X=1$—enough to graph the function. Then, we were to find the area bound between the plotted curve and a line at $Y=0$. The rest of that class was filled with explaining how to plot points on a graph, and other stuff leading up to this problem.

John and the other students took the problem home, and when they returned to class the following week, they found that everyone had answers ranging from .3 to 1/3. Everything seemed too simple and elementary.

I remember first taping together several sheets of graph paper
in order to be more accurate. I could tell the answer was .333
repeating. That was it? That was my big calculus introduction? What
a waste of time, this kid's stuff that everyone was able to figure out
for themselves. We didn't even need a math book for it!

The students discussed their results and how they arrived at them.
The teacher then suggested that they think about what would happen
if the squares got really small. It was obvious to everybody at that
time that it would produce an even more accurate version of .3333,
perhaps .3333333. But what would happen if they got really, really,
really small?

Somewhere along the way, we switched to rectangles stretching from the Y=0 to the X=Y² point instead of squares to make things easier. We set up a simple math problem to calculate the area of these rectangles (width times height). But then the teacher suggested we quit making the rectangle width smaller, and just make it zero, or rather approach zero! Pretty cool!

The assignments each week introduced new concepts, and new problems to solve, without the help of the calculus, such as proving the formula for calculating the volume of a sphere. The result was a class on calculus where the actual math was explained after the fact. While John enjoyed the class, he was anxious about whether it sufficiently prepared him for college-level math.

At the end of the course, I was glad I took the class, was happy with what I learned, but was a little nervous about the monster lurking in college calculus. After all, college calculus meets for an hour every day, and has lots of homework every day.

Fast forward to my sophomore year in college. I signed up for first year calculus. After a review of some algebra, we started working on real calculus problems. The short story is that I already knew all this stuff. What they taught me in college calculus was a bunch of shortcuts to doing things like finding a derivative of a polynomial.

The instructor held me after class one day to discuss my test results. He found my work hard to grade because I would find my own way of solving the problem as opposed to remembering the way it was solved in the book. To be perfectly honest, I was a little flattered by this reprimand, and I knew my teacher at Open School would be proud if he knew. My guess is that everyone in that college calculus class that didn't continue using what they learned forgot it faster than they learned it. But I still remember the content of individual class sessions from my high school calculus class twenty years later, and I use the problem-solving techniques I developed in that class to this day. This personal way of solving problems has helped me deal with changes in my adult life.

Not bad for a few days of class time in 1987.

This problem-solving orientation is what alumni go back to when they are preparing to learn new concepts or skills or anticipating the unknowns they may encounter in the future. Knowing how to learn is the key to being prepared for new challenges.

Schools that want to develop problem-solving skills in their students must first present them with problems. Programs that do not deviate from a set curriculum present students with little to choose from and even less to deal with. How can we prepare students for the future when we don't even allow them to make simple decisions?

The ability to question—whether it be questioning the status quo, anticipating the future, or assessing the direction of their own lives—was another skill cited by many alumni as useful in preparing for the world that might be. One alumna who has lived and worked around the world put it this way:

> It is almost impossible to question what is, without imagining what might be. In this, I think most Open School students are more likely than others to think of the future and to imagine many possible outcomes.
>
> In addition, the fact that we were taught to question ourselves and our own lives creates a kind of built-in adaptability. When you question yourself, you change yourself, and when you are used to changing yourself, you more easily adapt to the changes that occur around you.
> *—Jean Anne, class of 1979*

Quite a few alumni say that as advertising, political propaganda, and the global dissemination of information become more sophisticated, the ability to question, filter, and analyze information becomes essential in dealing with the world as it evolves. Their education, they say, encouraged them to be discerning and to think critically about things.

> I developed this confidence in my inquiry skills that I use now to cope with changing circumstances. I'm a lawyer, and I need to be prepared for the unknown and unexpected. By learning how to formulate my own questions, I am used to finding answers that deal with a "what if?" outcome. It really helps in being ready for the complexity and multiplicity of problems in an uncertain world.
> *—David, class of 1984*

Too often schools seem afraid to let their students question the status quo. If public schools want to encourage their students to become adaptive to change or become change agents themselves, then they will need to extend their trust and cut back on their control. Real education means constant questioning and searching in an unpredictable world. If we are not helping our kids to become critical thinkers in our schools, what exactly are we doing?

Alumni frequently have a way of looking at the experiences and challenges of life as quests and adventures. Through developing their own learning plans and completing their Passages—particularly their Adventure Passages—students become prepared to encounter the unknown in all aspects of life. Some element of the quest can be introduced into any school curriculum—just set the challenge, then get out of their way.

Rafting the Ticos River, Costa Rica

Kerry (class of 1990) says that she appreciated having the attitude that, "Life is your great big adventure!" Another alumnus remarks:

> As a lifelong learner, the key is that every situation, every book, class, job, and relationship is a learning opportunity. There is something to be learned from a breakup, from a new friend, or any new event. I am always eager to learn new things. I am also very adaptable and creative in the business world because I not only do well with change, I expect and look forward to it. There are always new ways to do things, new languages to learn, and new challenges to confront.
>
> *—Ted, class of 1994*

Profile of Success

Abby Ruskey, Class of 1979

Schools should be places where kids get a diversity of opportunities to make a difference in the world. They need to feel that they can be part of the future!

So says alumna Abby Ruskey, the Executive Director of the State Environmental Association of the state of Washington. It was at her school, after all , that Abby got her chance to feel empowered to get ready for a new world. It was 1974, and the country was just beginning to get a glimpse of a future of oil shortages and environmental decay. At the Open School, Abby pounced on her chance to get involved. She began working in the Sundance Project, a program that asked students to design and build a greenhouse and develop new renewable energy sources.

Abby Ruskey (class of 1979) working with leaders for a better world

Abby remembers learning how to build solar hot water panels and parabolic collectors. She also recalls that part of the project was to go door-to-door in the local community and ask families if they could help design and install some of the new energy saving technology in their homes. It was an exciting time of feeling like she was on the cutting edge.

We were community engineers and valued consultants! We had certificates and badges that proved we were experts. We were

teenagers, and we were not only allowed but encouraged to develop
our expertise and help people prepare for the future. We went to the
state fair and had a booth on our project; we went to other schools
and shared our information. We even went to teacher training in-
services and taught young teachers about what schools could do to
help students get involved. It was all very empowering!

Abby acknowledges that all of this would not have been possible without a
supportive community and a loyal, committed advisor guiding the curriculum. It
was the freedom to pursue passions without the pressures of grades and credits
and the interdisciplinary nature of the learning that propelled her. She decided
early on that all schools could do the same with their students by providing them
the opportunities to get involved and take some responsibility for their own
educations and for dealing with a rapidly changing world.

At the Open School through trips and projects and community
action we could all feel like we were drawing from our experiences
and finding our places in the world. We could feel like we were our
own facilitators and seekers of knowledge. The future became just
another great challenge, one more opportunity to learn something
more about ourselves, our skills, and even our fears.

As an adult, Abby has been following her heart. She has carried that sense
of power with her as the organizer and designer of the very first Earth Day K-
12 curriculum in 1990. She also helped elect the first student to the Berkeley
City Council. Abby's involvement even ranged from working for a small energy
company to becoming heavily involved in the nuclear freeze movement after
the Love Canal debacle. Now, after years of travel, work, and college, she has
returned full circle to the Sundance Project.

As director of a large state organization that is focused on helping educators
with a comprehensive environmental curriculum, Abby has put her Open School
values into practice. She is constantly trying to forge new alliances among
economic, educational, and environmental groups to provide an interdisciplinary
approach to environmental education. Her vision is a powerful one that reflects
the hope for a better world.

I am using the Open School model to provide a sustainable
education for a sustainable society and world. I'm trying to support
teachers, kids, and administrators who are willing to try alternative
methods such as experiential project learning and interdisciplinary
approaches to problem solving. This current atmosphere of teaching

to the test is undercutting our students' abilities to perform in the global theater.

Abby Ruskey's dedication to the Open School model demonstrates the power of opportunity, freedom, and empowerment. Preparing students to cope with the increasingly dangerous and complicated uncertainties of our world requires educators to involve them in creating solutions now, and making such involvement a central part of their education.

Putting Things into Perspective

There are, however, some alumni who are not happy with how the school prepared them for the world that might be. One student said that the school gave her an unrealistic, idealized vision of change always being a good thing.

> I found that change is not always so great. I wish they had taught me to be more ready for the hard times instead of just the good ones. Plus, the school gave me the idea that the future would be great if only we lived up to our ideals.
>
> *—Joann, class of 1980*

Several others felt that a stronger background in traditional academics would have better prepared them to engage the future.

> As I prepared myself for the future, I wished that I had had more training in the fundamental disciplines such as math and science instead of all of that "learning to learn" stuff. I think you need a stronger academic foundation to meet the future.
>
> *—Laura, class of 1985*

Still, most of the alumni (over 80 percent) thought that the preparation for the future was more than adequate. They frequently reported that they felt that the skills required in to face the future demanded that they be proactive and creative. They say the supportive environment of the school encouraged them to be constantly attuned to the changing world by accepting

Penny Greeley (class of 1996) recovering marshlands in Maryland

that change was one of life's few constants.

Just as the futurists predicted, the rate and intensity of change have accelerated exponentially in the last few decades. Accordingly, it is of paramount importance for our schools to help prepare our children for an uncertain future. According to the alumni, the Open School has shown the way by helping them think about the world that might be in creative, positive ways. The future always tends to be less daunting when it is viewed as an important part of one's journey to find one's way in the world.

We need our schools to provide the foundation for kids to cope with the storms of change. It is only when we begin to trust kids to explore, experiment, and even fail, that we can provide the practice ground for dealing with the world that might be.

Being Part of the Solution: Helping to Create the World that Ought to Be

●●●Eighty-nine percent of the alumni report that the school had a positive effect on their ability to create the world that ought to be.

●●●Eighty-five percent say that they volunteer an average of six hours a month for local community and/or global organizations.

I think that the Open School taught me that I had the power to create change in the world and in myself.

—Aaron, class of 1995

If we are not encouraging our kids to be revolutionaries, we are not doing our job as educators.

—Brian, class of 2000

Creating the world that ought to be is the jewel in the crown of the Open School. The worthiness of this goal is such that if the school were judged simply on the ability of its graduates to serve as positive agents of change, it would justify the entire program. Almost universally, alumni praise the school's focus on transforming the world we live in. Most say that they learned that they could really make a difference and that their opinions and skills were valued by the community. A full 89 percent say that the school influenced them strongly in their ability to effect change in the world and their desire to want to be involved.

> Because of the Open School, I actively fight against becoming
> passive and ignorant. There is always so much to know, to change,
> and to create!
> *—Stephanie, class of 2000*

The aspiration of any worthy school program should be to encourage the growth of people who can make a difference in the world. An effective education turns out adults who participate fully in a democratic society, and even become leaders who contribute to the positive growth of others in family, work, and community settings.

Giving back to others is the cornerstone of much of what takes place at the Open School. Community service, participation in school governance, and playing an active role in advising groups and other students' Passage committees are not merely seen as requirements to dispense with; they are integral to students' education.

All six Passage areas are connected to creating the world that ought to be. Whether it is the self-expression of a Creativity Passage or the deeper understanding of oneself in the Adventure quest, all Passage work calls on the student to understand her place in the world and her possibilities for improving it.

Some Passage areas are more obviously related to effecting positive change. The Global Awareness Passage, wherein one explores an issue that affects the world and then does something about it, is the most pertinent. As an accompaniment to this Passage, the student educates the school or local community on the issue and thereby helps to inspire and empower others to do something to help.

Students begin their Global Awareness Passage by learning about the complexities involved in the issue they've chosen and then thinking critically about effective solutions. This usually includes a lot of brainstorming and problem solving. One alumnus, who has gone on to a life of public service, describes some of the steps involved in his Global Awareness Passage.

> I examined issues of public access and the rights for disabled citizens for
> my Global Awareness Passage. I was encouraged to challenge the status quo
> and problem solve for the world that ought to be. First, I had to be able to
> hypothesize a better world for the disabled and come up with a better plan.

Then, the key for me was to educate others about these issues. Now, I do this for a living. I might be in the same place if I had gone to a conventional school, but I doubt it. The Open School is where I was allowed to do this as part of the program, not just as some after-school, extra-credit kind of thing. I believe that I will always be involved in creating the world that ought to be due to my successful experiences at the school.

—*Ian, class of 1997*

For her Global Awareness Passage, Morgan (class of 2001) explored women's reproductive rights. She quickly saw that this issue had enormous relevance in the Third World, where she had spent extensive time studying Spanish and Latina culture.

> I started to see how many of these global issues were threaded together. I saw how women in Third World countries sort of carried their cultures on their backs, how they were the ones who had to work hard and sacrifice just to keep things going.

Morgan (class of 2001) with President Clinton in the Dominican Republic, 2007

Now that she has graduated college, Morgan is in the Peace Corps in the Dominican Republic, where she works with women and their families as they struggle to make ends meet. At the Open School, she did a home stay with a family on a school trip to the Dominican Republic. She says that she has an added sensitivity to the issues at hand because of her head start in gaining global awareness in high school.

Responses from alumni about creating the world that ought to be suggest a circular model of development that regenerates their confidence and the ability to effect positive change.

Self-Awareness

Vision of What Ought to Be

Reflecting on Action

Circular model of effecting change within a supportive learning environment

Feeling Empowered to Act

Taking Action

Sid O'Connell

This model shows the continuous cycle of development that enables one to be an effective change agent. Alumni say that self-awareness increases their confidence to take action and that each experience reinforces the need to stay involved and try again, usually with new insights about the issue at hand. Early experience with this process at the Open School helps prepare students for a life of being involved in social change.

Know Thyself: The Starting Point

As do the other goals of the Open School, creating the world that ought to be starts with self-knowledge. One cannot begin to think about effecting change in the world without a clear sense of one's own strengths, weaknesses, and goals.

When I first came to the school as a thirty-five-year-old adult, I was unsure of my own abilities to create the world that ought to be. Like many students coming from the conventional world of education, I was buried in self-doubt and sorely out of practice with even trying to make a difference in the world. As I gradually grew into the idea of self-assessment and personal growth as important parts of the educational process, I began to discover my own potential for helping to create a world that was better than the one that existed. For example, I learned that by sharing my passion for African-American music and culture, I could help turn kids on to working for Habitat for Humanity and other service programs in the deep South.

The advantages of having a continuous K-12 school community are also evident when it comes to helping students see their effect on others. In an all-ages community of learners, students begin to see that their actions affect the community—that they don't act in isolation. If someone's behavior harms the community, it is addressed in advising meetings or even in an all-school governance meeting.

> We were encouraged to look deeply into ourselves and always be mindful of our being part of the whole community, whether that meant watching our language in front of younger kids or respecting others' privacy. I always saw the effects of my words and actions.
> *—Willow, class of 1998*

Furthermore, students who have experience with self-assessment are more apt to embrace the practice of honestly assessing whether their actions are in line with their values and goals. One alumna observed that students were expected to be "the ultimate critics and observers of their own behavior" vis-à-vis the community's ideals.

Another related this process of honestly examining one's behavior in terms of one's ideals to the Jewish principle of *tikkun olam*, which refers to repairing or perfecting the world. She observed that to rebuild or repair the earth, one has to look into one's "heart's eye." Thus, only knowing oneself can lead to the possibility of change in this world. Another alumnus describes it as "feeling comfortable with oneself and one's ability to change and be changed." Others say that an important thing they learned about themselves was that serving and helping others made them feel good.

> I went on the flood relief trips to Missouri and the trips to Florida
> where we helped build animal environments at a zoo. I learned that I
> really got a lot of pleasure from helping others and making the world
> a better place. It became a big part of who I was as a person.
> *–Harlan, class of 1997*

Many former students said that that finding out more about the ordinary lives of people in the Third World made them realize more about their own relatively privileged lives.

> I realized how cushy I had it in this country. A hot shower, plenty
> of food, and the rest, they were all really luxuries. Could I live in
> survival mode like most people on this planet? At least I started
> thinking about it in those terms. The Open School helped open my
> eyes at a time when I really needed to be woken up!
> *–Mike, class of 1982*

Vision: Students Who See the World that Ought to Be

Once students' eyes are opened, a picture of the world that ought to be becomes clearer. Many former students said that as they learned more about how people lived in other parts of the country or the world, such as the Mississippi Delta or the refugee camps of Gaza, they began to see what changes needed to be made to make the world a better place.

Kim (class of 1986) said that her city trip experience working with homeless people changed her life. She described the experience as humbling, and instrumental in shaping her idea of what the world ought to be like.

The use of simulations is another valuable tool to raise lasting awareness in students. Kim recounts this experience she says she will never forget:

> I remember a lunchtime in Munchie [the student-run cafeteria
> program] when the floor was divided into countries with masking
> tape, each country getting the area proportional to its actual size.
> Then, all the students were divided into countries by (proportional)
> population. For lunch, we got what our countries (proportionally)

consumed. People were carefully dividing up their lunches of
carrots and rice while the few embarrassed Americans were given 80
percent of the total food, mainly in the form of junk food. It was my
introduction to the phenomenon of globalization. I certainly got a
better idea of what the world ought to be like from this experience.

When exposed to the world outside their comfort zone, students frequently
develop concerns that go beyond fulfilling their personal needs as adolescents
growing up in a powerful country. They may develop a sense of compassion
for others because they start to see that the world is bigger than the local
mall, and that helping others less fortunate can be part of their vision of a
better world.

I picked chilies in the hot sun in Mexico next to nine-year-old kids
who were helping their families to just scrape by. I think I got a
pretty good idea of what ought to be as far as living wages and
exploitation went. As an adult, I always keep this experience in mind
as I try to help with the world that should be.
—Laura, class of 1997

On one of the Middle East trips, where students stayed with Palestinian and
Israeli teenagers and their families, many kids discovered the real world of fear
and terrorism for the first time. On their peacemaking mission, they discussed
ways to make the world a better place with the real people who face the problems
that, for most teenagers, exist only in newspapers or on TV.

We were in the middle of one of the biggest conflicts in the world
today, working with young people to make things better. This was
our education! How can you measure the effects of a trip like this
on a test? We got the best insight into what can be done to create a
better world.
—Andrew, class of 2000

Other alumni worked at senior centers and food programs as a regular
part of their curriculum. They often used their self-planned days to do their
service work.

I worked at the soup kitchen every Friday. I quickly discovered there
was another America out there. Now I try to help out whenever I can
because I realize that the world that ought to be should not include a
bunch of disenfranchised, homeless people on the streets.

The Open School as a Model

Should a school be a model of the ideal world? It's a worthy undertaking, but I wonder how many conventional school graduates would use their high school experience as their vision of the way the world should be.

> As an adult, I am amazed to find that most people don't even think about the world that ought to be or even that the world can be a better place. I have the Open School as my model. I found that the school, while not perfect, provided me with an example of a place that was nurturing, supportive, and democratic. My education set very high standards for me, but at least I have a vision for what is possible.
>
> *–Ashley, class of 1999*

Alumni say their school valued and promoted the very ideals that would make the world a better place. Their responses indicate that these values stood out when they thought about the school community: fairness, accountability, compassion, activism, courage, and responsibility to a community.

For Carissa (class of 1995), the school was a place where you "were taught not to judge other people." Her ideal world is one where people are not pigeonholed or divided into cliques. Elizabeth (class of 1979) says that the school helped her become a caring and just person, and she tries to promote those values with her students and clients in order to create a better world.

It's a living testament to any good school when its alumni try to reproduce its program elsewhere. Some alumni are doing just that. Tamara (class of 1996) is starting a school that employs a working farm focusing on action, adventure, and real work. It is based broadly on the Open School ideals of interdependence and self-direction. Tim (class of 1988) is exploring the use of adventure and challenge as the driving forces in an alternative middle school. John (class of 1986) is deeply involved with the Sudbury School that his kids attend in Massachusetts. Several others are also involved in projects to promote open, democratic schooling for children.

Heidi (class of 1978) said that by modeling high ideals and values, the school gave her something to shoot for:

> The school set the bar high. The staff never expected anything less than my very best effort. By demonstrating day-in and day-out how adults ought to behave, they helped me to now expect no less of myself. I know the ideal because I have lived it. I know what human beings are capable of, and I expect the same from family, friends, and coworkers. I have seen over and over again that if you set your

standards high, people will meet the challenge. The Open School
taught me to expect the best.
–Heidi, class of 1978

So a school can serve as a model for the world that ought to be by consciously emphasizing the values of community, collaboration, and responsibility among its students. In fact, it's essential that a school practice what it preaches. For many alumni of the Open School, their education did just that by encouraging them to act as valued, needed community members. As Robert (class of 1980) said, "One could not help but be empowered by this vision of how things could be."

Students Who Have the Confidence and Ability to Create Change

Since all Open School students can vote on important issues and are encouraged to participate in leadership classes, alumni say these opportunities were good practice for creating the world that ought to be.

I remember when we started a movement to change the entire
schedule to better fit our needs. It was like being part of a revolution.
We, the people, actually had the power, not some phony hierarchy of
leadership that didn't represent us at all.
–Jenni, class of 1991

John (class of 1987) recalls that if there were serious problems in the school, such as physical or mental abuse, students were sufficiently empowered that they did not hesitate to address them.

If something was going wrong at the school and enough people were
concerned, something was done about it long before it became more
of a problem. The community did not stand by like sheep and make
itself believe that things were okay the way they were. Action was
taken by students who felt some real ownership in their community.
If things had worked that way at Columbine High School, fifteen
people might still be alive today!

Other alumni say that they had lots of practice creating the "school that ought to be" by constantly revisiting the vision of the ideal school.

We were always encouraged to help create a better school. In fact,
we were expected to do something at one level or another according
to our abilities and our styles of learning. Some painted murals,

others cultivated gardens, and some attended leadership conferences.
In any case, everyone had the opportunity to contribute and, in their
own way, be leaders.
–Corrine, class of 1996

One alumnus says that he learned a sense of empowerment from being a
minority in an all-white environment.

As a Japanese American, I never really fit into the conventional
school paradigm. Mainstream schools were just not working for me.
When I came to the Open School, I was allowed to feel a sense of
power and self-direction regarding my own life. I was not pounded
into submission like I felt I was at conventional school. I started to
find my identity, and I began to establish a strong experiential base.
I took off when I realized that I really did have the power to change,
not only my own life, but the world as well. As an adult I am
constantly using this sense of power to help create sustainable and
democratic communities while still maintaining my own
ethnic identity.
–Derek, class of 1995

Nick (class of 1992), an outdoor education instructor, says that in his
work with his students, he "empowers people every single day." He notes that
he passes along the "magic of the Open School"—the idea that everyone can
be leader.
Some alumni from the 1970s remember being involved in the Sundance
Project, a greenhouse program and a self-sufficient community project
initiated by staff and students. The students started a greenhouse and garden
from scratch. They did most of the planning, building, and ongoing work. One
alumna recalls:

We were creating projects for the future that would have major
effects on how people lived in harmony with their environment.
Through developing our projects all year long and touring around
to schools and industries, learning and sharing information, I got
a strong sense of being part of a bigger picture. I started to see the
possibilities of being involved on a larger scale, and I realized that I
had the confidence and power to create a world that ought to be. I'm
still fighting for it today by being involved in environmental groups
and community-action committees.
–Sue, class of 1976

Action: Students Who Get Involved

Alumni say they have learned that they have to do more than fret and complain about injustice and suffering in the world, they have to do something about it. Whether they were completing and demonstrating competence with a Passage or doing service work as part of trip, Open Schoolers were always required to act decisively and get their hands dirty.

One alumna recalls learning to be proactive in her Career Exploration Passage about the logging of redwood trees and its effects on bird habitats and species survival, a skill she uses today in her continued work with endangered species.

> My Career Passage was directly related to creating a world that
> ought to be and taking the initiative to save birds and their habitats.
> My life as an adult has followed suit. My job at the moment focuses
> entirely on preserving the habitats for the Northern Spotted Owl. I
> think I am making a difference by finding these owls and effectively
> protecting their habitats from logging operations.
>
> The irony is that I am working for a logging company! I feel like I
> am making changes from the inside out by educating loggers as well
> as the general public about rare birds and their survival. I realize
> how important it is to find a balance in the world between economic
> and environmental concerns so that conservation is possible. At the
> Open School, I learned to be resourceful and assertive in helping
> create the world that ought to be.
>
> *–Heather, class of 1999*

For other alumni, their social action in the world has taken them far and wide. Shannon (class of 1997) went to a state university and quickly realized that she wasn't discovering anything new about herself or the world. She remembers her fellow students and how unhappy they were with their high school educations and their college lives. She finally realized the extent that they had sold out when a girl across the hall would reward herself for each page she had read of a biology book by taking a shot of tequila. In a recent

Shannon (class of 1997) with her students in Sri Lanka

letter, Shannon credits the many trips she took with the Open School for reviving her commitment to serving the global community.

> I am writing this to you from Mahavilachchiya, Sri Lanka, where I am assisting with English in a school that is teaching rural kids [how to operate] computers. If that doesn't speak to the Open School's effect on me, I don't know what will.
>
> The organization is called Horizon Lanka, and it was started by a local man who wanted to help give children in his village some of the same opportunities open to the rest of the world. Since my time at the Open School, I have found enormous value in giving back to the community; I am happy to say that my community is now a global one.
>
> *–Shannon, class of 1997*

Chankaroon (class of 1982) recalls her introduction to the school and how it influenced her desire and ability to help others. Arriving without parents or friends in Denver as a refugee from war-torn Ethiopia, Chankaroon was initially placed at a conventional high school in the area. She did not know how to read, write, or speak any English. What happened next, she describes as "striking gold." A teacher at the Open School intervened and convinced her host family to send her there.

> I was so fortunate! The Open School saved my life. I knew no one and had hardly any English. The school climate was perfect because I could relax and be myself while I learned a new culture and language at the same time. People went out of their way to help me. I would have been put in some special program and have been isolated at a regular school.

She remembers the Mexico work trip of 1982 as a turning point. This three-week trip to help build a school in Mexico showed her that the school was like one big family: "We worked together, slept together, and went through good and bad times together. It was real and wonderful, especially for someone brand new to this country."

Chankaroon says that the compassion, warmth, and encouragement she received provided the foundation for learning how to create the world that ought to be. She says she learned "kindness, speaking truth to power, collaboration, and being a good citizen in a democracy" at the school. She also says that she learned to be a good role model for others and how to work for the common good. These are values that Chankaroon continues to hold onto as she helps other immigrants struggling to find their way in a new culture.

A full 98 percent of alumni say that they are taking action to create the world that ought to be in their work or in their personal and community lives. Examples of their work are included in Appendix G.

New Consciousness: Students Who Assess Their Experience and Renew Their Efforts with Greater Insight

Some alumni describe the assessment and evaluation stage of their education as having given them a new consciousness about the world. After having had some firsthand experience with trying to effect change, students learn what issues need more attention and what ways and means are best suited for effective change.

Many former students say that, after they have worked for some time in one vehicle for progressive action, they see that things are just not working as expected or that avenues of change have been shut off. They then recognize the need to seek out new directions.

> I found that my attempts at forming self-sustaining communities
> were being stymied by the political and economic climates in this
> country. I decided to join the World Wide Organic Farmers network
> and create a model for change elsewhere. I think I learned to adapt
> to different circumstances through my work at the Open School. I
> found that you have to reevaluate your work for change on a regular
> basis and then follow your vision on a different path.
> *—Adam, class of 1998*

Others say that they have also learned methods of change that are better suited to their personal styles.

> What I really learned at the Open School was how to make decisions
> based on new ways of seeing things. I learned that the only way I
> could effect change was by influencing one person at a time, not
> through group action. I started to focus more on my personal life
> and how it modeled the world that ought to be. Then, I used my
> own model to educate others about protecting the environment and
> finding new sources of energy.
> *—Brenda, class of 1983*

David (class of 1990) worked for change with the Dalai Lama, setting up coffeehouses and community centers in India. After some time, he returned home to process and regroup. Then, he went in different directions, working with a local charter school and a university library. He credits the school with keeping him on his toes and his not becoming stagnant when it comes to being involved with social change and activism.

> We discovered that new ideas sprang from having a new
> consciousness based upon past action. In my adult life, I have gone
> through lots of cycles of action, reevaluation, and [setting] new goals
> and strategies based upon a changed consciousness about things.
> *—Dave, class of 1990*

Alumni say that this final stage of reevaluation and rejuvenation is an important one. It is at this point, they note, that they realize that there are many different routes and means available for creating the world that ought to be. They often start a renewed cycle of effecting change, this time with fresh eyes and new strategies.

There are some striking examples of what happens to adults who have had experience with creating the world that ought to be.

Profile of Success

LA MADRE OF THE URBAN OPEN SCHOOL

Kristen Nelson, Class of 1991

"The ripple effect"—that's what Kristen calls it. As one of the youngest principals in a large urban school district, Kristin Nelson simply passes on the joy of life, learning, and community to several generations of Mexican-Americans. What she has accomplished is truly remarkable: reaching out to and nurturing 650 students, their parents, and their neighbors in ways that have made her school the center of life in the community.

Creating an urban, ethnic version of the Open School, Schenk Elementary has become the cornerstone of this redheaded wonder's life. She has become *la madre* for *los de abajos* (the underdogs) by providing a gateway for the Mexican-American community, a portal for them to access literacy, dignity, and self-respect.

Kristin says it all goes back to the Open School. The *mecha,* or fuse, was lit when she returned to its caring environment for her junior year of high school. Disillusioned with her stint in conventional school after an elementary education at the Open Living School and smarting with grief from the early death of her father, Kristen needed to come back home: "I needed a place where I could grieve and get myself back together."

Kristen Nelson (class of 1991) with her kids

It took her two years to do all the work needed to graduate, but it was during this time that Kristen says she began to shape her life as an educator and Latinophile. Two school trips to Mexico made their mark.

In Mazatlan, Kristen did a home stay with a Mexican family. During the day she took Spanish lessons and learned about everything from local culture to cooking. The family's two boys helped Kristen acculturate. Her house parents treated her like one of their own. She fell in love with all things Mexican, the warmth of their family life, and the *carino*, or caring, that people had for their communities. Kristen decided then and there that somehow her life would be flavored with Latin spices.

Another trip to the Yucatan followed shortly thereafter. There, Kristen taught English to Mexican students. She became even more certain of her future path: "The Yucatan trip fossilized what I wanted do with my life: work with kids of Hispanic descent and help them build their communities in America."

Still another powerful school trip to Miami to consult with the Dade County School District about providing meaningful alternative school programs helped Kristen see that she could, even at this early age, be listened to and make a difference. When she heard repeatedly from the school officials that a school like the Open School would simply not work for "those kids," Kristen became determined to someday prove them wrong.

As her college years progressed, Kristen kept her dreams close to her heart. After majoring in Spanish, she pursued her teacher's license and a master's with a bilingual emphasis. After some time as a teacher and a social worker, Kristen decided that administration was the most powerful vehicle to drive her dream.

She entered a leadership-administration program at University of Denver. Taking her first administration position as an assistant principal, Kristen realized that she loved taking kids to the doctor, filling out immigration forms with the parents, and just generally being a community liaison and leader.

> I saw my role as an administrator as being similar to that of an advisor
> at the Open School. I was constantly influenced by the modeling
> of my advisor as to how to approach the problems of the Latino
> community with joy and compassion. I had practice being a mentor at
> the school. Now, I saw that I could put my practice to work.

Kristen decided that the bilingual program she was working in was just not working. Her personal preference was for a dual immersion program where students could learn English and Spanish together. She put together a proposal for a dual immersion school, the manifestation of the dream that had its genesis in those school trips to Mexico.

The proposal was accepted in 2002 and Kristen was ecstatic. She was already off and running, trying to create the ideal school program for a Chicano community in which most of the population was Spanish speaking only.

Her first principalship soon followed. In her first year at Schenck, Kristen was already selling nachos to stop graffiti, providing E.S.L. classes to parents and families, holding immigration seminars and "promoting literacy in English from day one." Her student body is 96% Hispanic and 100% of her kids receive free and reduced lunches.

> I wanted to create a culture like the Open School where students,
> families, and community members could come to the school for
> nurturing and support. I wanted everyone to feel not only comfortable
> at the school, but also like they could be respected and valued.

Kristen's relationship with her staff is also indicative of the Open School influence on creating a school that ought to be. She takes new teachers on a Wilderness-Trip-like retreat to discuss philosophy and goals. She also partners with a teachers' education program so she can "grow her own" leaders and even takes some of her teachers to Mexico to work on their teaching methods by helping Spanish speakers learn English.

The influence of the school also comes alive in this ironic vignette. During her budding days as an educator, Kristen ran into her old advisor from the Open School who was looking for a part time Spanish position in the district. Here was her mentor, the one who had lit the Latino fire for her, still trying to contribute to a better world for the Hispanic community. Furthermore, here was a teacher who himself was turned on to Mexico and the Latino world when he had transferred to the Open School in his late thirties.

The irony was not lost on them as their eyes met. They both began to weep with joy with the recognition that their paths had somehow merged once again. Kristen raced back to a staff meeting to share her experience and talk about what it meant for creating a powerful Hispanic community. Now, her former advisor volunteers at Kristen's school teaching English to neighborhood families. Mentor and former student are joined again in a worthy cause.

It seems that the ripple effect has come full circle. Even Kristen's two young sons have been immersed in Spanish and English. They, too, are part of the effect.

As I watch Kristen smile and hug kids, parents and neighborhood volunteers, I realize just what a wonderful job she is doing. The school culture is welcoming and supportive. It is a place where people come first, before tests, standards, and everything else. Creating the world that ought to be is never easy, but the challenges seem well worth the effort for Kristen.

> There is not a single day that goes by that I don't learn, grow, and
> have fun. Success for me is continuing my work in the community.
> It means developing amazing relationships and providing lots of joy,
> laughter, and learning.

Kristen's story shows that schools can start the ripples that reverberate throughout a student's life as an adult. Kids who are provided with the opportunities to change the world never stop trying. It is their reason to be, and it affects everyone around them. Pass it on.

Putting Things into Perspective

Overwhelmingly, alumni feel that the school had a profound influence on their ability to help create the world that ought to be. Most of them say they feel an obligation to give back to their communities and their world. Many say they learned to enjoy service work as part of their Open School experience.

Every day, the teachers at the school impart the message that it is incumbent upon each of us to help to create a better, more socially just world. My experience taught me that we each have particular gifts that we can contribute to this process. Mine, I hope, is to help spread the word about real possibilities for educating the next generation in a humane, joyful way.

As a young adult, I began to see the value of service work. From my colleagues and the students, I learned the joys of giving one's time and energy to help those less fortunate. As a result, service has become an important part of my life since I retired. I have worked in Haiti with a medical group, and I have taught at a peace camp for teenagers from some of the most troubled conflict areas of the world.

I also think that having a distinct idea of the world that ought to be has helped me to stay involved. For me, the school has served as an example of what could be in a world that often seems in conflict and pain. It's inspiring to know that, after thirty-nine years, the school remains a beacon for positive change and public service.

The idea that schools can be breeding grounds for change is nothing new. Dewey and other progressive thinkers have argued this cause for a hundred years. Still, more often than not, education has gone the other way—toward more testing, more dissemination of facts, less focus on human activities and experiences.

If we are looking for a new paradigm for education in the twenty-first century, then we need to pay attention. The Open School alumni tell us that schools can have a lasting effect on lives by providing a safe, supportive practice ground for changing the world in positive, meaningful ways.

Do the Right Thing: Did We Emphasize the Important Things?

●●●Ninety-five percent of the alumni report that the school had a positive influence on their lives.

It is with the heart that one sees rightly; what is essential is invisible to the eye.
—Antoine de Saint-Exupery, Le Petit Prince

Things which matter most must never be at the mercy of things which matter least.
—Goethe

Learning how to take tests, study, and get good grades is easy! The hard stuff is what the Open School addresses; it's the stuff that most people never or rarely get to learn. Thank goodness that I was able to acquire such wonderful skills for life. I consider myself a very prepared and able citizen.
—Rosia, class of 2000

Did we teach the right skills, emphasize the right values, and provide the right kinds of experiences at the Open School? These are the questions that all schools should ask of themselves.

Seventy-five years ago, a group of educators wondered whether public schools were doing the right things: whether they were, in fact, educating students for a demanding future and imbuing them with the life skills to cope with the changes of the industrialized world. In 1932, the Commission of the States, a progressive group of educators inspired by John Dewey and others, embarked on their historic Eight-Year Study, which compared experimental school graduates with those from conventional schools and followed them for eight years after high school. I discussed the study earlier in this book, but want to revisit now since it's the only study of alternative education ever done in this country, as far as I know, and I think it offers valuable information.

The results indicated that success in the adult world depended on more than just grades and test scores, as the experimental school alums not only outperformed their conventional counterparts in college (higher grades and more positive feedback) and career goals (higher levels of goal achievement and job satisfaction), but were also happier with their adult lives and relationships.

In 1952, Margaret Willis, the principal of one of the most successful experimental schools, the Ohio State Lab School, conducted a follow-up to the Eight-Year Study, called "The Guinea Pigs After Twenty Years."[17] In it, she asked the alumni of the school if they felt that the school had stressed the "right things, the important things." The majority of the 1932 graduates answered in the affirmative. The Lab School alumni said that they appreciated the unique qualities of their school and its emphasis on building confidence and encouraging personal growth. A summary of the important things, as deemed by the 1932 graduates of the University Lab School, are revealing:

• Warmth and human atmosphere

• Learning as discovery

• Concern of school for individuals

• Cooperative work in learning

• Trips

• The arts

• Life skills

For me, this question of stressing the right things became an essential part of the investigation of alumni attitudes about the school. Has the school really succeeded in its mission? Has it stressed the things that are really important for a happy, satisfying life as an adult? This is an intriguing question, one that goes beyond the bounds of a conventional way of looking at one's education.

As I look back on my own life as an educator and student of life, I see that my idea of what exactly the important things are has changed over time. I definitely feel that my understanding of the values of success and happiness have evolved as a result of my Open School experience. I see now that the important things for me are less material and less superficial than they once were. As I grow older, I find myself thinking more about the spiritual and humanistic values I learned to appreciate at the school, such as the value of my relationships with family and friends and the pure joy I get out of learning something new.

The school places importance on the central values and capacities essential to leading a full, satisfying life. Before coming there, I had somehow come to see my working and family lives as completely separate entities. After working there for some time, I started to see how the school's philosophy incorporated everything I did in my life, such as building meaningful relationships and searching for relevance, into a more comprehensive whole. The school sparked in me a holistic integration of self-discovery, developing my passions, and the various aspects of my work, community, and family lives.

I found that my fellow alumni agreed that we certainly did the right things. The focus on critical thinking, discovery, and learning practical life skills was powerful. The idea that one's education should be an integral part of one's personal growth seemed to be the key to the school's success. Again and again former students credited the school with the development of confidence, curiosity, and compassion— all wonderful assets in becoming healthy, productive adults.

Finally, a public school that can impact adult lives should be the norm, not the exception. As did the lab schools of the 1930s, education can make a real difference for kids today, especially by giving them a sense of hope and a belief that they can change the world.

Anything Missing?

Although the vast majority of alumni reported that the school did emphasize the right things, there was a distinct minority that wanted something different. Approximately 10 percent of the respondents reported that, though they were generally happy with their education, they wanted more of the following:

• Structure and sequence to academic subjects

• Courses in mathematics

• Academic rigor

• Basic grammar

• Test-taking skills

• Study skills

• More experience with the competitive aspects of the work world

• More training on forming support groups in the outside world

David (class of 1996) said that he felt "coddled" at the school. He said his advisor should have pushed him more. Another reported that she wasn't challenged enough academically. Some even say that they should have been made to take certain classes like calculus or advanced chemistry. After following up on some of these alumni with their former advisors, it became clear that some of these students were not exactly the kinds of kids who could be forced into anything and that their most important needs, at the time, were actually in the social and personal domains. Nevertheless, these alums felt that they had missed out on more demanding academic classes.

Other alumni discussed their college experience in terms of being out of touch with preparation for exams and writing formal papers. Some alumni blamed their deficiencies in spelling on the school. Interestingly enough, the alumni who complained the most about a lack of preparation for college had some of the highest grade point averages. Apparently they had the ability to quickly learn the skills they needed in college or, compelled to catch up with their peers, they did whatever it took to make the grade. For most alumni, however, facing their deficiencies for college work was taken in stride. One alumna recalls:

> Once I decided to go to college, I made an appointment to have an interview. I clearly remember walking into the office of admissions feeling strong and confident with my huge portfolio and transcript in hand. My mom and I entered a smaller office with an older bald man sitting behind a huge desk. He asked my mother and me to sit down and he began the interview by saying "Jefferson Open School… It's good that there are places like that for dropouts like you."

> I am not sure who was more enraged, me or my mom. I remember having to explain to him verbally what was clearly written in my personal statement: I had attended the Open School for twelve years; I started when I was four years old. It is not a place for dropouts; it's a place for young people who want to learn. Looking back, I think my sole purpose for going to that college was to change that man's idea of the Open School and me.

> Academically, I was afraid I was going to be light years behind other students. I entered the university under a type of window for students who had low GPAs in high school (or, in my case, no GPA and low scores on the ACT). This was a source of insecurity for me. My math skills were not up to par, and I was placed in a remedial class. I was somehow expecting to be the only student on campus in this situation, and, at the time, I put a lot of blame on the Open School for allowing me to go to college so ill prepared. It was a

surprise and a good lesson when I entered that class to find it full
of students from traditional high schools from all over the state and
country. I still can't do algebra under pressure, but I have discovered
that it has nothing to do with the Open School. And I am probably
not supposed to tell you this, but I turned in my Global Awareness
Passage research paper in my freshman biology class and got an A:
an A for affirming my education.

When I transferred to another college, I became an art-education
major. I got to be the topic of conversation in many of my education
classes. Sharing our own educational experiences often took place
in the education department. Mine always stood out. I always felt
lucky. I always felt proud, and I always made it a point to let people
know that my education looked different. I turned out okay… better
than okay. Now I am a teacher at an urban school, and I carry my
Open School values proudly and prominently.
–Katie, class of 1996

Another alumna concurs. Although she did well in college, she also went
through a stage of doubting her preparation for a conventional educational
setting. Now, two years after graduating university with honors, she sees things
differently.

The doubters will say: what about the test scores? Now I see that
learning how to take the tests and play the game are easy. Try studying
nematodes in Mexico and then explaining in Spanish what you are
doing to curious locals! A true education is learning about life, not
taking a test that says nothing about who you are as a person.
–Morgan, class of 2001

Yet another alumna adds:

Do I think I missed out on something because I wasn't taught
the methods of taking standardized tests in a Machiavellian high
school setting? No. I think the Open School teaches the right things,
because the whole point is that each student chooses which things
should be emphasized in her curriculum and in her life.

Occasionally, yes, my life has been harder because I didn't have
a yearlong chemistry class in high school, and, perhaps, I needed
to study harder for the GRE. However, the real difference in my

education is that it resulted in a higher-than-average delight in
learning, trust in and compassion for others, and a dedication to a
search for meaning in my life.
                              —Steph, class of 2000

Other alumni concur. The school, they say, emphasized being happy with
oneself and feeling free to express it by being engaged and involved and most,
importantly, not afraid.

The school stressed the really important things: how to feel good
about yourself, how to be independent. I learned that everyone has
something to contribute, that it's okay to be friends with people who
aren't just like you, and to open your mind to new ideas. I learned
not to be afraid to travel and try new things, and that it's okay to let
your freak flag fly! These are the important things for being involved
in your community and the greater world. For me, the Open School
got it just right.
                              —Shea, class of 1985

Another alumna says that although she came out of high school with less
math than her conventional school counterparts, she knew how to teach herself
the basics. More importantly, she also had something that conventional school
couldn't (and didn't even want to) touch: "how to live your life with passion and
knowing you have the ability to make a real difference in the world."

So, for a few alumni, the school was not structured or academically focused
enough. For most, however, what weaknesses existed in the program were more
than made up for by the strong emphases on the important things like personal
discovery, following one's heart, developing and using creative and critical-
thinking skills, working with and as mentors, personal responsibility, and
belonging (and giving back) to a supportive community. In fact, almost all of
the alumni surveyed said the school had a positive effect on their lives as adults.
Further, many stated that they used the framework of the school (with its focus on
the social, personal, and intellectual domains) to live their lives by. I wonder how
many high school graduates would say the same about their alma maters.

Bringing It All Back Home

When my only child entered the school, despite my own experience as a devoted
Open School teacher and advisor, I did not hesitate to ask the question: is this
the right kind of education for my child? As I mentioned earlier, I had my own
doubts about the school when I first started as an advisor. When my daughter
entered the school, those doubts began to haunt me again.

Like most parents who are sending their kids to the Open School, I examined the balance of emphasis given to the three domains; the social, personal, and intellectual. I wondered how well the reading, writing, and math fit in. I asked questions about basic skills and academic foundations.

Of course, because I had seen the wonderful results of the school with my advisee graduates and other alumni, I had insider information. I had heard the stories about how kids caught up with academic skills when they needed to because they had learned how to learn at the Open School. I also knew and admired those alumni who had gone off in other directions without college or any further formal education.

But with my own kid, I wanted to be sure that the school was right for her. Over the years, as she progressed, I learned an awful lot about my own ability to trust and let go. I found that having a child at the school is a perfect microcosm of the parenting process itself, the constant struggle between being too directive or too lax in one's approach. Like all parents, I was trying to find a balance. This experience alone made me a better, more understanding parent.

I began to see some trends and patterns emerge as I struggled with the process of letting go of my control over my child's education, and her life, really. The inevitable and natural ups and downs, the leaps and lags in developmental growth, became apparent as my daughter grew up at the school. Turning points for trust included project presentations, parent conferences with teachers (who actually knew our kid), and the changes in attitude toward school at home. I began to appreciate, all over again, the wonderful aspects of the Open School: its focus on trust, relationships, and the effervescent joy of learning. A fellow parent put it this way:

> When my son came home and proclaimed that he loved school, I almost dropped dead! We had struggled for years just to get him to show up. This was enough to sell me on the place right there!

Finally, I realized that my daughter's enthusiasm was the key to it all. Her teachers allowed her to go deeper into her interests, and by doing so she started to expand her world. When I learned to relax a little (not exactly my style) and allow things to happen, I began to see the synthesis of all of the domains. Music and performance became the center of her life. Everything else seemed to come from the center: the friendships, the skills, and the self-concept. We learned not to interfere with the self-assessment process. This was key.

We also saw that her intellectual development took a latent path. Once her interests were identified, she had the confidence and motivation to learn the skills required to explore them. She learned how to read music, she performed in plays and concerts, and she began to develop a sense of herself that is rare in youngsters.

We started to see the values of the school shine in our daughter's life. She was not only bright and curious; she was becoming a real *mensch* (a Yiddish word for a warm, compassionate human being). Our development as parents paralleled our daughter's growth at the school. We became better parents as we learned to let go and just be there when needed. We also learned to look at our own lives in a more meaningful context. We saw that we could learn so much from our daughter.

When she came out with her homosexuality at the age of twelve, we saw her struggle with her identity. Once again, the school provided a safe, nurturing place where she could just be herself. To this day, we are grateful that the "village" was so supportive.

I must say that I see some differences between our child and other people her age. She has a sense of confidence and identity that kids from conventional schools just don't have. Perhaps it is an attitude cultivated from advanced social acumen and self-exploration. I see it in other alumni as well.

As she went off to Africa to work at an AIDS orphanage or explored the Boundary Waters in a canoe, she was developing into a parent's dream: a well-rounded human being. Of course, we'd like to take all the credit for our parenting, but the truth is that the school acted as another set of parents. I think the entire community helped raise our child. Today, my daughter shines as brightly as ever as she graduates college this spring. I'm proud to say that she will always be a child of the Open School.

Looking back at my time as a parent, I see how naturally things developed, not just for my daughter, but for me as well. I, too, grew up at the school. I certainly wouldn't be the person I am today without my Open School experience.

I love this alumna's take on the school and how it can change lives.

> All of the right things were emphasized from day one. The wilderness trip and the first Passage were the foundation of all those things. The school is like an ecosystem, each thing building on and depending on the others. From the foundation in the values of loving life and learning comes other projects, and soon, even sitting in class and learning math becomes a way to build on all those things. It was stressed in the classroom, stressed during our team meetings with the advisors, and became the entire basis for the program.

> I watched wayward teens contribute in a worthwhile way to society. I watched straight-A bookworms begin to interact with others and feel more confident about themselves. I watched overachievers adjust their priorities so that they were happier.
> *—Maggie, class of 1991*

I can't think of a better tribute to a school that has changed so many lives: the village of the Open School. Schools that want to create similar villages need to pay attention to the things that really matter. They can be places where personal growth and meaningful transformation take place if they focus on all three domains of learning. Alumni of any good school should report that their school stressed the things that were not only useful but meaningful as well. An authentic education can stick with students forever.

Hope for the Future?
Let the Alumni Point the Way

Hope is a waking dream.
—Aristotle

I'll know there's hope in this world when I see the other schools copying the Open School.
—Open School parent

B e careful: sometimes you get what you ask for! In the 1990s, school boards and state education departments began to explore outcomes-based education and a standards-based approach to their district goals and mission statements.

As alternative educators, we at the Open School thought this was a move in the right direction. We had always talked about outcomes as true measures of growth. We often discussed the social, personal, and intellectual attributes we were looking for in our students and what we wanted kids to be able to do when they graduated from high school. When we saw discussions about outcomes occurring in the wider education community, we were excited. Our long-standing methods of developing whole, well-rounded people, we imagined, might finally be vindicated. Now, we could actually have a discussion with mainstream educators about demonstrated competence, self-evaluation, and experiential education.

Alas, our hopes were quickly dashed as we discovered that the outcomes the politicians and bureaucrats were talking about were only standardized test scores in a limited number of academic areas. Once again, kids were being shortchanged. Their wonderful individual gifts, their creative spirits, and their unique learning styles were being dismissed and demeaned.

This was just the beginning. High-stakes testing in the name of making our schools more accountable quickly became the calling card for politicians and ideologues. Somewhere along the line, the idea of what constitutes success also began to change. We were back to competing with other countries for narrowly defined technical expertise, especially in math and science. Good students were the ones who performed well on the tests. Good schools were the ones with the highest test scores. Good teachers were the ones who could get more students to perform well on the tests, while a successful graduate from high school was an academic overachiever.

The whole idea of a well-rounded education was put on the back burner. Kids started to feel the pressure. Dropout rates increased, especially for minority students, who once again felt pushed up against the wall. The disassociation between one's education and one's life became more pronounced. According to a Gates Foundation survey, 88 percent of the so-called dropouts left school not because they were failing or unable to keep up with the work, but because they were bored and felt that school had nothing to do with their real lives.[18]

As a culture, we began to reward achievement without substance, good test takers rather than good human beings. Recently, some of the so-called good students have been plotting to bomb their schools, killing their classmates, or stabbing their least favorite teachers. Meanwhile, studies following successful students (ones who had above-average grades) into adulthood have found them to be less satisfied with their work, their families, and their lives than average students.[19] The connections, then, between conventional measures of academic achievement and life satisfaction are dubious.

Is there hope for our schools? These days, it's easy to get discouraged. High-stakes testing, the narrowing of the curriculum, and the demeaning of the very essence of what it means to be educated could make anyone feel hopeless about our schools. Indeed, it seems that every sort of child is being left behind in one way or another in our depersonalized, increasingly standardized school systems.

It's ironic that some countries that have made this prescriptive adjustment in their educational systems are now complaining that their students have become too robotic and compliant and that they lack creativity and the ability to innovate. The educational minister for India recently lamented the dearth of critical thinkers and innovators among the graduates of a system that was trying so hard to get ahead of the others in math and science.[20]

Meanwhile, dropout rates of 32 percent nationwide have not improved at all over the past twenty years of the so-called school reform movement, and dropout rates have worsened among some populations and in some regions.[21] Indeed, a system that "marches students through an increasingly uniform curriculum" puts almost all of the kids at risk for feeling left out, bored or generally disaffected. Some call it the "college prep charade": by trying to prepare all students for college, schools are ignoring the fact that many students take different paths and have different interests. In any case, it comes as no surprise that so many kids are becoming turned off to learning.

Many educators now fear that the dropout rate is growing in proportion to the narrowing of the curriculum. They see the risks in the new standardization movement as growing more substantial over time. Not only are we in danger of creating a permanently disenfranchised underclass of dropouts, we may be producing a mean-spirited elite of alienated, angry, and creatively stifled graduates.

A group of conventional school students interviewed at a prestigious high school in California voiced their concerns that, although they were considered "successful and popular students" at their school, the curriculum was not relevant to their lives.[22] What they really needed, they said, was a more flexible structure that gave them some practice with making their own choices and real-life decisions, perhaps even failing sometimes, and learning from their mistakes. They also felt they needed more exposure to the real world, to getting along with different kinds of people, and to what it means to adapt to a rapidly changing world. In short, they felt ill prepared for the next steps in their lives, whether it would be going to college or entering the workplace.

Instead of working on the things that really mattered, their school focused almost solely on academic achievement and competition for grades. These students (many of them consistent honor roll students) began to feel the tremendous pressure from the high-stakes testing at their school. Some even talked about nervous breakdowns; others talked about the four hours of homework per night taking away from the social and personal sides of their lives. One high school senior said:

> As a senior, I have felt under so much pressure to get good grades
> and get into the best college that I have neglected my personal
> wellness, my friends, and even my family life. It's easy to lose
> focus about what's really important in life when you are constantly
> scrambling to keep up.

Other students lamented the lack of opportunity to talk about the important issues they face in their lives as young people about to become adults. What was absent in school, some reflected, was any focus on the search for meaning in their budding lives.

> Why can't we just talk about what it's like to be a teenager going
> through all these changes in a crazy world? We don't seem to have
> the time to discuss the things that really matter to us; everything

seems to be content-driven, when what we really need is to learn
how to become our true selves.

—High school junior, northern California, 2001

Other students[23] talk about how all the fun of learning has been pounded
out of them by having to adhere so strictly to a curriculum that was designed by
others, who thought they knew best what the students needed to learn. There was
little importance placed on being creative or designing one's own projects from
one's own curiosities or interests. Students never had to take the initiative; risk
taking was not only devalued, it could actually be dangerous. Thinking outside the
lines was not conducive to test taking or getting good grades.

Anaka (class of 1999), an Open School alumni who took a year off from
the school to attend classes at the conventional high school in her neighborhood,
found the expectations to be low and the experience to be quite mechanical.

> I just went to school and did my work. I didn't have to do anything
> hard, like make decisions about what classes to take or what I
> wanted offered. It was easy and boring. I got straight A's, and
> that was all that mattered. I never felt I was part of the place or
> responsible for anything that went on there.

It's also easy to get lost in the shuffle at large conventional schools. Cliques
are a natural way for kids to acquire some kind of identity, a way of battling the
lonely anonymity. More often than not, students don't have any adults in the school
community who really know who they are. Many become alienated and angry. Dean
(class of 2002), who came from Columbine High School, put it in these terms:

> I'm not saying that the school caused the murders to happen, but
> there is no doubt that many of the kids felt angry at the cliques and
> the teachers for treating them as if they didn't even exist. Nobody
> really cared about each other, so why would they expect us to care
> about the school?

Another alumnus, Jaime, 1994, who came from a conventional school, noted
the difference between the conventional school's attitude of isolation from the
wider world and the Open School's emphasis on global awareness as a central
part of its curriculum:

> When I came to the Open School, I went on as many trips as I
> could. I was surprised to realize how little I knew about the world at
> large. At conventional school, I think most of the students felt that

the world revolved around them; they had no idea how most of the world lives. It's frightening to think that many of these people will be future politicians and decision makers when they know so little (and don't even care) about the wider world.

Because the funding for, and very survival of, schools today depends on their annual test scores, the pressure to have a narrowly focused and standardized curriculum is increasing. Although students' feelings of alienation, boredom, and anger are increasing, as are school violence and social isolation and disaffection even among straight-A students, it remains very difficult to convince conventional schools that they are going down the wrong road.

Still, there is hope. The alumni of the Open School are living proof that schools that pay attention to the confluence of heart, mind, and spirit can help foster confident, competent, and compassionate adults. Their stories and reflections about the influence of the school on their lives point to the need for change in that most important of democratic institutions: public schools.

Hope for Change in the Conventional School System

When we are presented with the stories of the alumni from a public school that has dared to buck the system for thirty-nine years, we should feel encouraged. After all, here are people who say that their school experience has had a profound influence on their lives as adults. Many say that the school was not just a place to learn, but more—it represents a way of life. In fact, some say that they live their lives according to the basic principles of the school.

If we are inspired by the power of a program that has treated kids like human beings for nearly four decades and produced a joyful, dynamic, creative group of adults, what do we do now? Tell your school officials that the current research on effective, successful people calls loudly for a paradigm shift in our approach to education.

My Open School colleagues and I realize that this call for a change in consciousness can be. quite daunting. When I was in Arizona recently consulting for an alternative school that had grades and credits, I asked the kids a question: if you had the choice of doing a self-directed project or taking a class for a grade or credit which would you choose?

Almost to a person the students said that they would pick the class. "Even if it was a boring class with a bad teacher?" I asked. "Yes," they replied, "because it would be a lot easier; we'd know what to do just to get by." I immediately thought about what strong impediments to intrinsic motivation were represented by grades and credits. It's hard to crack the culture of external evaluation. So the lesson could be to take an incremental approach. Attention to the personal and social domains is a good start.

Instead of focusing solely on narrowly defined academic skills, we can emphasize the skills and traits people need to lead satisfying lives, such as those Stephen Covey identifies in his *Seven Habits of Highly Effective People*.[24] Covey begins with being proactive. Open School alumni tell us they learned to be proactive by being self-motivated and self-starting in their school environment. A second characteristic, leadership, is something that alumni say they got to practice through governance and the sense of ownership and personal power they exercised in their advising groups and project work. Calling on our schools to provide such opportunities to practice these skills is an important step.

Covey's third trait, self-management, is apparent in graduates' commitment to personal responsibility. Covey also emphasizes interpersonal skills, clearly an asset of Open School alumni. Being able to empathize and cooperate with others is another habit of effective people that alumni say they have developed at the school from all of their work in groups. The ability to synthesize information is another important trait that Covey identifies, and one that alumni have developed well. Covey also lauds the principle of synergy, which he defines as the power to put the different parts of one's life together in an effective, well-rounded whole. Alumni are particularly adept at this kind of integration. Finally, Covey's seventh trait, self-renewal, is one that alumni practice naturally as they continually examine their lives, reevaluate their goals, and continue to learn.

Although most schools are still ignoring what psychologist Daniel Goleman refers to as the emotional and social fabric of young peoples' lives[25] and what education scholar Howard Gardner refers to as the most important life skills, recent research finds that educational programs are much more effective when they teach a core of emotional and social competencies, such as anger management and dealing creatively with social problems and moral dilemmas.[26] Talking to school officials about new research and alternative approaches is a good place to begin.

The changes we want to initiate in our public schools will require some challenging problem solving and a healthy measure of determination and courage. It will have to start with parents and students, and include teachers, administrators, and community leaders. Putting pressure on school districts might include running for school board, getting involved in parent-teacher organizations, organizing student and parent forums at school board meetings, or gathering and networking teacher and administrator allies. Regardless of the approach, advocates must focus on the American tradition of community-based decision making concerning our schools.

Here are two approaches to working with existing conventional schools to make them more humane, engaging, and relevant:

Try to change the culture of existing schools through advocacy groups that attempt to put pressure on school boards and individual schools to change their approach to learning and teaching. Getting homeroom teachers to be more involved with their students and act as mentors and coaches is a start. Allowing time for discussions about personal and social issues would also help. Opening up student councils to student volunteers might also give students more power and ownership in their school community. By encouraging more kids to get involved in school governance and offering opportunities for decision making and choice, this can enable students to learn what it means to be engaged citizens in a democratic society—something the Eight-Year Study commission recommended nearly seventy years ago.

Create a school-within-a-school. The idea is to break down larger schools into smaller "houses" or programs based on special interest areas (such as the arts) or educational philosophy (self-directed learning). In this configuration, groups might insist on student choice for each house and the inclusion of an advising program wherein each student would have a personal counselor or mentor to coach and guide her progress in the three areas of human growth (intellectual, social, and personal). Remind school boards and your neighborhood schools that you want a well-rounded education for our children.

However we approach changing public school culture and practices, Open School alumni have told us that the following features should be stressed in the schools of today and tomorrow if we want to create the best of all possible educational worlds for our children. Even if we feel we cannot create a new alternative program and must work within an existing conventional school framework, there is still much we can do.

Authentic assessment. Advocate for an advising and evaluation system that promotes students' abilities to be self-assessing and to pursue development in all areas of their lives. As the alumni of the Open School have stated, this is the starting point for personal growth and responsibility. Talk about authentic assessment in terms of demonstrating competence. As the alumni have stated, a genuine sense of self-confidence and competence comes from showing what you can do, not just giving the right answers on a test.

Meaningful outcomes. All parents want their kids to become confident, empowered adults. Tell your school administrators what outcomes you think they should strive for that will help produce the kind of person you want your child to be when he leaves the program.

Accountability. Ask your schools to be more accountable by connecting students with at least one adult who is at once accountable to the student and encourages her to develop self-responsibility.

Freedom to pursue self-directed learning. Talk to your school's administrators and teachers about encouraging youngsters to identify their passions and use their natural curiosity to inform and motivate their learning. Advocate for more room for self-directed projects and experiential learning: allowing kids to design, carry out, and defend individualized projects as part of their curriculum. Open School alumni say that the freedom to follow their hearts' desires, both inside and outside of the classroom, was crucial to their development as lifelong learners.

Critical thinking skills. As we are increasingly bombarded by information, the ability to sift, evaluate, and process information effectively is crucial for making aware, informed decisions. We need our schools to help students develop critical thinking skills in real-world settings; delivering the right answers on tests is not enough.

Acknowledgment of different learning styles. Encourage schools to appeal to the multiple intelligences that young people possess.[27] Remind administrators and teachers that kids have different learning styles and unique strengths and challenges. There is no one way of teaching or learning. Schools should be charged with the task of reaching all of their students, not just some at the expense of others.

Social skills and social responsibility. Advocate for social skills development in everything that takes place at the school. Service projects, collaborative projects, and small group discussions all are important environments in which social skills and social responsibility can develop. Remind your schools that you value the focus on interpersonal relationships and giving back to one's community.

Awareness of the wider world. Try to get the kids out of the classroom to see the larger world that surrounds them and its diverse social, political, economic, and cultural realities. Open School alumni say that they are grateful for all of their travel experience: that this is where they learned about the world, their place in it, and their responsibilities as global citizens.

Pushing for change in entrenched bureaucratic systems is difficult. It requires personal fortitude as well as a strong sense of solidarity with others working for change around what should be our biggest concern: the welfare of our children. Fortunately, there are some highly successful alternative schools out there that can give us hope and serve as models.

Hope for Change from Alternative Schools

It is this author's hope that the Open School can serve as a model and template for alternative schools—both those that already exist and those that are being developed. With the recent proliferation of charter schools, more students and parents should be able to choose open types of schools. However, the enormous pressures of No Child Left Behind and high-stakes testing have resulted in less progressive, more conservative kinds of charter school offerings, such as back-to-basics programs (Core Knowledge Schools) and college preparatory academies.

This is not to say that there are not other successful progressive schools like Jefferson County Open School in other districts around the country. There are some, like the Harmony School in Indiana and the Ithaca Community School in New York, that have been around as long as the Open School. The Coalition of Essential Schools and the Big Picture programs have helped to keep the alternative school fires burning, but we need more alternative school options now more than ever before if we are to stem the tide of standardization and the further erosion of what it means to be educated in a well-rounded, humane way.

There are many alternative programs that have come and gone, suffering from a lack of either local support or strong leadership to keep them going. It takes a lot of determination and integrity to keep an alternative school going; many good schools have wilted in the face of the pressure to conform. The alumni of the Open School would remind us that it takes time, patience, and courage to develop a sustainable program.

What new and existing alternative schools can gather from this book are lessons about what makes for a sustainable education: an education that sticks with its students and continues to serve them as they grow and change in their adult lives. Alumni responses about the effects of the school can be boiled down to five "Cs": confidence, curiosity, caring, creativity, and competence.

What can alternative schools do to encourage these qualities in their students? Almost overwhelmingly, alumni say that the advising system was the critical starting point in their education, and sometimes reeducation. Everything, they report, begins with this positive, trusting relationship with an adult. From here, the student's world starts to expand to the wider community and, hopefully, the world.

The second key to their education, alumni say, is discovering oneself and one's goals, and this has its genesis in advising. It is the advisor who helps the student gain the insight and understanding needed to recognize what she is passionate about.

Also of primary importance is the fact that students are asked to evaluate all of their experiences in the personal, social, and intellectual domains. Alumni report that the self-discovery and self-knowledge that come from authentic assessment ultimately lead to enhanced self-confidence the feeling that one can do anything if one is excited about it.

Self-directed and experiential learning is clearly a pillar of the Open School that other alternative schools make part of their curricula. As we have seen in the graduates' accounts, the freedom to explore areas of interest in their Passages, trips, apprenticeships, and other self-directed learning experiences were central to their becoming engaged, proactive, lifelong learners.

Creating an environment of support for risk taking and growth is also essential. Learning from one's mistakes is a hallmark of the Open School experience. Looking back, many alumni say it was the best way to internalize their learning.

Alumni also recommend the consistent attention to social skills and encouraging students to get along with different kinds of people and develop compassion for others. Further, according to the alumni, the focus on ownership and personal power was key. Alternative schools should pay attention to the principles of self-governance and the building of democratic communities in their school design. Alumni also note that the idea of giving back to their communities was an important part of their education that they carry with them as adults who are actively engaged citizens.

Alumni recommend having students demonstrate their competence as part of their school program. Former students of the school say that they built competence from their presentations in governance and advising groups as well as other forms of hands-on demonstrations of skills they had learned. Schools that offer these kinds of opportunities will provide a compelling alternative to the mainstream.

Finally, the best way to show that something really works is by example. It is the responsibility of progressive, alternative schools to share their wealth of knowledge and experience with other public schools. It is through this kind of networking and modeling that significant change can begin. It is ill advised to be arrogant or isolationist about the alternative approach. Open School alumni would say: be proud, but be open to criticism and change if you want to influence

Jaime (class of 1993) National AAU Snowboarding Champion 1999

the mainstream. There is not just one way to educate our children.

Any school that gives high priority to these elements of a holistic education can expect positive results. The idea is to allow kids to grow up with the joy of life and learning and a confidence to follow their hearts. We want our children to be able to both adapt to and change the world. Open School alumni say that they still live by the school's philosophy and that all they needed was the support and opportunities that the school offered them. As adults, they see themselves as capable, confident, and caring people who continue to be guided by what matters most to them. And now, their success offers us hope and encouragement that we really can make our schools into places where our children can thrive as they become well-rounded, happy, satisfied adults.

Afterword

I learned how to be myself at the Open School.
–Robert, class of 1980

*Going to the Open School was the first time
I ever felt safe in a school environment.*
–Jeni, class of 1990

As I write this, the news of the day is about a student in Virginia who murdered thirty-two people at his college. I'm reminded that violence and desperation are still a part of the landscape of American educational institutions. As sad and frustrated as I feel about the news, I can't help but feel grateful that I found the Open School: a place where I felt valued and inspired. Like so many of the alumni you have heard from in this book, I too am as proud and passionate about the school as I was at the start. It changed my life in so many ways that I could have written the whole book as my own journey of self-discovery and growth. As I expected, many, many alumni offered their own joyful, loving accounts of how the school changed lives forever, and how they, like myself, are trying to live their lives according to its values and goals.

Since I began writing this book, many sad and wonderful things have occurred within the Open School community. Tragically, three alumni died well before their prime within the last year. One was drowned in a boating accident in the Boundary Waters, which is a sacred place in school lore. He died doing something he was excited about. This alumnus was also a young educator who was planning to start his own Open School-style charter school in Arizona. His dreams have not died; others have taken up his banner and are carrying on with his project.

Two of the families of the alumni who passed away chose to have their memorial services at the school. Both drew large crowds of former students who came to celebrate these young lives in the context of the extended family of the school. These services were meaningful reminders of the importance that the students and their families placed on the school's nurturing, healing, life-affirming spirit. That these were not recent graduates made these memorial services an even more profound testament to the vital role a school can play in one's life.

At one of the services, the young woman's grieving father spoke about her days there as the happiest of her life. It was a place, he said, where she could be comfortable just being herself. Our sadness was infused with a deep respect for how the school inspires lives. Talking with my colleagues and many alumni after the service, we all noted the feeling of love and support that we continue to feel for each other, as well as the sense that we are part of something bigger than ourselves—something resilient and beautiful. The grieving family felt it too as we talked about our fond memories of trips and other experiences.

Other, happier, events in the past year also attest to the school's ongoing influence on graduates' lives. These include a grand reunion of all the graduates during its full thirty-five years of service, and a major conference on authentic learning hosted by the school. The reunion, of course, warmed my heart because I saw many of the respondents to my surveys for this book. I was overwhelmed by the feelings of love and connection that tie alumni of all ages together into one extended family. We didn't need to have the clipped, awkward conversations that often occur at reunions; sometimes all it took to connect was a wink or a smile as we thought back to some funny or poignant thing that had happened on a trip we were on together. The conversations explored students' latest interests and the continuing influence of the school on their adult lives.

At the Conference on Authentic Learning, Open School teachers and alumni who are now teachers themselves shared with others, who are establishing alternative education programs of their own, the fruits of their experience. After more than thirty-nine years of remaining true to its open educational philosophy, the school has both the privilege and the responsibility to serve as a beacon to other alternative schools. During the conference, a panel of alumni presented their thoughts and feelings about what it means to be a success. I was proud of the articulate, passionate way that alumni expressed their genuine love for the school. It is obvious, even after many years, in some cases, that the spirit of creativity and giving back to one's community was alive and well in the hearts of these graduates.

Certainly, the school became the center of my life. I sometimes wonder if, without the support and inspiration of its goals, I would have run marathons, gone on challenging trips, gotten my Ph.D., or become a confident parent. Perhaps, but I do know that the school helped me to become a better person by opening me up to growth and change. My daughter feels the same; we both thank our lucky stars everyday for the opportunity to have been part of such a life-changing place.

My father passed away while I was working on this book. For many years, he did not understand my choice to be a teacher or to work at the Open School. I am grateful that, before he died, he was able to come to the school and meet the staff and many of my former students. He came to understand my love for the place, and now, I appreciate that what I learned from my experience there helped me to mend some family fences.

Writing this book, including the extensive research it required, is another example of a Passage. As most students experience while undertaking Passages, I intermittently felt inspired, frustrated, and challenged—but ultimately satisfied—by the act of following a vision. For that's what this project was for me: a dream that one day I would tell the story of these extraordinary people whom I so love and respect. Like my fellow alumni, I'm still doing my Passages, and I guess I will continue to do them for the rest of my life. We alumni never seem to graduate. As Aaron (class of 1997) puts it:

> The values of the school stayed with me as I transitioned through
> my adult life. I knew that I always had the school with me as a
> foundation of support, and I learned to build support groups of my
> own. I'll never feel like I graduated from the Open School. I'm
> a student of life, forever!

So here's to the alumni of the Open School! May your lives serve as examples of what is possible when a school inspires its students to become passionate, loving, lifelong learners.

APPENDICES

Appendix A
Passages: The Walkabout Program

JEFFERSON COUNTY OPEN SCHOOL, a school of choice, pre-kindergarten through twelfth grade, emphasizes self-directed experiential learning, shared responsibility, and the development of life-long learning skills. Every student has a staff advisor and an individualized learning program.

WALKABOUT, inspired by an Australian rite-of-passage, is the final phase of the program in which each student demonstrates readiness to function as an adult by doing six Passages, the actual transition to adulthood. Passages are begun when the advisor agrees that the student has the foundation of skills, knowledge, attitudes, and behaviors necessary to succeed and has demonstrated the ability to set meaningful goals and attain them. Passages are personally challenging projects developed by each student in six different areas to demonstrate the ability to apply his or her skills in the real world. The Passage process includes the writing of a proposal which is approved by a committee of peers, the advisor, and a staff consultant. Mentors and parents may also participate. Upon completion of the Passage, the student reconvenes the committee and presents a written summary for final approval. The six Passage areas are:

- *ADVENTURE: A quest, a personal and meaningful challenge, the pursuit of which requires courage, endurance, self-reliance, and intelligent decision-making.*
- *CAREER EXPLORATION: A broad investigation of a field of employment, including an in-depth study of at least one job within that field, with particular attention to possibilities for the future.*
- *CREATIVITY: The development of a product that is an expression of one's personal imagination, together with a detailed analysis of the process by which it was created.*
- *GLOBAL AWARENESS: The identification of an issue having global impact, followed by a study of how one's own culture and at least one other culture deal wit h this issue, culminating in a service project designed to influence the issue on a local level.*
- *LOGICAL INQUIRY: An investigation which includes the generation of an hypothesis, the development of a systematic approach to data collection, and sufficient documentation to allow replication of the study.*
- *PRACTICAL SKILLS: The development of proficiency in a skill or set of skills for which one was formerly dependent on others and which has the potential for life-long usefulness.*

GRADUATION from the Open School is based on successful completion of personal goals related to the Graduation Expectations (personal, social, intellectual), the Walkabout, and a written transcript in which the student describes his or her learning experiences and accomplishments as a high school student.

PASSAGE PROCESS

THE PROPOSAL
❏ Develop on IDEA (a dream). Consider your readiness in terms of past experiences, skills, motivation, resources, and personal strengths.
❏ Meet with your ADVISOR and TRIAD to talk about the idea. Take notes on responses and suggestions.
❏ Meet with your chosen PASSAGE CONSULTANT. Take notes during the meeting. Ask for help with anything you do not understand.
❏ Write a ROUGH DRAFT using the guidelines below, along with specific Passage guidelines.

HOW TO WRITE A PASSAGE PROPOSAL
1. Describe your Passage in the opening paragraph. You could use the "newspaper format of who, what, when, where, why and how. Try to make your statements as clear as possible – write them as if someone who knew nothing about the school were reading your proposal.
2. Tell why your Passage is a challenge to you and what risks (physical, financial, social, and intellectual) you expect to experience.
3. Describe your preparation for this Passage. Include your strengths, past experiences, and training you plan to pursue prior to beginning.
4. Describe the resources you have (personal strengths – motivation, knowledge, skills, abilities; people; books; materials; etc.), the resources you will need, and how you will obtain them.
5. What do you anticipate to be your greatest obstacles and how do you hope to overcome them?
6. Identify possible peripheral learning.
7. Describe your first step in beginning this Passage and list your steps, in order, toward completion. A timeline with checkpoints may be helpful.
8. How will you document this Passage? How will you show changes in skills, attitudes, behaviors, and knowledge?
9. State how you will know when this Passage is complete and the proposed date of completion.

❏ Give the rough draft to your advisor, triad, and consultant and ask for FEEDBACK. This will need to be at least two weeks prior to the planned meeting.
❏ Make revisions and write a FINAL DRAFT of the proposal. This process usually occurs more than once. It often takes more than two weeks for the re-writing process.
❏ Ask people to be on your PASSAGE COMMITTEE. The committee needs to include the following people: Advisor, Passage consultant, and triad members. You may also invite other students, parents, or community mentors as appropriate.
❏ Schedule a PASSAGE MEETING TIME. Inform all members of the committee of the time and place for the meeting.
❏ Give a copy of the final polished draft of the proposal to each member of your Passage committee at least one week prior to the meeting time.
❏ At the PASSAGE MEETING, seek approval and suggestions from the committee; take notes to use in making further revisions or in carrying out the Passage and writing the wrap-up summary.

THE PASSAGE
❏ Your Advisor, Passage consultant, triad, and members of our committee are available to help. If you need to change what you are doing, they need to be consulted. Meet often with you consultant.
❏ Document **everything** you do – journal, notes, photos, receipts, letters, or other relevant records. Be sure to date and sign all important documents.

THE WRAP-UP
❏ Schedule a demonstration/display.
❏ Organize the documentation.
❏ Write a ROUGH DRAFT of the Passage summary with the help of the guidelines below, along with specific Passage guidelines.

HOW TO WRITE A PASSAGE WRAP-UP

1. Describe your Passage as you proposed it. The description should be written clearly, with attention to main events and/or highlights, so a person unfamiliar with you and/or the school could understand this experience. Balance a need to "summarize" with the equal need to detail the process you used to successfully complete this Passage experience.
2. Tell what you accomplished and how you know you reached your goals.
3. Describe turning points or highlights within the experience. These can be documented with excerpts from your journal.
4. Describe what obstacles, challenges, and risks (perceived and real) you encountered in this Passage and how you dealt with them. Describe unexpected events, setbacks, and opportunities. Explain whether or not your initial expectations were realistic.
5. List all the resources you utilized (personal strengths – motivation, knowledge, skills, abilities; people; books; materials; etc.). Be specific.
6. Describe peripheral learning or unexpected learning that occurred in this Passage.
7. Describe how you have documented this Passage.
8. The closing statement could include the following: how you feel about yourself and the completion of this Passage, why this Passage has made a difference in your life, where you will go from here with further exploration or experiences.

❏ Refer to specific Passage guidelines for additional information required for each wrap-up.
❏ Meet with your advisor for feedback and help.
❏ Meet with your triad for feedback and help.
❏ Meet wit h your Passage consultant for feedback and help. (This needs to occur throughout the course of the Passage.)
❏ Submit your rough draft of the wrap-up at least two weeks before you intend to have your wrap-up meeting. Be sure to include a summary of things that you learned which were peripheral to the Passage or that were unexpected.
❏ Revise and write and FINAL DRAFT of the wrap-up based on notes, suggestions, and feedback.
❏ Schedule a WRAP-UP MEETING TIME on a Walkabout Day. Inform all members of the committee of the time and place for the meeting.
❏ Give a copy of the final polished draft of the wrap-up to each member of your Passage committee at least one week prior to the meeting time.
❏ Present your accomplishments to your committee and CELEBRATE YOUR SUCCESS!

ADVENTURE: *The Quest*
PASSAGE GUIDELINES

OVERVIEW: The focus of the Adventure Passage is a personal quest. This Passage is like the mythical hero's journey. After the quest becomes clear, the hero prepares for a search or journey. Leaving a familiar environment (physical, emotional), he or she is tested by facing the risks and challenges, known and unknown, internal and external. In the end, transformed by success, the hero returns to the world ready for a new role.

BACKGROUND AND PREPARATION: If the Passage includes a trip, the usual "reasonable and prudent" procedures for school trips apply. These include informing parents and the principal of potential risks and describing how they will be dealt with. The Advisor and Consultant will help each student develop appropriate safety procedures.

STEPS IN WRITING THE PASSAGE PROPOSAL
❏ Identify your *quest*. State the quest in terms of a personal goal that involves challenge and risk. Tell why this is an appropriate quest for you.
❏ Tell *how* you will reach your quest. Be specific.
❏ Describe experiences that have prepared you for the challenges and risks you will face. Include the following:
• **Courage** – attempting to reach a goal in spite of fears. Identify the fears you have about this Passage and describe ways you can confront and overcome them.
• **Endurance** – the ability to withstand difficulty, with finesse. You must go beyond merely "surviving" to demonstrate strength and perseverance.
• **Intelligent Decision-Making** – responsibility in action. Show that you are able to consider important factors such as safety, support systems, itinerary, emotional and physical self-preservation and contingency plans to deal with the unexpected. Show that you are able to do what you *need* to do, not only what you *want* to do.
• **Self-Reliance in an Unfamiliar Environment** – the ability to apply skills and knowledge to new situations. Show how you will apply learning from past experiences to your quest.
❏ Describe you personal strengths and weakness in the following areas: self-concept, motivation and follow through, relationships with people and the environment, self-directed learning.
❏ Develop a detailed plan which includes itinerary with check-in dates, budget, equipment list, emergency procedures, contact names, addresses and phone numbers, needed resources, other relevant information.
❏ Indicate *HOW YOU WILL KNOW IF YOU HAVE REACHED YOUR QUEST.*

DOCUMENTATION: Keep a portfolio to document significant events, challenges, risk-taking, problem-solving, and decision-making throughout the Passage. Show how you have changed and become more self-aware.
DEMONSTRATION: You will be expected to describe your newfound vision resulting from completing your quest.

IDEAS / POTENTIAL PERSONAL QUEST:
CONSULTANT:

CAREER EXPLORATION
PASSAGE GUIDELINES

OVERVIEW: For this Passage, you will explore a career related to your interests, passions, talents, and experiences. You may choose a vocation that would allow you to carry out your mission in life or "create the world that ought to be". Essential parts of this Passage are a personal profile, interviews, hands-on experience in the chosen career, a résumé, an investigation into the training or education necessary to enter the field, and an exploration of related fields.

BACKGROUND AND PREPARATION: You will prepare for this Passage through classes, trips, experiences, community service, internships and apprenticeships.

STEPS IN WRITING THE PASSAGE PROPOSAL
❑ Meet with a consultant to discuss your idea before you start writing. Make a schedule for checking in with your consultant.
❑ Explain what you have already done to prepare for this exploration. Describe classes, trips, experiences, community service, internships, apprenticeships or jobs. Show how these activities motivated or inspired you to investigate this career field even if they involved different areas.
❑ Prepare a Personal Profile of your strengths and weaknesses in the personal, social, and intellectual domains.
❑ Describe methods you will use to complete this Passage. Possibilities include interviews, job shadowing, apprenticeships, internships or on-the-job training.
❑ List people to interview and tell why you selected each one.
❑ Prepare a questionnaire to use in interviewing people to get information about the necessary skills, attitudes and personal characteristics necessary for this career. You may also want to find out what preparation is needed and what the rewards and challenges are.
❑ Explain what education or training might be involved in order to prepare for this career, including specific schools or places that you might investigate.
❑ Describe how you will explore related fields.
❑ Set up a timeline with dates for completing specific tasks.

DOCUMENTATION: Documentation options could include records of interviews, feedback from supervisors or teachers, a journal, a résumé, a portfolio, college or training information, and letters of recommendation.

DEMONSTRATION AND WRAP-UP: The Wrap-up will include all your documentation. Show how this career matches your Personal Profile by describing how your skills, attitudes, and characteristics fit or do not fit this field. Tell how you feel about doing this Passage and what the next steps for your career exploration will be.

Sample Interview Questions
• How did you become interested in this career?
• What schooling or training was necessary for this career?
• What schools would you recommend to someone interested going into this field?
• What is the average beginning salary in this field?
• What is the potential highest salary in this field?

• Does this career require on-going training/education?
• What personal characteristics are optimal for this field?
• Are there any geographic constraints to this career?
• Do you belong to any professional organizations/unions?
• What are the rewards and challenges of this career?
• Do you enjoy your job?
• What freedoms/constraints are inherent in this career?
• What advice would you give to someone interested in this field?

**CREATIVITY
PASSAGE GUIDELINES**

OVERVIEW: For the Creativity Passage you will explore a concept, develop a design, and carry out a process to make a unique personal final product. The intent of the Passage is to help you understand the creative process, yours and others. The ability to create is not "mystical" or a natural gift possessed by only a few. It is a process of generating ideas, planning, solving problems, and making changes and understanding **WHY** you made them. **Creativity is not limited to the arts!**

Creativity involves the following elements:
• Challenging assumptions, "make the familiar strange"
• Making new combinations of "old" knowledge
• Seeing in new ways
• Recognizing patterns and connections
• Taking risks
• Solving problems / Analyzing and making changes
• Taking advantage of chance

BACKGROUND AND PREPARATION:
❑ An essential component of this Passage is to extend skills and interests to a *level of excellence* in an area in which you have previous experience and expertise. Experience and expertise may have been acquired in a variety of ways including classes, independent studies, or apprenticeships.
❑ Seek out and study creative works that appeal to you.
❑ Become actively involved in the creative process with a finished product as an outcome.
❑ Deal with an element of risk, striving to complete the project in spite of difficulties, such as scarcity of materials, lack of time, overestimating skills and abilities, and losing interest.
❑ Be responsible for finding and purchasing materials as well as making arrangements for use of school equipment or space, if needed.
❑ Allow for spontaneity and change while involved in the creative process, but remember, major changes in direction will require the approval of the Passage committee.

STEPS IN WRITING THE PASSAGE PROPOSAL
❑ Include the following in the proposal:
• Cost estimate
• List of materials and equipment, with possible sources
• Estimated amount of time needed for completion

- Work location
- Expected date of completion

DOCUMENTATION: Keep a record of the creative process you utilized throughout the Passage in the form of a journal, portfolio, photos, slides, film, videotape, drawings, notes, audiotapes, or other forms of documentation. Document the processes involved in creating, such as brainstorming, deciding, planning, and changing directions. Documentation of the ideas you disregard is as important as documentation of the ideas you pursue.

DEMONSTRATION: Present a completed project or a product in finished form along with process documentation and a summary for your final wrap-up committee. Consider a show or performance for a larger audience.

My previous experience with creativity:
Ideas for taking one of these skills to a level of excellence:

GLOBAL AWARENESS
PASSAGE GUIDELINES
Think Globally, Act Locally

OVERVIEW: This Passage gives you the opportunity to help "create the world that ought to be." This is your chance to see that education truly does exist outside the walls of the school building. The process of completing this Passage will help broaden your global perspective. One person truly *can* make a difference!

BACKGROUND AND PREPARATION:
❏ Choose an issue about which you are passionate – one that affects your life and that you believe you can affect.
❏ Try to find a topic that you have been exposed to in the past, through classes, trips, or personal life experiences.
❏ Before attempting this Passage, you should have had experience in research, community service, and personal risk-taking. You should be able to demonstrate your ability to follow through with commitments.
❏ A suggested requirement for this Passage is the Research Paper writing class.

STEPS TO COMPLETION: There are three major components of this Passage: **a research paper, community service, and the education of others.**
- **The Research Paper** – The research paper is a formal paper using resources and documentation to support a thesis (a statement of your opinion). Your Passage should keep a *global* perspective, but the research paper should focus on a *particular* aspect of the issue. The research paper should be written in MLA style and contain a clear thesis statement, a title page, an outline and a Works Cited page.

> Potential Resources:

Research Paper class	Opposing Viewpoints Series
MLA Handbook	Internet, EBSCO
Writer's Inc.	Research Paper packet (copies in the library)

- **Community Service / Action** – Get involved in a community service project,

apprenticeship, or other action, which you believe will help make a difference with your issue. Documentation is necessary.
• **Education of Others** – Educating others could include a Governance presentation, organizing a Day of Dialogue, teaching a class, creating a website, initiating a letter writing campaign or in some way raising the awareness of the issue in the affected community.

DOCUMENTATION AND DEMONSTRATION: Demonstration of the Passage should be in the form of a portfolio that reflects the three components: research paper, community service, education of others.

Global issues I am interested in:
Thesis ideas:
Community Service ideas and contacts:
Ways I might educate others:

LOGICAL INQUIRY
PASSAGE GUIDELINES

OVERVIEW: A Logical Inquiry Passage is a mental challenge, following a process to discover an answer to a question or problem that has personal meaning and relevance to you. This Passage is about thinking and rethinking a problem, introducing a variable and measuring the effects of that variable. The process demands the use of reasoning, problem-solving, research, investigation, data collection, analysis, synthesis, conclusions, and self-critique.

BACKGROUND AND PREPARATION
❏ Preparation includes both in-school experiences, such as science, cooking, and art classes or trips and out-of-school experiences, such as PLAID Days, IEP goals, reading, observations, and work. It may also include formal activities, such as seminars and apprenticeships, as well as informal life experiences, such as babysitting, problem-solving in relationships, animal training, car repair, etc.
❏ Include documentation in your portfolio to show how you have developed skills in problem-solving and applying the scientific method.
❏ Extensive consultation over a long period will help you understand logical inquiry in a variety of environments, prepare for the final demonstration, and assist you in overcoming the numerous obstacles and difficulties inherent in any Passage.

WRITING THE PROPOSAL AND THE PASSAGE PROCESS
❏ Share documentation of your preparation with your Advisor, triad and the Consultant to help determine your expertise and an appropriate level of challenge for the Passage.
❏ Identify a topic or problem to study and research.
❏ Conduct a Review of the Literature related to you inquiry to help solidify your understanding of the topic and identify an appropriate course of study. This critical step will help eliminate obstacles.
❏ Identify the best approach to studying your topic or problem. You may pick from the following.
• **Research through scientific literature.** Review and evaluate scientific literature on a chosen topic. Show your findings in a research paper.

- **Explore the effects of science on society.** Research and show how a particular aspect of science affects society and people's lives. Show your findings in a paper.
- **Integrate or apply science.** Explain how something works or why something happens by integrating scientific concepts or principles from two or more fields of science. You may also create a working model. Show you findings in a paper.
- **Conduct experimental research based on a hypothesis.** Carry out a study or experiment using a hypothesis, control, variables, and experimental design. The type and scope of analysis will depend on the data collected. Results from research involving surveys or opinion or attitude polls are usually derived from some type of statistical or numerical analysis.
- **Conduct naturalistic research based on case studies.** Select a field of study. Observe and record observations over time, then draw conclusions. Report findings in a paper.

DOCUMENTATION AND WRAP-UP: Documentation for the wrap-up will include:
❑ A research paper if required for your chosen approach
❑ A journal documenting the process you followed
❑ Appropriate graphics and displays of data collected and information gathered
❑ An analysis of the data and information you collected.
❑ A write-up detailing your conclusions, a self-critique of your experimental design or process, a description of peripheral learning, and self-reflection on why this Passage is a passage from adolescence to adulthood for you

Logical Inquiry
"The important thing is not to stop questioning. Curiosity has its own reason for existing. One cannot help but be in awe when he contemplates the mysteries of eternity, of life, of the marvelous structure of reality. It is enough if one tries merely to comprehend a little of this mystery every day. Never lose curiosity."
Albert Einstein

Logical Inquiry Passage Proposal Template for the Experimental Design Approach

Introduction: (What you want to do? Why do you want to do it? Why this is a Passage for you i.e. what are the risks and challenges for you? What experience you have with the Scientific Method?)
Review of the Literature: (What have other scientists studied to give you insight into this particular Passage? What were their results? How will your Passage be similar/different?)
Hypothesis: (Stated in measurable terms – one sentence)
Test Group: (What or who are you testing in your experiment?)
Control: (In order to know if your test has had an impact, you need to have a group you *do not* test to see if there is a difference in results.)
Method: (Very specific: Who or what will you be testing? Give all the specifics

here of your Experimental Design, including facts such as where you will conduct your experiment, what variables you will be testing, what variable you will be introducing, a timeline, etc.)
Resources: (What are the print and human resources you will use? How will you acquire those resources?)
Materials List:
Data Collection Method: (Who will gather data and how – Make a sample data collection form to be discussed in your Passage meeting)
Analysis: (Once you get your data, how are you hoping to analyze it? Graphs on Microsoft Excel are a great way to both display and analyze your data)
Conclusion: (This will be the conclusion for this Passage, not just the experiment. It is here that you will analyze your entire methodology and see if there are things you would have changed.)

*We would hear about **Logical Inquiries** into such questions as, How does a starfish bring about the regeneration of a lost arm? What does one experience when meditating that he doesn't experience just sitting with his eyes closed? What is the most effective technique in teaching a dog obedience? How do you navigate in space? Does faith-healing work, and if so, how? How many anomalies, such as the ancient Babylonian battery, are there in our history and how can they be explained? What folk and native arts and crafts have developed in this area? What are the 10 most important questions man asks but can't answer? What is insanity -- where is the line that separates it from sanity? and, What natural means can I use to protect my crops most effectively from disease and insects?*
From Maurice Gibbons article "Walkabout"

PRACTICAL SKILLS
PASSAGE GUIDELINES

OVERVIEW: Generally speaking, for a Practical Skills Passage you do something for yourself that ordinarily someone else has done for you, such as baking bread or building a 747. Often this involves a manual skill and will yield some product besides a journal or written description of what you have done. If you are a "hands on" person, you may want to do this Passage first. However, you should not limit your thinking to manual skills exclusively. For example, students have completed this Passage by mastering such activities as learning a second language, living on their own, and improving communication skills.

BACKGROUND AND PREPARATION: To begin, show that you are ready to take on the Passage process and demonstrate the ability to be a self-directed learner.

WRITING THE PROPOSAL
❏ Identify and list the practical skills you will master and demonstrate through this Passage. Be specific.
❏ Indicate your current skill level and how you have depended on others in the past.
❏ Tell how you will demonstrate an increased level of proficiency.
❏ Identify the RISKS you will be taking and tell how you will deal with them.
❏ Describe what you think your biggest obstacle to completion will be and how you plan to deal with it.
❏ List all the resources you intend to use (such as books, magazines, or people).

❏ Include a proposed budget and a list of materials. Consider including a statement concerning how you might conserve materials.

DOCUMENTATION
❏ Indicate what kind of documentation you will use. It is essential that your documentation be detailed, clear, and specific. Possibilities include: photographs, journals, videos, portfolios, letters of reference.
❏ The best documentation is actual performance of the skills.
❏ Describe the peripheral learning you may have gained from this Passage.

DEMONSTRATION: Make this a display of excellence and share with more people than just your Passage committee. Some examples could be to act as a guest speaker in a class, present to advisory groups, or share in Governance. Invite your parents, teachers, friends, supervisors, or any other significant people who helped make this a successful experience. If there is a more appropriate setting to demonstrate your skills, have the meeting there.

List of **Skills** I would like to master:

Passage Progress	Adventure	Career Exploration	Creativity	Logical Inquiry	Practical Skills	Global Awareness
1. Idea						
2. Talk with advisor						
3. Talk with consultant						
4. Proposal–rough draft written						
5. Feedback on proposal from triad						
6. Proposal–final draft written						
7. Proposal accepted by committee						
8. Passage work complete						
9. Wrap up; rough draft written						
10. Feedback on wrap-up from triad						
11. Wrap-up; final draft written						
12. Wrap-up accepted by committee						
13. Celebrate in Governance						

Appendix B
Trips Open School Classes Have Taken

This only a partial list of the trips that students, parents, and staff have taken over the past thirty-nine years.

Domestic Trips

Archeology:
 Arizona
 Colorado
 New Mexico
 Utah—Arches and Zion
  National Parks

Bears:
 Churchill, Alaska

Biking:
 California
 New England
 Oregon

Blues:
 Memphis
 Mississippi Delta
 New Orleans

Canoeing:
 Boundary Waters,
  Minnesota

Civil rights:
 the South

College exploration:
 Northwest and Colorado

Service:
 Mississippi flood lands
 Pine Ridge Reservation,
  South Dakota
 Tallahassee Junior
  Museum, Florida

Winter camping:
 Rocky Mountains

Wolves:
 Michigan

Boston, MA
Chicago, IL
Hawaii
Los Angeles, CA
Mississippi River
New York, NY
San Francisco, CA

Foreign Trips

Australia
China
Colombia
Costa Rica
Cuba
Europe
France
Germany
Italy
Spain
Guatemala

Honduras
Japan
London and England

Mexico:
 Desert and sea
 Mexico City
 Teacapan
 U.S.-Mexican Border
 Yucatan
New Zealand

Peace-making:
 Middle East
 Northern Ireland
 Peru
 Russia

Domestic & Foreign Trips

Diving:
 Dominican Republic
 Florida
 Mexico

Sailing:
 Bahamas
 New England

Whales:
 Baja, Mexico
 California
 Oregon

Appendix C
Graduation Expectations

<u>**JCOS Graduation Expectationa and Outcomes Inventory**</u>

	Exposure (E)	Experience (X)	Competence (C)	Excellence (L)
PERSONAL				
1. **Wellness -** the ability to assess and enhance emotional, mental, and physical wellness.				
1.1 Emotional Wellness - learn to understand yourself and live in harmony with your deepest feelings, impulses, and intuitions.	❏	❏	❏	❏
1.2 Physical Wellness - maintain a healthy physical lifestyle; your positive self concept and self confidence depends on physical wellness.	❏	❏	❏	❏
2. **Self-Directedness -** demonstrate the ability to be self-directed by meeting commitments to yourself and others, setting goals and priorities, managing time effectively, and completing tasks on schedule.	❏	❏	❏	❏
3. **Risk and challenge -** demonstrate willingness to take risks and challenge yourself.	❏	❏	❏	❏
4. **Work Experience -** experience work as an integral part of your high school education.	❏	❏	❏	❏
5. **Values / Moral Decisions -** Recognize and define values and principles, and develop skills and abilities to make moral decisions.	❏	❏	❏	❏
6. **Sense of Humor -** students understand and utilize humor as a source of health and joy	❏	❏	❏	❏
SOCIAL				
1. **Individuality / Relationships -** an understanding of individuality within relationships and development of a meaningful relationship with another person.	❏	❏	❏	❏
2. **Confrontation -** resolve conflict with others effectively and engage in conflict resolution in a positive manner.	❏	❏	❏	❏
3. **Flexibility / Resourcefulness -** demonstrate flexibility and resourcefulness in accommodating differences of opinion or dealing with unexpected obstacles, changes in plans, and/or bureaucratic red tape.	❏	❏	❏	❏
4. **Community Involvement / Contribution -** will demonstrate contribution to the school community, expanding to the world beyond.	❏	❏	❏	❏
5. **Cultural / Ethnic Awareness** – develop cultural/ethnic awareness within a global perspective, and experience another culture besides our own.	❏	❏	❏	❏

	Exposure (E)	Experience (X)	Competence (C)	Excellence (L)
6. **Ecological Awareness** - a developed sense of inter-relatedness and respect for environments.	❏	❏	❏	❏
7. **Family** - develop an understanding of family patterns as well as the responsibilities of members within families.	❏	❏	❏	❏

INTELLECTUAL

1. **Communication** - a process of self-growth through communication.	❏	❏	❏	❏
1.1 Reading - *ability to comprehend and interpret written language*	❏	❏	❏	❏
1.2 *Writing* - *students effectively utilize writing as a tool for communication and self-expression.*	❏	❏	❏	❏
1.3 *Speaking* - *learn to use oral communication skills effectively.*	❏	❏	❏	❏
1.4 *Listening* - *listening is an essential element of effective communication.*	❏	❏	❏	❏
1.5 *Non-Native language* - *be able to effectively speak and comprehend a non-native language.*	❏	❏	❏	❏
1.6 *Literature* – students will develop an appreciation for literature and the analytical skills necessary to encourage continued life-long growth in that appreciation.	❏	❏	❏	❏
2. **Analytical Reasoning** - students graduating from JCOS will be able to demonstrate mastery of the foundational math skills described in this document.	❏	❏	❏	❏
3. **Practice Research / Problem Solving** - be able to solve problems effectively utilizing a variety of resources. Practice research in order to find needed information.	❏	❏	❏	❏
4. **Science -** students graduating from JCOS should develop an appreciation for the beauty and wonder of the natural world and its phenomenon.	❏	❏	❏	❏
5. **Technological Literacy and Morality** - effective and ethical use of current technology and the ability to make informed choices for the development and application of future technological advances.	❏	❏	❏	❏
6. **Creative Expression** - students explore aesthetics and creative expression, such as art, theater, dance and music.	❏	❏	❏	❏
7. **Sense of History / Political Awareness** - acquire a sense of history and knowledge of politics in order to practice active global citizenship.	❏	❏	❏	❏
8. **Financial Literacy** - application of these skills are necessary to manage one's own finances, including the skills for a financially responsible lifestyle.	❏	❏	❏	❏

Appendix D
Colleges, Universities, and Professional Schools Attended by Open School Alumni

Alaska Pacific University
American University (DC)
Antioch College (OH)
Arapahoe Community College
Arizona State University
Augustana College (IL)

Bard College (NY)
Beloit College (WI)
Bemidji State College (MN)
Bennington College (VT)
Berklee School of Music (MA)
Bethany College (MO)
Boise State University (ID)
Boston Architectural College
Boston University
Brown University (RI)

California Institute of Art
California State University at
Monterey Bay
California State San Diego
Chapman College (CA)
Chemekata Community
College (OR)
Clark College (MA)
College of Santa Fe (NM)
Colorado College
Colorado Institute of Art
Colorado Mountain Colleges
(Glenwood and Steamboat
Springs)
Colorado School of Mines
Colorado State University
Columbia University (NY)
Community University of New
York
Concordia Lutheran College
(WA)
Cornell University

De Vry University

Earlham College (IN)
Edinboro University (PA)
Evergreen State College (WA)

Fairhaven College
Fordham University (NY)
Fort Lewis College
Friends World College (NY)

George Mason College (VA)
Guilford College (NC)

Hampshire College (MA)
Harvard University (MA)
Heartwood College (ME)
Humboldt State University
(CA)

Hunter College (CUNY)
Ithaca College (NY)

Lewis and Clark (OR)
Linfield College (OR)
London School of Journalism
Loyola College (CA)

Macalester College (MN)
Marymount Manhattan
College (NY)
Massachusetts Institute of
Technology
Mesa State University (CO)
Metro State College (CO)
Michigan State University
Mills College (CA)

Naropa Institute (CO)
New College of California
New England Conservatory
of Music
New England Culinary
Institute
New York School of Film
New York University
New York University

Ohio University
Okinawa University (Japan)
Oregon State University
Oxford College (UK)

Parks College (CO)
Pfizer College (CA)
Portland State University (OR)
Prescott College (AZ)

Red Rocks Community
College (CO)
Regis University (CO)
Rider University (NJ)

San Francisco Institute of Art
San Jose State University
Sierra Nevada College (NV)
Southern California Institute
of Architecture
Southern Illinois University
St. Johns College of Santa Fe
(NM)
St. Johns University (NY)
Swedish Royal Conservatory
of Music, Stockholm

Texas Christian University
Texas Tech University
The Boston Conservatory
Trinidad Junior College (CO)

United States International
School at San Diego
University of Arizona
University of California–
Berkeley
University of California–Santa
Barbara
University of California–Santa
Cruz
University of Chicago
University of Cincinnati
University of Colorado
University of Denver
University of Dijon (France)
University of Hawaii
University of Houston
University of Iowa
University of Massachusetts
University of Melbourne
(Australia)
University of Miami
University of Michigan
University of Minnesota
University of Northern
Colorado
University of Oklahoma
University of Oregon
University of Puget Sound
University of San Diego
University of South Carolina
University of Southern Maine
University of Torino (Italy)
University of Turku (Finland)
University of Utah
University of Vermont
University of Washington
University of Wisconsin
Madison
University of Wisconsin
Stevens Point
University of Wisconsin Stout
University of Wyoming
Utah State University

Vanderbilt University (TN)
Vassar College (NY)
Vermont College

Washington University of St.
Louis (MO)
Western New Mexico State
Western State College
Westminster College (MD)
Whitney Museum College
William and Mary (VA)

Yale University (CT)

Appendix E

Fields of Study and Types of Degrees Earned
by Open School Alumni

Fields self-reported

Includes double majors and minors

Disciplines	Percentage of Alumni
Education	19
Arts	16
Psychology/Sociology	9
Sciences	8
Business	7
Math/Engineering	6
English	6
Languages and Cultural Studies	6
History	4
Anthropology	4
Nursing	2
Political Science	1
Philosophy	1
Aviation	less than 1
Archeology	
Culinary Arts	
Communications	
Computer Science	
Criminal Justice	
Divinity Studies	
Geography	
Healing Arts	
Human Services	
Journalism	
Law	
Library Science	
Medicine	
Museum Studies	
Trades/Technical	

Appendix F
Careers of Open School Alumni

Addictions counselor
Air Force
America Corps
Anthropologist
Archeologist
Architect
Army

Banker
Bike mechanic
Biological consultant
Biological researcher
Biologist
Booking agent

C.E.O. and owner of a
    telecom company
Certified public accountant
Chemist
Chiropractor
City planner
Custom home builder

Dancer
Director of student services
Early childhood specialist
Ecologist
Editor
Elementary school teacher
Emergency medical
    technician
Environmental educator
Environmental manager
Environmental Protection
    Agency
Executive chef

Fiber optics technician
Film director
Film producer
Financial consultant
Fire and rescue team
Flight dispatcher
Forester

Game designer (computers)
Geologist
Germanic historian
Germanic languages
Graphic designer

Healing arts
Holistic health practitioner
House painter
International relief fund
    administrator
Investment broker

Law enforcement
Leadership consultant
Librarian

Marines
Master plumber
Mediator
Message therapist
Midwife
Mineralogist
Minister
Montessori school teacher
Mortician
Museum curator
Museum educator
Museum preparer
Musician
Naturalist

Navy
Novelist
Nurse
Nutritional consultant

Organic farming
Osteopathic medicine
Outward Bound instructor

Painter
Peace camp director
Peace Corps
Photojournalist

Physical therapist
Physicist
Pilot, commercial airlines
Poet
Political lobbyist
Professor of Arabic
Professor of cultural
    studies
Professor of ecology
Professor of law
Psychiatrist
Psychologist
Public health administrator
Publisher

Recording engineer
Registered nurse
Residential counselor
River conservationist
River guide and canoe
    maker

Secondary school teacher
Sheriff
Skydiver
Snowboard champion
Social worker
Speech pathologist
Surveyor

Travel agent
Truck driver

Web designer
Natural foods restaurant
    specialist
Wildlife instructor
Windows and glass
    technician
World hunger program
Writer for a snowboard
    magazine
Yoga instructor

Appendix G
Alumni's Social Action Work

Here are some examples of social activism that alumni report being engaged in both in volunteer capacities and in jobs.

I am an attorney in Helsinki, Finland who works for underprivileged people. I help with their legal problems with getting social benefits.
–Vappu, class of 1990

I am an eighth grade teacher. I encourage and challenge my students to think outside of the box and to speak their minds about issues that are important to them. We are very active in community theater and music. I have started a string group in rural Maine. I give scholarships, raise funds, and build confidence in kids. I am trying to help my students become more self-directed like the Open School taught me to be.
–Alice, class of 1979

I am active in advocacy groups and organizations that represent my interests and beliefs. I recently started my own political action group as a response to the most recent election.
–Anne, class of 1990

My job with a world relief organization is to create a better life for abandoned children, poor people, and those involved in natural disasters such as earthquakes, tsunamis, etc.
–Antonella, class of 1982

I am involved in anti-capital punishment groups and am thinking about starting a Christian organization supporting abolishment of the death penalty.
–Benjamin, class of 2001

I'm a youth pastor for my church. I try to shepherd kids through some of the toughest challenges in life.
–David, class of 1997

I have been active in peace organizations in India, sustainable communities, and school boards. Plus, I always try to lead by example.
–Dave, class of 1990

I volunteer for a nonprofit tutoring program for kids. I think all the time about how to raise children to be happy, secure, and good community members.
–Liz, class of 1997

I work in social science research and as a therapist to alleviate issues facing the mentally ill and foster children.
–Effie, class of 1988

I work in a healthcare facility to provide care for women who can't afford to seek care elsewhere. My goal is to better advocate for the cessation of medical treatment and the introduction of more palliative care for those who are dying and in pain.
–Emmie, class of 1995

I'm living on a small homestead farm learning about sustainable agriculture and ethnobotany. I have learned to hunt, knit, and create my own tools. We are creating our own sustainable community.
–Harlan, class of 1997

I am the program director of the Georgia O'Keefe Museum's Art and Leadership Program. In the face of a society that often ignores boys rather than nurtures them, I try to help preteen boys develop a sense of self-worth like I was able to do at the Open School.
–John, class of 1992

I work at the Amnesty International's Women's Rights Program and I am planning to return as a counselor for the Urban Studies Team, teaching and sharing about poverty and inequality in the inner city.
–Jonna, class of 2000

I work as an assistant to a program called Building Bridges for Peace that unites Palestinian, Israeli, and American teenage girls in a community peacemaking process.
–Molly, class of 1999

I am in the Peace Corp in the Dominican Republic. I first got interested in the area when I went there on an Open School trip. I also focused on Spanish and culture at the school.
–Morgan, class of 2001

Alumni report that they volunteer between two and ten hours a week. Groups that they are involved with include:
• Natural Resource Conservation Center
• Peace Corps
• Business Alliance for Local Living Economies
• International Scholarship Leadership Camp
• Parents, Families, & Friends of Lesbians and Gays
• Ecological Architectural Association
• Face-to-Face Peace Camp
• "I Have a Dream" Foundation
• Earthville Environmental Program, India
• Seeking Common Grounds (a peacemaking group)
• Ocean Conservatory
• Delta Blues Educational Program
• Environmental Protection Agency
• Poaching Prevention Association
• Authentic Learning Network
• Coalition of Essential Schools
• Buddhist Peace Fellowship

Appendix H
Notes

[1]Art Combs. 1984. *The six principles of learning*. Greeley, CO: University of Northern Colorado.

[2]John Dewey. 1916. *Democracy and education*. New York: The Macmillan Company.

[3]Joseph Kahne. 1995. Revisiting the Eight-Year Study and rethinking the focus of educational policy analysis. *Educational Policy* v. 9(1) March 1995: pp. 4-23: Corwin Press Inc.

[4]Carl Rogers. 1951. *Client Centered Therapy*. Boston: Riverside Press.

[5]Art Combs. 1988. The risk of 'A Nation at Risk.' *Rocky Mountain News,* November 26, p. 61.

[6]Maurice Gibbons. 1974. Walkabout: Searching for the right passage from childhood and school. *Phi Delta Kappan* v. 555(9): pp. 591-600.

[7]David Brooks. 2006. Stressed for success. *The New York Times*, Tuesday, March 30, 2004.

[8]Abraham Maslow. 1954. *Motivation and personality*. New York: Harper.

[9]UNICEF Innocenti Research Centre. 2007. *An overview of child well-being in rich countries*. Report Card 7: February 14.

[10]Alan Wagner. 2006. *Measuring up internationally: developing skills and knowledge for the global knowledge economy*. (National Center Report #06-7). The National Center for Public Policy and Higher Education. Online: www.highereducation.org/reports/muint/index.shtml.

[11]David Brooks. 2006. *op. cit.*

[12]D. Chamberlin. 1942. *Did they succeed in college? The follow-up of the graduates of the thirty schools*. New York: Harper & Brothers.

[13]Daniel Goleman. 1995. *Emotional Intelligence: why it can matter more than IQ*. New York: Bantam Books.

[14]Malcolm Knowles. 1975. *Self-directed learning: a guide for learners and teachers*. New York: Associated Press, in addition to the works of John Dewey and L. Piaget.

[15]Alfred Toffler. 1970. *Future shock*. New York: Random House

[16]James Hillman. 1989. *A blue fire*. New York: Harper & Row.

[17]Margaret Willis. 1961. *The guinea pigs after twenty years*. Ohio State University Press.

[18]Nathan Thornburgh. 2007. Dropout Nation. *Time Magazine*, Sunday, April 9, 2007. Online: www. dfoy.org/2007/research%20and%20reports/Time%20Dropout%20Nation.htm

[19]J. Felsman & H. Valliant. 1987. Resilient children as adults: a fifty year study, in E.J. Felsman and B.J. Cohler, eds., *The invulnerable child*. New York: Guilford Press.

[20]Thomas L. Freidman. 2005. *The world is flat: a brief history of the globalized world in the twenty-first century*. London: Allen Lane.

[21]Nathan Thornburgh. 2006. *op. cit.*

[22]Al Mayberry and Mary De Lave. 2001. *A Clear View*. Video documentary produced and directed by A. Mayberry and Mary De Lave. Stinson Beach, California.

[23]Al Mayberry and Mary De Lave. 2001. *op. cit.*

[24]Stephen R. Covey. 1989. *op. cit.*

[25]Daniel Goleman. 1995. *op. cit.*

[26]W.T. Grant Foundation. 2006. Sponsored research project on life skills and education.

[27]Howard Gardner. Gardner, Howard. 1983. *Frames of mind: the theory of multiple intelligences*. New York: Basic Books.

_____ 1993. *Multiple intelligences: The theory into practice*. New York: Basic Books.
_____ 1999. *Intelligence reframed: multiple intelligences for the 21st century*. New York: Basic Books.

About the Author

Dr. Fredric Posner began working for the public schools as a bus driver and custodian. He went on to become a special education teacher, consultant, and alternative school teacher and administrator. Receiving his Ph.D. in 1989, he established his expertise in the fields of self-directed learning and the modern rites-of-passage curriculum.

During his time at Jefferson County Open School in Colorado, one of the longest standing public alternative schools in the world, he took students all over the globe, including the West Bank, Gaza and, when the Wall came down, to Berlin. Dr. Posner also taught a wide range of classes that reflect his eclectic personal passions, ranging from Willy Mays, James Joyce, and Muddy Waters to ethnic cooking and marathon running.

He is a proud "graduate" of the Open School (retired in 2001) who has maintained his penchant for lifelong learning by doing service work in Haiti, consulting for alternative schools around the world, and writing this book. Like so many of his fellow Open School alumni, Dr. Posner claims that the school saved his life.